Technoliberalism and the End of Participatory
Culture in the United States

Adam Fish

Technoliberalism and the End of Participatory Culture in the United States

palgrave
macmillan

Adam Fish
Lancaster University
Sociology, Bailrigg, Lancaster,
United Kingdom

ISBN 978-3-319-31255-2   ISBN 978-3-319-31256-9   (eBook)
DOI 10.1007/978-3-319-31256-9

Library of Congress Control Number: 2016949072

© The Editor(s) (if applicable) and The Author(s) 2017
This work is subject to copyright. All rights are solely and exclusively licensed by the
Publisher, whether the whole or part of the material is concerned, specifically the rights of
translation, reprinting, reuse of illustrations, recitation, broadcasting, reproduction on
microfilms or in any other physical way, and transmission or information storage and retrieval,
electronic adaptation, computer software, or by similar or dissimilar methodology now
known or hereafter developed.
The use of general descriptive names, registered names, trademarks, service marks, etc. in this
publication does not imply, even in the absence of a specific statement, that such names are
exempt from the relevant protective laws and regulations and therefore free for general use.
The publisher, the authors and the editors are safe to assume that the advice and information
in this book are believed to be true and accurate at the date of publication. Neither the publisher nor the authors or the editors give a warranty, express or implied, with respect to the
material contained herein or for any errors or omissions that may have been made. The
publisher remains neutral with regard to jurisdictional claims in published maps and institutional affiliations.

Cover image © John Turner

Printed on acid-free paper

This Palgrave Macmillan imprint is published by Springer Nature
The registered company is Springer International Publishing AG
The registered company address is: Gewerbestrasse 11, 6330 Cham, Switzerland

To Io and Robin, creators.

Acknowledgements

I wish to thank the following colleagues at the University of California, Los Angeles, for their support and guidance during the early days of this research: Sherry Ortner, Chris Kelty, John Caldwell, and Ramesh Srinivasan.

The work would not have been possible without the contributions of the interviewees but I'd like to thank the following participants, whom I feel became friends: Jason Silva, Sarah Penna, Giselle Diaz Campagna, and Don Rojas.

I've learned much from discussions with the following colleagues at Lancaster University: Graeme Gilloch, John Urry, Robert Crawshaw, Sylvia Walby, Adrian MacKenzie, Robert Jessop, Monika Büscher, Lucy Suchman, Brian Wynne, Tim Dant, Bron Szerszynski, Imogen Tyler, and Bruce Bennett.

It would be remiss of me not to thank two mentors who have advised and encouraged me: Henry Jenkins at University of Southern California and Tom Boellstorff at University of California, Irvine.

Most importantly I'd like to thank my family and close friends who have been with me throughout: Mary, Dick, Jennifer, Emily, Richard, Heidi, Rich, Levi, Bradley, Nat, Ellie, and Ramesh.

CONTENTS

1	Introduction: Liberalism and Video Power	1
2	Histories of Video Power	21
3	Liberalism and Broadcast Politics	57
4	Corporate Liberalism and Video Producers	85
5	Technoliberalism and the Origins of the Internet	107
6	Technoliberalism and the Convergence Myth	129
7	Silophication of Media Industries	165
8	Neoliberalism and Terminal Video	181
9	Toward the Beginning of a New Participatory Culture	203
Index		213

CHAPTER 1

Introduction: Liberalism and Video Power

Buoyed by the marketing and academic hype surrounding Web 2.0, the trendiness of the term "democratization" peaked in 2005, according to Google Trends. Since then, the term has lost much of its original punch, as what was once radical about blogging, vlogging, tagging, commenting, and uploading has become mainstream and commodified. We are now quite familiar with the exaggerated claims of media democratization: amateurs aided by laptops, free time, cell phone cameras, and affordable internet connections would challenge politicians and professional journalists. Wikipedia, open-source software, Reddit, YouTube, and other instances of volunteered value creation illustrate this golden era of user-generated content. Books like Henry Jenkin's *Convergence Culture* (2008), Yochai Benkler's *The Wealth of Networks* (2006), and Clay Shirky's *Here Comes Everybody* (2006) offer quintessential celebrations of this emergent form of digital sharing, caring, and business "disruption." These authors were not responding to scholars such as Mark Andrejevic (2003) and Tiziana Terranova (2003), who earlier claimed that this volunteerism was a new form of "free labor" and worker exploitation. Regardless of the critique, the user-generated economy flourishes to this day. Networked amateurs are now taking on transportation (Uber) and lodging (Airbnb), as old industry figureheads like Kodak—destroyed by online photosharing and Facebook's Instagram—file for bankruptcy. The claim made by the chief executive officers (CEOs) of these companies is that the internet has manifested the values of Western liberalism—individualism, democracy, and a free market.

© The Author(s) 2017
A. Fish, *Technoliberalism and the End of Participatory Culture in the United States*, DOI 10.1007/978-3-319-31256-9_1

2   A. FISH

Sometimes it is difficult not to believe the hype. New technologies have the potential to animate political action. We have seen the political impacts of citizen-collected videos of police brutality that, once uploaded, have galvanized social movements. Footage of Eric Garner being choked to death by Daniel Pantaleo after selling cigarettes on a New York street was announced online in 2014. A video of Walter Scott being gunned down in the back by South Carolina police officer, Michael Slager, was released in April 2015 by *The New York Times*. The civil rights movement constellating around the Twitter hashtag #blacklivesmatter emerged online and in the streets, motivated in part by these deaths and the video evidence of police brutality. One need only consider the footage of Neda Salehi's blood pooling on the streets of Tehran in 2009 to understand how graphic video can motivate protest movements. But while the capacity for citizens to use internet video to bring transparency to corruption will continue, the industry of internet video has become less of a free-for-all since 2005. Major old and new media players—Netflix, Amazon, Apple, AT&T, Disney, Discovery, and Google—are consolidating their video power. It did not have to be like this.

Writing in *The Nation* in 1972, Ralph Lee Smith advocated that the USA should be committed to "an electronic highway system to facilitate the exchange of information and ideas." He continued, "[T]he stage is being set for a communications revolution ... audio, video, and facsimile transmissions ... will provide newspapers, mail service, banking and shopping facilities, data from libraries." He was inspired by the new networked technology of the time, cable television, which was supposed to empower the multitudes. While this type of utopianism could have been heard during the dotcom period of the late 1990s or the heyday of the Web 2.0 hype of 2005, it was being proclaimed in 1972. More circumspect than utopian, Smith also warned "short term commercial considerations will dictate the form of the network" (Smith 1972, 83). Monopolization, mediocrity, market fundamentalism, and other ills were possible with the new networked technology of cable. Local vigilance to keep cable in the hands of activists, educators, and the state was needed if the socially beneficial attributes of cable were to be realized. Similar cautions were uttered about the future of the internet.

J.C.R. Licklider, a psychologist who was in charge of the Information Processing Techniques Office at the Pentagon, foresaw what was to become the internet years before its arrival. An innovator of cybernetics, Licklider described in classics such as "Man-Computer Symbiosis" (1960) how networked computers would, one day, supplement human cognition, memory, and mental work. In the 1967 essay "Televistas," commissioned by the Carnegie Commission on Educational Television, Licklider criticized existing television for not being participatory. He wrote, "From an educator's point of view, the main intrinsic defects of broadcasting television are that it offers everyone the same thing and does not give viewers a direct way of participating." Computer networks, cable television systems, data storage, and multiple cameras, he believed, would enable viewers to engage with programming, producing a more diverse and less hierarchical television system. In this world of narrowcasting, "Community theater would have a chance to compete, if not with Broadway, with Hollywood" (Licklider 1967, 215). The internet circa 2005 appeared to finally embody this uploading dream.

This moment seems to have passed, however, as the internet is increasingly being designed around delivering not community theater but Hollywood. Control over expensive technical innovations such as server farms, colocation, IPTV, adaptive bitrate streaming, and edge caching has put major corporate forces in the driving seat. Focus is now on delivering professional content from the center of the once decentralized internet. This is big business. "Providing popular audiovisual content on the internet had quickly come to look more like a factory enterprise from the Industrial Revolution than the post-industrial future that had been promised," writes Christian Sandvig (2015, 232). "The internet," Sandvig continues, "is now, for the first time, centrally organized around serving video. [And] a particular kind of video from a very small number of providers to large numbers of consumers. The internet is now television, or it will be soon" (2015, 237). Netflix and Google account for more than half of the internet traffic in the USA at peak hour. While companies like Netflix may appear like newcomers in comparison to the major television networks, they exemplify the shift from a participatory, lean-forward, user-generated internet to a lean-back, spectator, professional internet. Lawyer Tim Wu (2010) calls "the Cycle" that historical process of media industries that begins with amateurism and ends in professionalization. Throughout the twentieth century, new communication technologies, media activists, and state regulation came together to create brief openings for amateur participation on television. While these moments of openness soon gave way to closure and capitalization, they offer insights into the struggle for democratic participation.

4   A. FISH

This book is the first cultural history and sociological study of how professional television broadcasting and amateur digital video met at the pressure points of new technology, regulation, and practice. Based on over 80 interviews collected within the television and internet industries in the United States between 2006 and 2012, this book critically examines the turbulent media culture of amateurs and activists using new video technologies and regulations in order to access an otherwise privatized television system. The book illustrates how the socially liberal ideals of equality and the neoliberal ideals of competition clash on the battlefield of participatory culture.[1]

Many of the project participants grew up in middle-class homes and were college-educated—many at top universities. While the majority is white, I endeavored to interview equal numbers of men and women. When I interviewed the project participants, they were employed in media industries. Although their work was precarious at times, most of the participants have become more successful since our experiences together, securing more prestigious and well-paid positions. Some made and sold video companies and became millionaires, and others joined major firms like Google and Twitter. The freedoms these privileged subjects experienced and were able to exercise in university manifests in the ideals of social media as a form of both public participation and economic prosperity. Doing well and doing good simultaneously, a concept that is inherent to some strands of West Coast liberalism, is not paradoxical for these subjects.

From its inception, liberalism has been rife with internal contradictions. A core premise that emphasizes individual freedom is bound to conflict with another core premise, that is, of social solidarity. No early liberal scholar better addresses these paradoxes than Scottish political philosopher Adam Smith. Taken together, his two primary treatises, *The Theory of Moral Sentiments* (1759) and *The Wealth of Nations* (1776), embody the intertwined concerns for social empathy and individual entitlement. In the first text, Smith designates the source of social solidarity as the "mutual sympathy of sentiments." Here Smith developed a theory in which individuals find positive confirmation in an internal voice, an "impartial spectator." Breaking with Thomas Hobbes and Jean-Jacques Rousseau, who saw humans as inherently selfish, Smith considered all people to have the capacity to sympathize and care for the other. This manifests, one could argue, in a sense of responsibility and a willingness to be charitable. He asks us to put ourselves in the shoes of the downcast and celebrates the humility and generosity that comes from that exercise in self-effacement

(Colato 2010). In short, the book is a study in the psychology of a prudent Christian welfare state guided by social liberalism and the idea that society should look after the less fortunate with whatever means necessary. *The Wealth of Nations* presents a different vision of society, one ruled by self-interest and commerce. Economics underlies politics, justice, and morality. It is the classic text of economic liberalism, one in which freedom and individuality are indivisible from deregulated economics. Taken together, the two books provide a view of a non-contradictory synthesis of economics and moral philosophy. This approach would need both the "mutual sympathy of sentiments" and the "invisible hand" of the market, without one or the other dominating. Considering both texts, a "single axiom, broadly interpreted ... is sufficient to characterize a major portion of the human social and cultural enterprise. It explains why human nature appears to be simultaneously self-regarding and other-regarding" (Smith. A. 1998, 3). To quote Isaiah Berlin (1969), true freedom for the majority of citizens requires both negative liberty—freedom from coercion—and positive liberty—social support—to maximize the freedom celebrated by both social and economic freedom.

This struggle for democratic participation on television can be understood through the political philosophy of liberalism. In the 1970s, early video and cable television activists, driven by a socially liberal desire for participatory media to augment democracy, accessed the new networked technology of cable television. In the 1980s, corporate liberal approaches regulated television to create thriving private industries with a small and tokenistic public participation. In the 1990s, television networks eyed the camcorder-enabled citizen as both a consuming audience and a source of labor. By the 2000s, the economic liberalism of the free-market internet made the niche programming countercultural dreams of the 1970s a lucrative reality for a few. In the 2010s, the neoliberal absence of internet regulations created a winner-takes-all economy for those willing to brand themselves as self-entrepreneurs. This struggle can be articulated in terms of video power—the capacity to speak and be seen on the present cultural form of television. This book tells this history and elaborates upon a new iteration of liberalism, technoliberalism, which sees Silicon Valley technology and the free market of Hollywood end the need for a politics of participation.

When they emerge, networked visual technologies are often politicized. Video, cable, satellite, camcorders, and the internet were seen not only for their entrepreneurial potential but also for their political impact.

6 A. FISH

Various players vie for this video power. The resources to acquire video power are unequally distributed and shift between amateurs, activists, and professionals. New technologies, new uses of old technologies, new ideas about convergence and participatory media, and new regulations may create openings wherein new players may gain entry. In these instances of disruption, amateurs and activists may secure a modicum of video power. Through time, however, these amateurs may become professionals and their politics may be obstructed; the professionals may take over through various means; or the video power secured by the amateurs may be shown to be illusory and the professionals have always been in charge.

The eventual direction this video power takes depends upon the political orientation of those who acquire the power. The tenor of this politicization varies but can be discussed as influenced by variants of liberalism—a multifaceted political philosophy whose emphasis on equality and liberty develops through time into conflicting ideals. Equality is often expressed as human rights and social justice and linked to the broader concept of social liberalism that is expressed through pro-state reformist policies and citizen-driven populism. However, contrary to this notion, liberty is often interpreted as economic freedom, the ability to buy and sell unperturbed by the government. Negative liberty and *laissez-faire* capitalism are celebrations of singular independence or individualism and align with economic liberalism. In this way, liberalism includes the economic freedom for corporations (capitalism), the role of the state in securing and defending social equality (progressivism), the rugged individual unencumbered by the state (individualism), and the rights and responsibilities of citizens to collaborate (populism). Technoliberalism advances these versions of liberalism into an age of powerful technology companies and neoliberal deregulation.

I base my definitions of technoliberalism on ethnographic and empirical studies of the political values of digital media producers. Based on their ethnographic research with hackers, anthropologists E. Gabriella Coleman and Alex Golub (2008) take liberalism not as a monolithic concept but as a "cultural sensibility with diverse and sometimes conflicting genres" (2008, 256). Other empirical studies of networked communication technologies use liberalism as a rubric through which to interpret the political aspirations of digital media producers. Anthropologist Thomas Malaby conducted fieldwork in the offices of immersive virtual reality world *Second Life* at Linden Lab, and discusses the workers he encountered in terms of "'technoliberalism,' which marks both its similarities to neoliberal thought but also its emphasis on contriving complex systems through manipulation of technology" (2009,

16). Technoliberals, like the workers at the San Francisco-based Linden Lab, engineered social interactions through the production of technological platforms. *Second Life* enables autonomous virtual individuals to explore a landscape and engage in libertine, collaborative, or economic pursuits. In this manner, technology generates the conditions for liberal subjectivity. At Linden Lab, developers mix economic liberalism and "left-libertarian" values (Malaby 2010, 60). This confluence of left and right politics emerged in an earlier history of digital media production in California. Historian Fred Turner (2006) analyzed how the social liberal values of the counterculture in the 1960s evolved into the economic liberal impulses of the 1990s. These left-libertarian technologists believed that the conditions for equality and liberty could be engineered with the right tools, and eventually saw capitalism as another decentralized network capable of empowering individual liberties. They exhibit what Evgeny Morozov (2013) calls digital "solutionism" or a belief that social problems can be solved by technology. Technoliberalism contains within it a belief that technology can ameliorate the contradictions of social and economic liberalism. They believe that asocially-just and an economically profiable world is possible with the right tools.

This book is about political theory in action. Its key contribution is a critique of contemporary liberalism and how it works through the technological practices of video and television producers and regulators. Technoliberalism is a form of self- and social governance that is mediated through technologies and regulatory bodies. The variations of technoliberal practice in action include video power, and other terms I will discuss, such as proformations, silophication, and digital discourse. Throughout its history, amateurs and activists have attempted to access television. New technologies—video cameras in the 1960s, cable and satellite in the 1980s, and the internet in the 1990s—often provided brief openings for activists to gain access to television. These openings, however, were often short-lived, with the interests of profit and professionals soon taking precedence over the interests of amateurs and activists. Beginning in the 1940s and proceeding to 2005 and the era of social media convergence, Chapter 2 provides a historical overview of how new technologies galvanized amateurs' and activists' pursuance of video power and television access. This history of video power engages the early commodification of amateur filmmakers in the 1960s (Aufderheide 1994; Zimmerman 1988) and video activists and artists from the 1970s to the 1990s (Halleck 2002; Luca and Wallner 1993; Mellencamp 1990; Merrin 2012; Oullette 1995a, b; Pierce 2003). In addition to speaking to the recent past, this chapter investigates earlier phases of

8 A. FISH

computer-made and network-distributed amateur video from the 1990s to the 2010s (Boddy 2014; Christian 2014; Parks 2004; Turner 2006). In the 1950s, 8mm cameras were marketed to lower social classes in such a way that precluded these amateurs using these cameras to challenge the hegemony of the film industry, while 16mm cameras were sold to higher social classes aspiring to professional projects. In the late 1960s, video challenged these earlier film standards and video activists emerged to exploit the new technology. Television networks adapted to exploit the new mode of production. For example, CBS hired Videofreex in 1969 to make a documentary on the counterculture and politics. Videofreex proceeded to interview Abbie Hoffman at the Chicago 8 trial, as well as Fred Hampton, a leading Black Panther member, just days before his murder, but CBS tabled the footage as being too "ahead of its time." Satellites too provided opportunities for activists. For instance, from its inception, Deep Dish TV used satellites to resist the Persian Gulf War. In 1989, the Nicaragua Network produced a live call-in show in Managua with the Nicaraguan president, Daniel Ortega, in order to counteract the US Administration's belief that the contras were "freedom fighters." In these instances, video and satellites provided opportunities for both activists and amateurs to reach television audiences. In the beginning of NBC's *I Witness Video* (1993), a program billed as an early installment in citizen video journalism, the camcorder was framed as a revolutionary tool. By the end of the first season, however, the radical potential of video-enabled amateurs had been severely curtailed and the program began to look more like *America's Funniest Home Videos*, a program featuring videos submitted by the American public. The early days of the internet saw a number of platforms for amateur video activists. Oxygen, the Digital Entertainment Network (DEN), and Pseudo.com created content with and for gender and racial minorities and were framed as empowering these underserved populations. In reality, however, this had little to do with diversifying the voices online, as it was more concerned with niche marketing in the age of diversified programming.

Claims for video power are enabled by the efforts of media reform organizations. Chapter 3 introduces the numerous models used by broadcasters and media reformers to articulate, motivate, and justify their media reform activism and broadcasting activities. Broadcasters' models are arrayed across the public sphere, guardianship, and commercial models. Guardianship and commercial broadcasting models are represented aesthetically through traditional news broadcasting featuring television

INTRODUCTION: LIBERALISM AND VIDEO POWER 9

journalists. The public sphere model, requiring the transformation of the audience into media producers, is a less prevalent yet more radical broadcasting model. These practice reveals how broadcast models are cultural interventions, flexible in their application of liberalism.

Most media reformers want serious reform and believe that media systems are public resources that have been erroneously given to commercial interests. Their project is to mobilize a suite of models to challenge the privatization of public media resources and defend public control over the scarce examples that remain of public interest media. A range of models are used by media reformers with entry points beginning in anti-monopoly, public interest, free speech, access, public resources, emergent technology, and democracy. These models are linked to a variety of liberal manifestations.

In addition to three years of fieldwork and interviews with television and internet video producers, I worked as a paid, contract-by-contract, freelance citizen video journalist, or a viewer-created content (VC2) producer, beginning in 2006, and eventually I produced 16 documentaries for Current before the organization ceased the VC2 program in 2009. Current was a global television network founded by former US Vice President Al Gore in 2005 and purchased by Al Jazeera in 2012. They had deals with satellite and cable companies in the USA, the UK, Ireland, and Italy and reached between 30 million and 50 million homes. The professional experience of working with Current provided valuable opportunities to observe the workings of the company and generate the contacts necessary to conduct interviews with more than 30 Current employees throughout a range of corporate departments. In addition to broadcasting television programs, Current endeavored to "democratize" the production of voice within the hegemonic public sphere. Current's effort in democratization embodied a social liberal pursuit of equal representation on television, while their ultimate goal was profitable market liberalism.

The second major fieldsite is Free Speech TV (FSTV). Artist and curator Jon Stout and radio spectrum entrepreneur John Schwartz founded FSTV in 1995 with the goal of providing progressive and independent news and documentaries via satellite, cable, and the internet. Receiving no money from advertising or the federal government, FSTV is a not-for-profit organization and finances its operations through viewer support and foundation grants. Workers at FSTV tend to be politically progressive, seeing media systems as public resources, and therefore they oppose the corporate control of media systems. From a small office in Denver, Colorado, FSTV broadcasts to potentially 30 million viewers on the DISH and DirecTV satellite platforms. FSTV produces live television coverage from progressive political events such as the National NAACP Convention, Netroots Nation, the National Conference for Media Reform, and Take Back the American Dream—the conferences I attended with FSTV in 2011. Attendance at these conferences allowed me to observe FSTV's television production and intersectional practices, as well as other partners in the field of media reform broadcasting. Preparing for these experiences, I participated in FSTV's office and television production practices in Denver for two weeks where I interviewed most of the non-profit television network personnel.

Throughout their history, media reform broadcasters have modified their broadcasting approaches, regarding how they address the public, and from which reformist model they draw. Their mission is to improve democratic dialogue on private media systems. Their broadcasting models oscillate through time from public sphere and guardianship to commercial broadcasting models as they address the public as participants, informed citizens, or consumers. FSTV follows the reformist models of free-speech, anti-monopoly, and public access. These models are most prevalent in FSTV. At Current, the dominant discourses are centered on how television and the internet can best be mobilized to increase democratic participation. As part of this technodemocratic modeling, the producers at Current also dialogue in utopian fashion on the positive role of technology in contemporary life more generally. In these manners, media reform broadcasters' models, frames and discourses are mobilized to articulate approaches to accessing and contributing to the hegemonic public sphere.

Chapter 4 introduces the media activist practice of proformation—a portmanteau of *pro* duction/re *formation*. It is technological and political action to gain public access to the means of production on information infrastructures, be they satellite television systems or the internet. The concept addresses the hybrid culture of information reform and information production at the interface of private information and media reform, infrastructural praxis, and communications rights. The theory of proformation developed from an analysis of qualitative material collected from FSTV. This network's job is made possible by corporate liberal policies that allocate the majority of media resources to private firms and the minority for public use. In this way, proformers reify and depend upon the pro-corporate policies they seek to transform. FSTV produces progressive content, has petitioned for "set-asides" for public media, and has modified its identity to secure access to a range of private information infrastructures,

INTRODUCTION: LIBERALISM AND VIDEO POWER   11

such as cable, satellite, and internet communication systems. During the course of my 2010–2012 participant research with FSTV, the company shifted their resources from regulated television to the deregulated internet, and entered a world where the policy protections afforded to them by corporate liberalism no longer existed.

Corporate liberalism is a form of governmentality by which corporate agendas are masked as social policies creating consenting subjects. Politicians enacting corporate liberal policies provision public media resources to corporations that are required to provide few channels for public use (Streeter 1996). Under corporate liberalism, the state performs a waning obligation to the "public interest." Increments of pro-public interventions into media monopolies are allowed under corporate liberalism, such as the small amounts of public media "set-asides" enjoyed by public television stations (Sterne 1999, 507). In this process, proformers become embedded within the capitalist world system, which the socially liberal content they produce often critiques. Put bluntly, within corporate liberalism, televised progressivism becomes complicit in its own domination. From this perspective, FSTV is an actor within corporate liberalism, allowing major cable and satellite companies like TCI, DISH, and DirecTV to comply with federal regulations, which profit from the privatization of public media resources. The internet era and its absent regulatory assistance for public media can be more accurately correlated not with corporate liberalism but with neoliberalism, which with its market fundamentalism denies statutory obligations to public media.

FSTV engineered and used access points provided by corporate liberal policy to expand its audience across a number of information infrastructures. In the form of The 90's, it was on seven cable networks (1989–1995) before being ejected by John Malone, an anti-public-interest telecommunication conglomerate CEO. For the next five years (1995–2000) FSTV was a "program service," packaging content that it "bicycled" to any public interest channel that would air it. Throughout, FSTV petitioned the US Congress and adapted itself to new policies regulating emergent information infrastructures. Under pressure to provide public access to its satellites, DISH gave FSTV a deal on an out-of-the-way channel, and the network was on its first satellite. Through the same process, a decade later, FSTV was on its second satellite, DirecTV.

FSTV's political identity is expressed through its programmatic choices. It reported critically on the lead-up to the 1990 Gulf War, the 1999 World Trade Organization (WTO) protests, the 2000 Democratic

12   A. FISH

National Convention, the 2003 Iraq War, and the 2011 Arab Spring and the Occupy Movements. FSTV's technological identity is also observable in the savvy ways it used amateur technologies in professional ways, such as being a pioneer in the use of online video in the mid-1990s and using MPEG-2 video compression and a T1 internet line for a daily television news production. It was also an innovator in citizen video journalism, beginning with the 1999 WTO protests and the 2000 Democratic National Convention.

During the 2008 global financial crisis, FSTV hired new management, rebranded itself, reformed its use of internet video and social media, began anew with in-house and live production, and orchestrated new partnerships with progressive media groups. The period of my fieldwork (2010–2012) represented a culmination of these efforts as I observed a two-pronged campaign, consisting of new studio news and live political event programming paired with efforts to maximize audience engagement through social media.

For FSTV, Current, and other discussed in this book, the internet is a key symbol in the discourse of contemporary liberalism. It stands for individual innovation, economic freedom, civic collaboration, and political potential. In political rituals on the campaign trail, the internet's symbols are mythologized and fetishized by many including politicians such as former US Vice President Al Gore and former US President Barack Obama, both claiming for themselves or their party a hand in inventing the internet. Chapter 5 focuses on technoliberalism as a digital discourse that attempts to mitigate the contradictions of liberalism through a discussion on technology. Four genres of digital discourse emerge: (1) technoindividualism; (2) technocapitalism; (3) technoprogressivism; and (4) technopopulism. The chapter concludes by considering the contemporary domination of technocapitalism and its eventual demise.

During the 2000 and 2012 US Presidential campaign trail, Gore and Obama, respectively, prominently celebrated how the US government had financed the development of the internet. In discussing the internet on the campaign trail, Obama defended the role of government against neoliberal anti-statism, Gore defined himself as a politician with visionary acumen. In associating themselves with the technology of immense economic, scientific, political, and social significance, politicians hoped to elevate themselves to higher political office. And yet, summoning the internet on the campaign trail produced two of the most catastrophic gaffes for both of these politicians as journalists willfully misinterpreted these claims. This

INTRODUCTION: LIBERALISM AND VIDEO POWER   13

chapter makes two points. First, these campaign trail events exhibit the rituals, myths, and fetishes of digital discourse. Second, this richly discursive field defines technoliberalism, a term that designates how digital discourses are mobilized to mitigate the contradictions of liberalism. The battle over who made the constitutive elements that became the internet—the Pentagon with ARPA; Xerox and Apple; the volunteer bevy of open-source coders; the "founding father" network engineers Paul Baran at RAND, visualizing packet switching, Vint Cerf at ARPA, engineering TCP/IP, Tim Berners-Lee at CERN, developing HTML, or Marc Andreessen at the University of Illinois, creating Mosaic—spread across four camps, each with their own classically liberal belief system regarding internet freedom, the role of the state, the legitimacy of business, the collective vibrancy of organizing without organizations, the sheer wit of gifted individuals, or the ideal confluence of state/business/citizenry/scientists.

Soon after the ruthless edits hit internet video sites, four arguments emerged about who really made the internet. L. Gordon Crovitz at *The Wall Street Journal* started the polemic by going against the accepted wisdom and saying that Obama was wrong, it was Xerox PARC, and therefore corporations made the internet. Farhad Manjoo of *Slate* rebutted that the President was correct, Crovitz's facts were not facts at all, and the state did fund and support what became the internet. Harry McCracken of *Time* added to the debate by bringing back an old idea that never gets old in technology journalism, that it was not the state or corporations, but brilliant individuals who should be thanked for the internet. Finally, Steven Johnson, writing in *The New York Times*, said it was not states, corporations, or smart individuals but a public of open-source coders who should be thanked for building the software with which states, corporations, and individuals access the internet.

Each makes impressive claims, but my point is to consider these statements as discourses that reveal at the same time as they attempt to conceal political persuasions in historical revisions. These four internet historiographical ideologies can be traced back to classical Western liberalism and its emphasis on freedom of the corporation (technocapitalism), to the state in securing and defending freedom and citizen responsibility (technoprogressivism), to the rugged individual unencumbered by tradition (technoindividualism), and to the collaborative citizen public (technopopulism).

14 A. FISH

Chapter 6 examines Current, the for-profit television network founded in 2005 by former US Vice President Al Gore and lawyer entrepreneur Joel Hyatt with the expressed goal of "democratizing television." By being a platform on which amateurs and activists could air their content on television, Current attempted to converge the participatory possibilities of internet-based affordances with the broadcasting power of television. A specific discourse manifests through the myth that internet and television convergence can solve democracy. In a study of the discourse on how technology is going to improve the life of the post-Fordist worker, Eran Fisher (2010) coined the term "digital discourse." According to this theory, worker subjectivity is empowered by networked technologies. Digital workers are not exploited by capitalists; their work is more creative, communal, and pleasurable. This post-alienation empowerment is the result of the flexibility and mobility of contract-based digital work. This is a discourse that mitigates through talk the social dysfunctions of technocapitalism. Current and its workers hoped to be associated with the positive qualities related to the internet (e.g. the creative economy, social media, open source, crowdsourcing, "sharing economies," "internet freedom" and the Arab Spring, Google, iPad, and Skype), while ignoring what might be suspect (e.g. surveillance, free and outsourcing labor, networked authoritarianism, cyberbullying, actual and virtual sweatshops, monopolies, offshore banking, and Wall Street algorithmic crime). Their moral technical imaginaries are examples of digital discourses that mitigate less favorable perspectives of the past through obfuscating and elevated talk on technologies. Digital discourses foreclose important issues such as user-generated and below-the-line labor. They relegate difficult and pragmatic work to other people or networked computers, believing that technology alone will fix problems that are social in origin. In technoliberal fashion, Current attempted to merge both progressive social liberalism and financially profitable economic liberalism. The digital discourse of convergence attempts to mitigate these contradictions of liberalism through talk on technology.

Within this broad mitigating digital discourse exists a convergence myth that the workers who are making the internet and television come together are improving democracy through bringing internet-enabled citizen voices into elite television production. As myths do, the convergence myth both obscures and reveals economic and political power. Current's convergence myth obscures the difficulties of digital labor and digital democracy with a digital discourse. In the end, Current reveals not

INTRODUCTION: LIBERALISM AND VIDEO POWER   15

only the difficulty of converging the internet and television into a political and profitable project but also the difficulties of operating pro-democratic projects within a milieu of global technocapitalism. The failures of the convergence myth are exposed through an analysis of the following: Current's programming schedule, freelance contracts, studio aesthetics, departmental competitions, commercialization of user-generated content, employee life histories, initial public offering (IPO), and its final sale to Al Jazeera. Idealistically, Current thought that convergence would solve the problems plaguing democracy by bringing diverse voices to television. This, however, was a digital discourse that claimed that democracy could be solved via the application of citizen video power.

Chapter 7 consists of a series of interrogations of media reform broadcasters' efforts to diversify voice within the American public sphere (Couldry 2010). One problem independent television producers attempt to overcome through "intersecting" with partner organizations is "silophication." Partnering practices reveal the precarious situation of media workers and media activists in an increasingly consolidated media environment. This analysis of the strategies of independent television networks exposes the contradictions within capitalist information work, namely the tensions between fluidity and fixity in employment and collaboration. Tensions between silophication and fragmentation are a metaphor for the desire and difficulties of convergence. The analysis of the challenges of diversifying voice with these practices reveals the frustrations of pro-democracy media activists working within a capitalist world system.

As illustrated with the evidence from Current, structural silophication is a synonym for corporate departmental balkanization. The data from Current illustrates the challenges of bringing together the affordances of the internet and television. This results in different "moral technical imaginaries" (Kelty 2008) associated with each technology. While Current illustrates structural silos, FSTV illustrates the economic potential and political risk associated with mental silos. Both Current and FSTV seek to address the problem of silophication. Anthropologist and journalist Gillian Tett suggests solving the issue through silo-busting, or what the media reform broadcasters call intersectionality.

Based on interviews with those leading the explosive internet video industry, Chapter 8 investigates the liberal politics—or the lack thereof—of several multichannel internet video networks and examines the practices of self-branding executed by video entrepreneurs. In 2011, Google

16   A. FISH

picked up an internet video company, Next New Networks, for $27 million. One of its biggest hits, *Obama Girl*, featured a scantily clad songstress serenading the former president. Discovery Communications picked up video network Revision3 for $30–40 million in 2012. Revision3's top-viewed video is entitled *Super Slow Mo Slap in the Face*. DreamWorks bought the video company AwesomenessTV for $100 million in 2013, featuring "your favorite beauty gurus, advice for teens, celeb gossip, teen pop stars." AT&T purchased a majority share in Fullscreen in 2014 in a deal that valued the video network at around $200–300 billion. On Fullscreen's roster is Shane Dawson, whose top video is a parody of Miley Cyrus's *Wrecking Ball* video. Disney acquired Maker Studios, a network of YouTubers, for almost $1 billion in 2014. Maker Studios' most viewed "influencer," PewDiePie, tells dirty jokes while playing video games. Many of these gamers, vloggers, sketch comedians, and make-up artists have become millionaires from product placement deals with the likes of Mattel, Kia, Target, Clorox, Pepsi, and Old Navy. The social liberalism lingering in technoliberalism has now disappeared as conglomerates invested in internet video. To make this point, this chapter links the neoliberal self-entrepreneurialism of internet video microcelebrities to the macroeconomics of conglomeration.

The conclusion charts how earlier desires that internet video would constitute a socially liberal public sphere for participatory politics and amateur production have been replaced by a gold rush of acquisition, conglomeration, and monopolization. Internet video now is less an open, generative, and democratized platform and increasingly one dominated by the logic of capital. If YouTube is the new television—and is not regulated—then how will we secure equity in access and visibility in the future of internet broadcasting?

My point throughout this book is that liberalism provides a guide for thinking about how to answer this question. Liberalism means different things in different places and times. There are studies of liberalism in Central America (Colburn and Cruz 2007), France, Germany (Vail 2014), and California (Turner 2006). Liberalism takes on a specific coloration in contact with the idealized applications of technology in and around Silicon Valley (Kelty 2014). Variously, liberalism can be "a concept, theory, ideology and political movement" (Rosales 2013, 1). In this book, liberalism is taken as a philosophical orientation with pragmatic applications in the field of politics and political representation. The field of cultural production surrounding television and internet video provides a fertile ground for the socio-technical manifestation of multiple liberal ideals.

This book is an experiment in the classification of diverse historical and cultural interventions into the liberal tensions between individualism and collectivism. Each modality of liberalism is situated in a specific cultural, technological, economic, geographical, and political context. Situatedness is important for video activists who link the power of self-representation to the locality of performances of political identity (Braidotti 1994; Haraway 1988). Likewise, the power to see or be seen is a key concern as well (Fish 2016). Visibility "lies at the intersection of the two domains of aesthetics (relations of *perception*) and politics (relations of *power*)" (Brighenti 2007, 324). Hegemonic power is enacted through vision and may be rejected through visibility. The histories and case studies that follow are situated struggles for video power along a liberal spectrum.

NOTE

1. In addition to interviews, other methods were used in the collection of data—business document analysis, historical studies, observation, and co-production of media. While my graduate training may have been in anthropology, this book is not a traditional ethnography. In addition to personal experience, I analyze and report on media content, policy documents, and historical accounts. These eclectic and mixed methods are like those used in other qualitative research on cultures of television (Dornfeld 1998; Caldwell 2008), software (Kelty 2008), and film production (Ortner 2013). I corroborate sociological theory derived from investigations into technological cultures to interrogate this historical moment of internet and television convergence (Fisher 2010; Jenkins 2006; Marwick 2013; McChesney 2013; Mosco 2005; Streeter 1996; Turner 2006). The research for this book came from fieldwork conducted in the United States with a primary focus on the media industries across south and central California. With Los Angeles being the capital of television production, and San Francisco leading the technology sector in the USA, California is an ideal location for the investigation into internet and television convergence. A nexus for multiculturalism, the counterculture, and progressive politics, California is a place to observe the mixing not only of new technology and capital but also of social ideals.

18 A. FISH

REFERENCES

Berlin, I. 1969. *Four Essays on Liberty*. Oxford: Oxford University.

Braidotti, R. 1994. *Nomadic Subjects: Embodiment and Sexual Difference in Contemporary Feminist Theory*. New York: Columbia University Press.

Brighenti, A.M. 2007. Visibility: A Category for the Social Sciences. *Current Sociology* 55(3): 323–342.

Caldwell, J.T. 2008. *Production Culture: Industrial Reflexivity and Critical Practice in Film and Television*. Durham: Duke University Press.

Colato, N. 2010. Adam Smith Moral Philosopher. *Oxonian Review* 11.1. Accessed December 13, 2015. http://www.oxonianreview.org/wp/adam-smith-a-moral-philosopher/

Colburn, F.D., and A. Cruz. 2007. *Varieties of Liberalism in Central America: Nation-States as Works in Progress*. Austin: University of Texas Press.

Coleman, E.G., and A. Golub. 2008. Hacker Practice: Moral Genres and the Cultural Articulation of Liberalism. *Anthropological Theory* 8(3): 255–277.

Couldry, N. 2010. *Why Voice Matters: Culture and Politics After Neoliberalism*. London: Sage.

Dornfeld, B. 1998. *Producing Public Television*. Princeton: Princeton University Press.

Fish, A. 2016. Mirroring the Videos of Anonymous: Cloud Activism, Living Networks, and Political Mimesis. *The Fibreculture Journal* 26(191): 85–107. http://fibreculturejournal.org/wp-content/pdfs/FCJ-191AdamFish.pdf

Fisher, E. 2010. Contemporary Technology Discourse and the Legitimation of Capitalism. *European Journal of Social Theory* 13(2): 229–252.

Halleck, D.D. 2002. *Hand Held Visions: The Impossible Possibilities of Community Media*. New York: Fordham University Press.

Haraway, D. 1988. Situated Knowledges: The Science Question in Feminism and the Privelege of Partial Perspective. *Feminist Studies* 14(3): 575–599.

Jenkins, H. 2006. *Convergence Culture*. New York: New York University Press.

Kelty, C.M. 2008. *Two Bits: The Cultural Significance of Free Software and the Internet*. Durham: Duke University Press.

Kelty, C. 2014. *Fog of Freedom in Media Technologies: Essays on Communication, Materiality, and Society*, ed. Tarleton Gillespie, Pablo Poczkowski, and Kristen Foot. Cambridge: MIT Press.

Licklider, J.C.R. 1960. "Man-Computer Symbiosis" Is Reprinted, with Permission, from IRE Transactions on Human Factors in Electronics, vol. HFE-1, 4–11.

———. 1967. Televistas: Looking Ahead Through Side Windows. *Supplemental Paper for the Carnegie Commission*.

Lucas, M., and M. Wallner. 1993. Resistance by Satellite: The Gulf Crisis Project and the Deep Dish Satellite TV Network. In *Channels of Resistance: Global Television and Local Empowerment*, ed. Tony Dowmunt, 176–194. London: BFI Publishing.

INTRODUCTION: LIBERALISM AND VIDEO POWER 19

Malaby, T. 2009. *Making Virtual Worlds: Linden Lab and Second Life*. Ithaca: Cornell University Press.

Marwick, A. 2013. *Status Update: Celebrity, Publicity, and Branding in the Social Media Age*. New Haven and London: Yale University Press.

McChesney, R. 2013. *Digital Disconnect: How Capitalism Is Turning the Internet Against Democracy*. New York: New Press.

Mellencamp, P. 1990. Video Politics. *Discourse* 10: 2.

Merrin, W. 2012. Still Fighting 'The Beast': Guerrilla Television, and the Limits of YouTube. *Cultural Politics* 8(1): 97–119.

Morozov, E. 2013. *To Save Everything, Click Here: The Folly of Technological Solutionism*. New York: Public Affairs.

Mosco, V. 2005. *The Digital Sublime: Myth, Power, and Cyberspace*. Cambridge: MIT Press.

Ortner, S.B. 2013. *Not Hollywood*. Durham, NC: Duke University Press.

Ouellette, L. 1995a. Will the Revolution Be Televised? Camcorders, Activism, and Alternative Television in the 1990s. In *Transmission: Towards a Post-Television Culture*, ed. Peter d'Agostino and David Tafler. London: Sage.

———. 1995b. Camcorder Dos and Don'ts: Popular Discourse on Amateur Video and Participatory Television. *Velvet Light Trap* 36(Fall): 34–44.

Parks, L. 2004. Flexible Microcasting: Gender, Generation, and Television—Internet Convergence. In *Television After TV: Essays on a Medium in Transition*, ed. Lynn Spigel and Jan Olson. Durham, NC: Duke University Press.

Pierce, S. 2003. DBS and the Public Interest Opportunity in Satellite Television. In *Public Broadcasting and the Public Interest*, ed. Michael P. McCauley, Eric E. Peterson, B. Lee Artz, and DeeDee Halleck. Armouk, NY: M.E. Sharpe.

Rosales, J.M. 2013. Liberalism's Historical Diversity: A Comparative Conceptual Exploration. *Contributions to the History of Concepts* 8(2): 67–82.

Sandvig, C. 2015. The Internet as the Anti-Television: Distribution Infrastructure as Culture and Power. In *Signal Traffic: Critical Studies in Media Infrastructure*, ed. Lisa Parks and Nicole Starosielski. Chicago: University of Illinois Press.

Smith, A. 1759. *The Theory of Moral Sentiments*.

———. 1776. *The Wealth of Nations*.

Smith, R.L. 1972. *The Wired Nation: Cable TV: The Electronic Communication Highway*. New York: Harper and Row.

Smith, V.L. 1998. The Two Faces of Adam Smith. *Southern Economic Journal* 65(1): 1–19.

Sterne, J. 1999. Television Under Construction: American Television and the Problem of Distribution, 1926–62. *Media, Culture, and Society* 21: 503–530.

Streeter, T. 1996. *Selling the Air: A Critique of the Policy of Commercial Broadcasting in the United States*. Chicago: University of Chicago Press.

20 A. FISH

Terranova, T. 2003. Free Labor: Producing Culture for the Digital Economy. Accessed December 5, 2015. http://www.electronicbookreview.com/thread/technocapitalism/voluntary

Turner, F. 2006. *From Counterculture to Cyberculture: Stewart Brand, the Whole Earth Network, and the Rise of Digital Utopianism.* Chicago: University of Chicago Press.

Vail, M.I. 2014. Varieties of Liberalism: Keynesian Responses to the Great Recession in France and Germany. *Governance* 27(1): 63–85.

Wu, T. 2010. *The Master Switch: The Rise and Fall of Information Empires.* New York: Knopf.

Zimmerman, P. 1988. Trading Up: Amateur ilm Technology in the 1950's. *Screen,* 17–29.

CHAPTER 2

Histories of Video Power

The Refusal of Activism Amateur Film Production in the 1950s

Photography was big business in the USA after World War II. When the high-resolution 16mm film cameras first came onto the market, they were made for the upper classes of the post-war era with the expendable income and leisure time to dedicate to learning the technology. Between 1947 and 1954, companies like Kodak, Keystone, Revere, and the Swiss company Bolex successfully marketed to amateurs cheaper and easier-to-use 8mm film cameras and stock. Cameras like the Revere 50, Bell & Howell 172b, and the Kodak Brownie 8mm were some of the first amateur-grade 8mm film cameras in this trend. Throughout the 1950s, amateur photography grew by 112.5%, the use of 8mm film cameras increased by 41%, and the shipment of these cameras swelled by 201%. By 1961, the annual market for amateur film technology was $700 million (Zimmerman 1988, 50). By the 1960s, 8mm camera sales had skyrocketed by 62% and 16mm camera sales fell by 43% (Zimmerman 1988, 46). Camera manufacturers had succeeded in finding the price point that would encourage not only upper-income consumers to buy 16mm cameras but also middle-income and lower-income families to invest in 8mm film equipment.

Through marketing and manufacturing, the 8mm and 16mm markets were segmented. Product differentiation was marked by an "ideology of professionalization" (Zimmerman 1988) in which higher forms of technical skill and expertise were associated with 16mm cameras and

© The Author(s) 2017
A. Fish, *Technoliberalism and the End of Participatory Culture in the United States*, DOI 10.1007/978-3-319-31256-9_2

21

22   A. FISH

higher-earning classes. The 16mm cameras enabled users to modulate exposure, focus, and lens lengths while 8mm cameras, marketed for lower-income households, did not allow for such creative agency. This class and product differentiation also had a geographical component. The cheaper, lower-grade 8mm cameras were sold in the suburbs while the more professional 16mm retailed in downtown shops. Through targeting lower-income households with cheaper and simpler film production technologies, Bell & Howell and their competitors did not encourage these social classes to aspire to professional standards and competencies. Through product differentiation designed to capture new consumers at affordable price points, these camera companies reiterated the boundaries between professionals and amateurs along lines of social class. This process, in turn, affirmed that higher classes had the capacity, technological prowess, and leisure time to make professional-grade products while the rest of the population could not.

In the 1950s, film technology companies sought to frame 16mm camera use and higher social class amateur film production as empowering, enticing these amateurs to emulate Hollywood and US television production but without providing them the correct format (35mm) or a realistic route to theatrical or television distribution. Thus 16mm cameras were "a form of play with technology in simulation of professional labor" (Zimmerman 1988, 51). By the 1950s, zoom lenses were available so that users could emulate the tricks of professional television producers. An advertisement for the DeJur film camera claimed that its zoom lens enabled users to achieve "professional style pans" and "television style zooms" (Zimmerman 1988, 48). Bell & Howell's Filmorama and the Dutch Vitascope cameras both mimicked the CinemaScope 35mm projection ratio but in substandard 16mm or 8mm formats so that users could aspire, in their minds at least, to the technical wizardry and spectacle of Hollywood (ibid.).

The expansion of professional-grade tools and tricks to amateurs was short-lived and unrealistic. No pathway to theatrical or television broadcast was available, they were shooting on substandard formats, and few if any networks or production companies were interested in the "user-generated content" of the 1950s. By the early 1960s, Bell & Howell and other companies had recognized that the surest route to increasing profitability was not in encouraging all amateurs to aspire to professional standards but in focusing attention on high-end 16mm cameras with zoom lenses and home projection-ready aspect ratios for the upper

HISTORIES OF VIDEO POWER 23

classes. While at the same time, these companies sold simpler, cheaper, and professionally unusable 8mm cameras to a clearly demarcated amateur class of suburban users, with less disposable income and little to no aspiration or potential for their films to gain a wider audience. While upper-class users of 16mm film cameras were encouraged to aspire to professionalism, but were destined to ultimately fail on technological grounds in these aspirations, the lower classes were neither encouraged nor provided the technical tools needed to ascend to professional status. For the most part, the film cameras of the 1950s marketed for amateurs were considered not as tools for journalism but as toys with which to simulate some aspects of professional practice while never actually challenging that category.

Unlike instances of video democratization that followed, the fluidity between amateurs and professionals provoked by amateur access to professional-grade equipment never came to be, as amateurs were instructed to use equipment incapable of producing theatrical or television quality images. New inventions from the 1970s till today—video, satellite, cable, and the internet—would eventually open small portals for short durations for amateurs to produce professional-grade content. With these technological innovations and marketing strategies came renewed discourses about democratization, empowerment, and citizen journalism. While the 1950s lacked the politics of user empowerment that existed in excess in the 1970s and 2000s, the links between technology, amateurs, and empowerment can be identified.

Communication systems like satellite, cable, the internet, and video capturing technologies have co-evolved throughout the last 35 years, further blurring the categories of amateur and professional video producers. By 2005, and with the development of 3CCD (three charge-coupled device) cameras, the rhetoric that amateur access to professional video technology was democratized and that the boundaries between amateurs and professionals was permeable, was to be heard again. Adding to the discussion of these blurring boundaries was something missing from discussions of the amateur film production in the 1950s: distribution. Today, amateur involvement in media production and distribution for substantial numbers of individuals in the West has been achieved. Along with the "democratization" of media production, comes a political discourse of empowerment and a diversification of the public sphere. This is a result of the shifts in media theory and media production that developed with the counterculture of the 1960s. In this discussion, the advent of video technology and

24 A. FISH

the expansion of television distribution on cable and satellite have created the conditions for a renaissance in citizen video production. This renaissance was short-lived and reemerged in the 1990s, 2000s, and 2010s, with the Web 1.0 and Web 2.0 technologies.

Throughout the history of amateur production, film and video companies, marketers, guerilla video and cable television producers, and television networks, have attempted to capitalize—economically and politically—on the increasing user productivity. This will become most obvious in the period from the 1960s to the 1980s.

Cybernetic McLuhanism in Television Video from the 1960s to the 1980s

[T]he term guerilla television, with its implications of aggression and subversion came to signify a specific kind of activist videotape, one that functioned as an ironic observation of the follies of the establishment against the conventions of television. (Sturken 1990, 107–108)

Jump-starting both artistic and political expression, the Sony Corporation released an affordable, portable, half-inch video camera for personal use in 1965. Nam June Paik pioneered video art with one. Documentarians like Les Levine shot seedy, serialized, and amorphous "street tapes" with New York's homeless with this camera. In 1967, Sony updated its earlier model by releasing the DV-2400 Video Rover that recorded 20 minutes of video on half-inch magnetic tape (Tripp 2012, 6). Chasing the growing market in portable video, in 1968, Sony released another model, a more transportable half-inch reel-to-reel CV Portapak. A handful of colleagues and friends used the Portapak as a tool for artistic expression, political documentation, and self-awareness. Paul Ryan, a research assistant for Marshall McLuhan, while McLuhan was in residency at Fordham University from 1967 to 1968, helped to form one of these early video collectivities. Borrowing equipment from Fordham, Ryan lent the gear to Frank Gillette, David Cort, Ken Marsh, and Howard Gustadt who formed Commediation. Gillette made a five-hour documentary on street life in New York City. Others made videos of a range of hippie life: activism, communes, drugs, and so on (Boyle 1992, 67). The group lasted only a few months, but catalyzed Gillette as a video artist and activist. In early 1969, together with Ira Schneider, Gillette produced the video art, "Wipe

HISTORIES OF VIDEO POWER 25

Cycle," which attracted Michael Shamberg, a *Time* journalist and eventual author of *Guerilla Television*.

"Wipe Cycle," Paul Ryan's interactive "Everyman's Moebius Strip," Nam June Paik and Charlotte Moorman's "TV Bra for Living Sculpture," and other installations were included in the genre defining the "TV as a Creative Medium" exhibit at the Howard Wise Gallery in New York City in 1969. Not a documentary film, Wipe Cycle was an early tape-loop installation with the goal being the "conversion (liberation) of an audience (receiver) into an actor (transmitter)" (Antin 1976, 176, in Hill 2012, 23). The multichannel installation included a live camera and nine different monitors. Upon exiting an elevator, visitors would immediately encounter a video of their own image delayed and repeated by each of the monitors. For Hill, Wipe Cycle's "conversion" or liberation of the audience recalls video activism of the late 1960s, namely Third Cinema. Fernando Ezequiel Solanas and Octavio Getino, write about audiences of politically charged cinema as no longer being mere spectators, but rather "the spectator made way for the actor, who sought himself in others" (1969, 54, in Hill 2012, 24). These notions of conversion via evocative cinema and video are akin to the notion of "political mimesis," or the way that cinema and video hail viewers to model themselves after the politically active individuals depicted on screens (Gaines 1999). Participation and feedback became hallmarks of the cybernetic video production of this era.

In 1970, Schneider, Gillette, and Shamberg formed Raindance Corporation, dedicated to collective video production. The name was a spoof on the military research subcontractor RAND Corporation, which became a household name because of ex-employee Daniel Ellsberg's leaking of the Pentagon Papers (Coffman 2012, 65). Schneider introduced to the group the video art journal *Radical Software* (1970–1974), edited by Beryl Korot and Phyllis Gershuny. The first issue of *Radical Software* contained Ryan's essay "Cable Television: The Raw and the Overcooked." In it, Ryan envisioned how video feedback systems would create a "two-way information system." Sounding much like his mentor McLuhan, Ryan wrote, "Film extends man as a spectator … video extends man as a cybernator" (Ryan 1970, 12). With lifelong interests in the overlaps between cybernetics, ecology, and media, Ryan led Raindancers to make and dispense tapes at the first Earth Day in 1970 (Coffman 2012, 68).

In November 1971, Shamberg and Raindance Corporation published what became the central text of the movement, *Guerilla Television*. By guerilla, however, they did not refer to left-wing guerilla warfare. Rather, they

26   A. FISH

redefined guerilla in post-political terms: "We ... believe in post-political solutions to cultural problems which are radical in their discontinuity with the past" (Shamberg and Raindance Corporation 1971, ix, in Merrin 2012, 100). Inspired by *Whole Earth Catalogue* editor Stewart Brand and Marshall McLuhan, and not Lenin and Guevara, guerilla television can be described as "Cybernetic McLuhanism [which] synthesized McLuhan's ideas on electric media, the futurist ideas of Buckminster Fuller, and the cybernetics rooted in the formulations of Norbert Wiener and reinterpreted though Gregory Bateson's systems theory ecological approach" (Merrin 2012, 200–201). Raindancers embraced the cybernetic notion of feedback as a way of emphasizing the importance of two-way and interactive communications systems to embolden a new generation of citizen video journalists and artists. Video producers would form "video data banks" that would challenge the class-based disparities of access to knowledge production in contemporary America. No longer would the disparity in the distribution of quality production equipment prevent all classes from being heard.

Post-politics describes a cynicism about working within the current system of democratic capitalism. Scholars like Alain Badiou, Slavoj Žižek, and Chantal Mouffe argue that the content of democratic capitalist policies is irrelevant, and the system is corrupt and will not achieve universal equity. This oppositional approach necessitates rigorous critique, a withdrawal from the present, and the proposal of alternatives. The editors of *Radical Software* were also "post-political" stating: "Unless we design and implement alternate information structures which transcend and reconfigure the existing ones, our alternative system and life styles will be no more than products of the existing process" (Korot and Gershuny 1970, 1). Guerilla television producers mixed technological determinism, technoutopianism, a de-emphasis on traditional politics, and an emphasis on media ecology. The process of experimenting with new communication formulas was more important than the content produced by the said experiments. The point was to create feedback loops capable of testing and elaborating upon Cybernetic McLuhanism.

One guerilla television producer who conducted a number of such experiments was Ted Carpenter. The mountainous regions around Johnson City, Tennessee, prohibited the development of broadcast television, as the signals would not penetrate the topography. Carpenter identified this as an opportune locale to experiment with cable television that was not dependent upon satellite signals but was transmitted through coaxial cables that could be laid under the ground through the riverine corridors. Broadside TV was the result and Carpenter and others trained local people to produce local programming. In order to participate, locals had to first watch a program and work with the video cameras and equipment. Carpenter had the local interviewers use a television-like monitor as a viewfinder so that the interviewee and interviewer could see the live recording. With no pedantic director, Broadside TV was conceptualized as a technology-assisted feedback practice. Interviews with midwives, coal miners, folk musicians, and storytellers were shown to neighbors in community halls and homes as well as cablecast. In this way, Broadside TV merged the feedback practices of Cybernetic McLuhanism with community development via cable television (Hill 2012, 22).

Ken Marsh, the co-founder of New York City video collective, People's Video Theater, did not mince words about the capacity of video to refresh democracy: "The people are the information ... Everybody could do it and everyone should do it. That was the mandate—pick it up, it's there. Like the power to vote—vote, take responsibility. Make it and see it" (Hill 2012, 21). Marsh, like other guerilla television producers, expressed remarkable faith in the ordinary citizens to make video. It is as easy as voting. What made video production easy was the shifting expectation for quality. Eschewing tripods, the videographers in these videos wandered like their subjects. Few videographers had editing equipment or could afford to store each half-inch tape, so few finished products were completed. Instead, unedited tapes were quickly screened and overdubbed. Emphasis was on process and the practice of video production not the product.

However, countercultural guerilla television was soon to be coopted by mainstream television. In 1969, CBS funded the production of *Now*, about the counterculture. CBS executive Don West heard about the work of guerilla television crew Videofreex and its founders David Cort and Parry Teasdale at the Woodstock Festival and commissioned them to rove the USA collecting video about the many facets of countercultural life (Tripp 2012, 9). Once they had received funding for travel, equipment, and rent, Videofreex proceeded to interview Abbie Hoffman, at the Chicago 8 trial, as well as Fred Hampton, a leading Black Panther member, just days before his murder. West wanted *Now* to replace *The Smothers Brothers Comedy Hour*. But despite this valuable footage, CBS declared it "ahead of its time" and rejected it without broadcasting it (Boyle 1992,

28   A. FISH

69). "Arrogant and naïve, they learned the hard way that television had no intention of relinquishing its power," claimed the video historian Deirdre Boyle (1992, 69). Undeterred or overly confident, in the 1971 manifesto, *Guerilla Television*, Michael Shamberg and Raindance Corporation outlined their plan to decentralize what they saw as the corrupt and banal American corporate television system and democratize its production through video technologies. The rejection of *Now* was evidence that television studios were not going to willingly give up their hegemonic position. Changes in technology emboldened the guerilla television producers. In 1970, the AV (audio/video) format that Portapak rolled out conformed to the international standard for half-inch videotape. This interoperability allowed tapes shot on one camera to play on any other AV format. In 1972, three-quarter-inch U-matic cassettes were made available. These technological advances encouraged the exchange of tapes and inspired videographers to think that their videos could now be broadcast on standard compliant cable systems. Along with the advent of cable television came federal mandates that cable service providers must provide television access to local producers. Guerilla television producers were ecstatic. In cable, they were going to be provided access to a newly decentralized television system (Boyle 1992, 70).

As in the 1950s, advances in film and video technology created an opening for amateurs to make professional-like content. In the 1970s, new magnetic videotape and portable batteries made it possible for creators to experiment with video production. Where in the 1950s aspirational upper-class 16mm hobbyists were hailed and sought to play with some of the tricks of professionals, the 1970s guerilla television producers saw new video technologies as a way to challenge the professionals. Unlike the 1950s, the 1970s amateur producers saw this opportunity as political. They were going to transform the public sphere through transforming television itself. Unlike the 1950s producers, there were few opportunities for the 1970s producers to distribute their content on newly developed satellite and cable systems. Emphasis on bottom-up empowerment through technology was quintessentially technosocial liberalism, a belief in technology to energize the grassroots.

Guerilla television emphasized participation, process, and immersion and was best embodied by the protest videos of the 1970s. With long takes and in-the-protest interviews, *Mayday Realtime* (1971), produced by David Cort and Curtis Ratcliff, documented anti-war protests in Washington, DC. In the video, activists speak directly to Cort, disregarding

HISTORIES OF VIDEO POWER 29

the camera. Police ambush a crowd that includes the videographer. He is hit by a policeman's billy club. The handheld camera pans and tilts wildly. Immersive and reflexive, this videographic technique personifies "performative non-fiction" (Fish 2007), a form that continued to be popular among adventurous journalists through the decades.

The video collective Top Value Television (TVTV) exemplifies the practice and discourse of guerilla television of the 1970s. With the new standardized videotapes and a commitment to decentralizing television production, TVTV went to the Republican and Democratic National Conventions of 1972. In producing *Four More Years* (1972), they immersed themselves in the goings-on, interviewing young Republicans and protesters on and off the convention floor. Without exclusive access to candidates, TVTV talked to "ordinary" people. TVTV's style was ironic, reflexive, and with little to no attention put on narration. This made for compelling programming and TVTV was commissioned to make more documentaries for public television. Again, new technologies made it possible to broadcast the type of high quality, half-inch videos TVTV produced. They had access to color video cameras and stock, editing systems, and a way of synching sound and video. Soon other video documentarians were producing with these new technologies.

Guerilla television producers mixed the individualism of the mobile video documentarian with a "mystical futurist metaphysics" (Mellencamp 1990, 199). The desired result would be "global salvation via access, circumventing institutions and going directly to individuals of conscience" (Mellencamp 1990, 199). TVTV member Michael Shamberg believed, "Cybernetic guerilla warfare means re-structuring communication channels, not capturing existing ones" (1971, 29). Guerilla television, "aimed at fighting analogue broadcasting with analogue videocassettes, yet it employs cybernetics and the language and concepts of computing (radical software) and develops a critique of broadcasting's features now common in commentaries on the digital ecology" (Merrin 2012, 106). Shamberg used terms like "broadband," "wired nation," and "pipeline" to reference a "personal and public access video data bank." In this "national knowledge grid system" there would be "grassroots television producers" (Shamberg 1971, 36, 95). In this way, Shamberg described a system not unlike the internet and YouTube. In a 2009 interview, Shamberg defends his 1971 vision:

> I think you need to look no further than iPod apps, Facebook, and Twitter to see that new media forms, like life forms, keep springing up organically. The great thing is that, like Guerilla TV, the corporations can't control it.

30   A. FISH

> What I saw correctly is that we were democratizing the means of production. What I didn't see was that you also had to democratize the means of distribution. I should have invented YouTube but there was no technology even to suggest it. (Merrin 2012, 109–110)

Though simplistic in its reading of power, "*Guerilla Television* is the seminal text of the user-generated-content revolution" (Merrin 2012, 110). Emphasis on feedback, democratic development, amateur production, and creative empowerment, continue into the later video and internet eras, for both activist and commercial video projects. While social liberal concerns were absent from the production discourses of amateur producers in the 1950s, social liberalism mixed with a discourse of technologically aided empowerment in the 1970s.

TVTV was in the movement of guerilla television that sought to use video technology to empower users to speak back to power. Others, like People's Video Theatre, made propaganda that invited viewers to "speak back to the news" and "become part of the news" (Shamberg 1971). Ant Farm and Videofreex carried a pronounced version of the guerilla television technological discourse centered on a belief in "liberation via the democratic pluralism of television" (Mellencamp 1990, 200). Marked by a denial of hierarchy, all of these groups eschewed celebrity by using shared pseudo-anonymity; as they wrote, "Ant Farm accepts only worker ants, and by regulation, no queen ant or leader ant is admitted" (Mellencamp 1990, 202).

Formed from a counterculture of young, middle-class, affluent, predominantly white, well educated people, guerilla television was not a revolutionary movement demographically or ideologically. Despite this homogeneity, the guerilla television producers drew their inspiration from socialism, anarchism, environmentalism, feminism, sexual liberation, and localism (Mellencamp 1990, 203). They were moved by the creations and theories of Marshall McLuhan, Buckminster Fuller, and John Cage—as well as chemical consciousness scholar Timothy Leary. Walter Benjamin's "Art in the Age of Mechanical Reproduction," first published in 1936 and translated into English in 1968, discussed access to information infrastructure as fundamental as access to water, gas, and electricity. Hannah Arendt brought Benjamin's theories to *New Yorker* readers a year later where it may have been read by guerilla television producers. In 1969, the Museum of Modern Art presented, *The Machine as Seen at the End of the Mechanical Age*, which put forth the argument that electronic and chemical media were now capable of simulating the

HISTORIES OF VIDEO POWER 31

human mind. Roland Barthes advanced the idea that meaning is co-created by texts and readers. Active, participatory audiences were not only a cause for media freaks, but also theorists. In this way, the pursuit of liberation through technology was not only a countercultural but also a theoretical quest.

In the spirit of the Soviet agitprop trains, guerilla television community Ant Farm traveled the USA proselytizing their video gospel in a "customized media van with antennae, silver dome, TV window, inflatable shower stall, kitchen, ... portapak and video playback system" (Mellencamp 1990, 201). Ant Farm produced some of the most memorable video installations and happenings of this era such as the Media Burn (which is featured on the cover of this book) in which they set on fire dozens of stacked televisions before driving a jet-powered car through the lot. The whole iconoclastic spectacle was filmed.

Guerilla television producers and countercultural computer researchers shared a language of "data," "software," "network," and "cybernetics." Both held a digital discourse that technologies would be empowering for self if not also society. Such countercultural computing centers included Douglas Engelbart's Augmentation Research Center (ARC) at the Stanford Research Institute (SRI), which worked on human and computer interaction. SRI was affiliated with Xerox's Palo Alto Research Center (PARC), the *People's Computer Company*, and the Homebrew Computer Club. Like the counterculture around them, these computing centers looked at how technology could provide the tools for individual transformation. The cybernetic video theories of the guerilla television producers were supported by the work of Stewart Brand, the editor of the *Whole Earth Catalogue*, and his work straddling both SRI and the counterculture between 1968 and 1972. Brand endeavored to bring together the ideals of counterhegemony, individualism, reflexivity, and interactivity that existed in the computing industry, the counterculture, and guerilla television. He introduced technologists like Bill English, inventor of the first computer mouse, Engelbart, the inventor of the Windows interface, and Dave Evans, member of ARC, to hippie parties, communes, and happenings in Mexico and the forests around Santa Barbara. Steve Durkee of the psychedelic video art, installation, and happening troupe, The Company of Us (USCO), visited the ARC offices. Media communities like USCO and media institutions like the Portola Institute where Brand worked were nodes around which these distinct tribes circulated (Turner 2006, Chap. 4).

32   A. FISH

In addition to his role as editor of the *Whole Earth Catalogue*, Brand was also a television guerilla. In 1968, he was hired by Evans to be a videographer for the "Mother of all Demos." In San Francisco, in December of that year, at the Computer Society's Fall Joint Computer Conference, Engelbart demoed the NLS system (oN-Line System). Brand filmed Engelbart, a projected computer screen behind him, as he worked through various computer tasks with a mouse and keyboard. This was the first time this now commonplace interface was performed in public and it was filmed on video by Brand and linked via telephone lines and microwave systems to a terminal at SRI (Turner 2006, Chap. 4). This was the beginning of individualized or "personal" computing and it was performed within a feedback system made possible by video and "video data banks." Brand claimed it was just a "gig," but the NLS system, the *Whole Earth Catalog*, Raindancer's McLuhanism, and the cybernetics underlying both guerilla television and computing cultures, linked together an emphasis on feedback, technology, and community. All of these systems strove to bring together individuals through technology while preserving individuality. In this way, the concerns of the cybernetic counterculture circulating around Stanford's SRI and Brand were echoed in the works and concepts of guerilla television.

Into the mid-1970s, Brand ignored the profit potentials of Silicon Valley, focusing instead on cybernetics, particularly the work of Gregory Bateson, and hoped to develop technologically sustainable farms and communities. Like the guerilla television communes, the Ant Farm, and others, Brand sought to use technology to bring people back to the land. By the early 1980s, however, Brand had abandoned the countercultural communal practices but retained the technology discourse, shifting to the computer industry and in particular, personal computing, as the repository of the values and capacities for individual liberation. Eventually, the ideology of the video guerillas too would shift from the countercultural to the corporate. Social liberalism took a back seat as the market fundamentalism and its emphasis on individualism were to triumph in the 1980s and 1990s.

Like computers, the guerilla video of the late 1960s and 1970s was soon to enter the mainstream. Guerilla television methods of handheld videography, man-on-the-street interviews, and collectivized production were quickly appropriated by a television industry not wanting to be left behind. First published for public television and later edited into an hour-long pro-

HISTORIES OF VIDEO POWER 33

gram for the American Broadcasting Company (ABC), *The Police Tapes* (1976), by Alan and Susan Raymond, took an insider's perspective on urban crime in the South Bronx, foreshadowing the spate of reality television and cop dramas that were to follow in the decades to come (Boyle 1992, 71). When not aping the style, the industry hired the personnel. TVTV's Michael Shamberg became a successful film producer, *The Police Tapes* was fictionalized as the *Hill Street Blues*, and other guerilla television producers worked for NBC's *Today Show* and *The Nightly News* (Boyle 1992, 72).

In the 1970s, New York City, cable television and portable half-inch video arrived almost concurrently. In Chicago, however, cable arrived late and so video activists had time to experiment with content instead of new forms of broadcast. In 1975, the independently produced *It's a Living* aired on WTTW. Tom Weinberg, formerly of TVTV, and other guerilla television veterans, produced this video that documented the voices of the working classes—a secretary, model, parking lot worker, among others. Studs Terkel narrated the six portrayals, and explained what he hoped would be the positive impact of the videos:

> "Remember, you said, 'What happens to people who are in [Terkel's] oral history books?' Remember that their relationship to their friends has altered and they become sort of celebrities in a way ... it occurred to me that's bad: But is it? Suppose two hundred million people were photographed ... I mean, suppose they were voluntarily in something, then all two hundred million would say, 'that's me. I am recognized,' you see? So then there is no celebrity. I'd like that. That'd be kinda good". (Chapman 2012, 45)

By empowering people through being seen, *It's a Living* attempted to create a public sphere of self-representation. Not the transformation of "media America" and its information infrastructure, but these more humble and local acts became the legacy of the guerilla television producers of the 1970s.

The political potential of video was discovered in the mid-1960s. Street tapes and video collectives with a distinct look drew from cybernetics, McLuhan, and individual empowerment. Pseudo-anonymous collectives like TVTV, Ant Farm, Videofreex and others were informed by and helped to propel the countercultural movement with their emphasis on interactivity, two-way communication, and praxis. Programs like *Four More Years* (TVTV 1972), *Mayday Realtime* (Cort and Ratcliff 1971), *Now* (Teasdale and Cort 1969), as well as the instance of Stuart Brand filming the 1968

34   A. FISH

"Mother of all Demos" with Engelbart, exhibit the cybernetic and participatory ethos of the counterculture. The event concluding this utopian moment was Media Burn, the explosive stunt of driving the jet car into the tower of exploding TVs (Ant Farm 1975).

In these early instances, video was the medium that delivered the message of empowerment. The guerilla television producers propagated through their practices a narrative of individual enfranchisement and alternative information storage and distribution. Produced without hierarchical organization, their handheld videos, complete with scan lines and choppy editing, coded an aesthetic of a movement. The politics tended to be post-political: the point was the transformation of the medium or of an individual's consciousness through new practices—not the transformation of society through radical content. While social liberal concerns were absent from the production ideologies of amateur producers in the 1950s, social liberalism mixed with a technological discourse of technologically aided empowerment in the 1970s. However, the desire for socially liberal progressive change met the early stages of individualism attendant with the later phase of neoliberalism.

As the decade continued and the dreams of social change gave way to business models, aesthetic innovation replaced experimental practices as the driving force of innovation. A more nuanced approach to video production was exhibited in the following videos and series: *It's a Living* (WTTW, Terkel 1975), *Image Union* (WTTW 1978, Weinberg [formerly of TVTV]), and *The Police Tapes* (Alan and Susan Raymond 1976). *Image Union* is a TV series that showcases independent film and video on WTTW-Chicago. It was created by Tom Weinberg in 1978, and he produced it until 1988. It is still on the air occasionally, although it is no longer the important force in the Chicago community it once was.

The first episode of *Image Union* aired on November 14, 1978. It was an hour-long show, broadcast 52 weeks per year in prime time. It aired at 10:00 p.m. Saturday nights to catch the pre-*Saturday Night Live* crowd, which was seen as the natural audience for the program. *Image Union* featured video and film, in every conceivable genre: documentary, animation, narrative, image processing, and other experimental forms. About half of the programs were theme shows, such as "working people," "Chicago labor history," "international women's day," "music," or "animation." The other half was a potpourri of styles and content, only limited by the producers' vision of what makes good TV. During the 1980s, it was one of the most popular shows on WTTW, reaching about

150,000 people per episode. Many now-established videomakers, filmmakers, and artists had early appearances on *Image Union*, including Jim Belushi, Melissa Leo, Joe Mantegna, and many more (Chapman 2015). A hybridization of professionalism and grassroots political content marks this transitional phase.

After Weinberg left *Image Union*, he created and produced a show called *THE 90's*, which was broadcast nationally on the Public Broadcasting Service (PBS) from 1989–1992. The show was a national expansion of the format of *Image Union*, being comprised of work by independent producers from around the world, some who worked under contract for *THE 90's*, and some who just sent in their work for consideration. The historical significance of *THE 90's* was acknowledged by the *Save America's Treasures* program of the National Endowment for the Humanities, which supported the preservation and digitization of the entire collection of shows and camera original materials (Chapman 2015). This example of early crowdsourcing exhibits the continuing legacy of amateur and activist involvement in the professionalization of video.

The last years of this period were marked by a return to the politics of content not just form. In the decade that followed, new technologies emerged on the market and the cycle that began in technological discourse and ends in a coopted pragmatism refreshes anew.

SATELLITE RESISTANCE AND VIDEO CONTAINMENT IN THE 1980s AND 1990s

By mixing the slick sophistication of music video style with the guerilla-like coverage of demonstrations, by juxtaposing the high-end quality of broadcast Betacam with the low-tech grit of home video camcorders, they have appropriated the full range of production tools and aesthetics and effectively rendered distinctions between low- and high-tech documentary video obsolete, further democratizing the medium and opening it up for creative and political possibilities. (Boyle 1992, 77)

Speaking in 1961, a few years after the first satellite launched, US President John F. Kennedy said that with the new communication technology of satellite "public interest objectives [would] be given the highest priority" (Pierce 2003, 110). Built upon the foundation of federally subsidized science and technology as well as amateur homemade receiving dishes, satellite was an act of social construction that involved both

36   A. FISH

professionals and amateurs. In 1962, the first commercial satellite capable of delivering television developed from a partnership between the National Aeronautics and Space Administration (NASA) and AT&T. Also that year, the Communications Satellite Act led to the creation of the Communication Satellite Corporation or Comsat. Its task as a private corporation was to privatize the new satellite system (Pierce 2003, 112–113). By the 1980s, thousands were making "large home-brew wood and wire mesh backyard dishes" so as to be able to pirate content from satellites broadcasting unscrambled content. The trade press was impressed with their fortitude saying that homemade dish owners were "a public so committed to television but so impatient with its progress that it took things into its own hands" (ibid.). At the same time, these "do it yourself" (DIY) dish-makers, or "signal pirates" as the satellite companies called them, were recipients of the "biggest electronic free lunch in history." This was a short-lived moment of openness, user-innovation, and public participation that the satellite companies soon closed through signal scrambling designed to lock users into inactive consumers. In essence, "The deregulated telecommunications environment of the late 1980s, combined with the exceptionally high capital requirements of adapting direct-broadcast satellite (DBS) technology for a mass consumer market, resulted in an oligopolistic industry that was interested in programming only as a commodity form" (Pierce 2003, 114). Nevertheless, in the early 1980s, there were so many satellites in orbit, and so many dishes on the ground, that satellite space/time was relatively affordable for media activists to rent.

In the 1980s, satellite space/time was rented by media artists and activists. For example, media artists and activists enacted "space bridges" which connected, both metaphorically and actually, Soviet bloc countries and the West. A group of activists known as the Nicaragua Network initiated "Project Satellite" in 1989 in order to counteract what they perceived as propaganda (Pierce 2003). According to US President Reagan, the Nicaraguan contras were "freedom fighters," which many activists thought was completely wrong. The result was a live call-in show in Managua with the Nicaraguan President, Daniel Ortega, that was broadcast using two satellites, one above North America, the other over Latin America. Viewers called in and asked Ortega questions directly, thereby routing around the corporate media blockade. Downlinking sites were established throughout the USA so universities, private households, and public access stations could broadcast the program.

HISTORIES OF VIDEO POWER **37**

While satellite space/time was becoming leasable, camcorders were proliferating. In 1985, camcorders were in the hands of approximately 500,000 Americans. Ten years later, 16 million Americans had camcorders. With the least-expensive camcorders in 1995 selling for $500, the gear was available to many. Camcorder ownership was surprisingly well distributed across economic classes, with 18% of all income levels owning a device. Panasonic, JVC, and other electronics manufacturers sold camcorders, but, as in the 1970s, it was the Japanese company Sony that helped to popularize the devices. Sony had no ties to US technology and television industries and made a camcorder that was not piracy-proof like the technologies sold by American companies CBS (Columbia Broadcasting System) and RCA (Radio Corporation of America). For these American companies, the camcorder was a mere extension of television. As media studies scholar Laurie Ouellette wrote, "Since television has been naturalized as beyond the realm of ordinary producers [for this reason], it was unlikely that participatory TV would be considered a viable marketing theme" (1995b, 34). For the Japanese companies, the camcorder was an open tool for creation. Sony's camcorder was a mobile tool, not merely a domestic technology. Seeking to capitalize on this mobile utility in a safe manner, commercial television programs sought to use the camera's potential, while finding ways to domesticate it. During the same time, social liberal activists and their technological discourse framed the camcorder and accessible satellites as political accessories.

Videotapes shot on amateur equipment can be transmitted by satellite without major problems. In the late 1980s and early 1990s, with reasonable funds, and the aid of satellites, video activists could make their content available to millions of homes without the need of approval from cable networks. Using a satellite to distribute activist video required a number of steps. First, one needed to rent a transponder, which is a transmitter and receiver, capable of receiving and transmitting satellite signals. Transponders situated on satellites owned and operated by multinational corporations could be rented from $250 to $800 (in 1993) per hour—a price not outside even the limited budgets of video activists in the late 1980s. Second, the video activists rented "uplinking" services that sent their signal to the rented transponder. Third, the program detailing what content and what time the downlink from the satellite would be available was advertised in national newspapers. Dish owners, both private and institutional like universities, could tune their dishes to the transponder, download the content at the right

38   A. FISH

time, store it, and rebroadcast it at their discretion. Including production costs, the entire operation of making satellite content available cost around $2000 (Ouellette 1995a, 180). Deep Dish TV received a grant to implement this strategy to deliver video content resisting the Persian Gulf War (Lucas and Wallner 1993, 170). To acquire this content, they solicited video from a network of amateur, politically active camcorder producers.

American troops and aircraft carriers began to congregate in the Persian Gulf in August of 1990. Video activists affiliated with Paper Tiger TV and Deep Dish TV, Martin Lucas, Marcus Wallner, and others, planned to argue against what they considered a war of aggression for oil that both the Bush administration and mainstream media thought inevitable. Eventually, the Gulf Project connected satellites, activist organizers, journalists, public television access stations, amateur and independent video producers, and engaged viewers to mount a critique of the 1990–1991 Persian Gulf War. Deep Dish received over 1000 pieces of video content and aired the content from over 100 producers. Deep Dish was an innovator in participatory television, engaging an audience to "speak for itself" and helping local stations to organize "wraparound" shows as well as call-in programs (Halleck 2002; Ouellette 1995a, 181). As many as 300 public access television stations and 5000 home satellite dish owners downlinked the programming for local broadcasting. Tapes were submitted in every format, from VHS and 8mm film, and converted to three-quarter-inch videotapes. Deep Dish did their own producing, interviewing activists on Hi-8 cameras. This format was inclusive, enabling amateurs who might be able to contribute a 5–10-minute piece but could not produce an entire 28-minute segment. Eventually, over 30 PBS stations aired the Gulf Crisis TV Project, potentially being viewed by as much as 40% of the PBS audience.

Using the contributions of proto-citizen video journalists, four programs in the first year's series included *War, Oil, and Power*, a critique of the connections between the US military and petro-energy. *Operation Dissidence* analyzed how the G.H.W. Bush administration, along with the mainstream media, had made the case for war in Iraq. *Bring the Troops Home Now!* gave audiences a look at anti-war protests emerging within the military. *Out of the Sandtrap* exhibited how the Cold War provided a framework for the Persian Gulf War. The four half-hour programs were dynamically edited with collision juxtapositions and other avant-garde tricks. The numerous formats, various qualities, and hybrid genres, added

HISTORIES OF VIDEO POWER   39

to the energetic and unrefined quality of the programming. These were *America's Angriest Home Videos*, according to one of the programming's organizers, Dee Dee Halleck (Lucas and Wallner 1993, 186). The programs were "tremendously successful" in provoking critical thought on the war, declared cultural critic Douglas Rushkoff (1996, 222). The second season consisted of six hard-hitting episodes. In their expansion, they hired a diverse staff of Arab, Asian, and African Americans. *News World Order* analyzed media complicity in drumming for war. *Lines in the Sand* studied the history of US and European policy in the Middle East. *War on the Homefront* revealed the economic benefits (for some) of war. *Manufacturing the Enemy* exposed the racism experienced by Arab Americans. *Veterans for Peace* was a live call-in program with Boston-based veterans. *Just Say No!* showed military personal resisting militarization. But the second season did not have the impact of the first primarily because Philadelphia's WYBE dropped the program. The Federal Communications Commission (FCC) had challenged WYBE's license, claiming it was jamming an FM radio station. This was in February 1991 and the US air bombardment was in full swing. WYBE may have self-censored the Gulf Crisis TV Project to avoid arousing the ire of the FCC (Lucas and Wallner 1993).

Regardless, the Gulf Crisis TV Project was a "watershed event in the history of community television: never before had so many activist products been assembled on such a short notice over such a wide area. Never before had the final product been edited so quickly and distributed so broadly; never before had public response been so widespread and favorable" (Pierce 2003, 117). By the early 1990s, the proliferation of video cameras and the accessibility of satellite transponder time made for a dynamic socio-technical opportunity for activist video power. Along with this was a progressive politics of social liberalism and digital discourse about empowerment through video cameras and satellites.

While Deep Dish TV encouraged to empower amateur and independent camcorder producers to challenge mainstream media and militarization, ABC and NBC were claiming that camcorders were tools for idiotic jokes, self-surveillance, and other light amusement to be shown on *America's Funniest Home Videos (AFHV)* (ABC) and *I Witness Video* (NBC). Beginning in the early 1990s, a number of prime-time programs were based on the exhibition of amateur video content on television. While it is easy to dismiss this practice as a gimmick, or worse, an exploitation of free labor, there is no denying that at least in theory it posed a significant challenge to professional labor and, by extension, capitalist

40   A. FISH

media industries. This is one of the many contradictions of capitalism, the very productivity of networks, markets, and technology makes it possible for the materialization of a technology that tests capitalism itself. In the 1990s, commercial television actively solicited camcorder content, signifying an "end to marginalization of amateur media and the birth of a true television democracy" (Ouellette 1995b, 33). Guerilla television of the 1970s too attempted to change the system from the inside.

AFHV began in 1989 on ABC and continues to base part of its programming on ludic family videos. But in order to get the right kind of content, viewers needed to be trained to value their camcorders and the videos they produced in a way favorable to ABC. The network encouraged camcorder manufacturers to distribute video cameras to affiliate stations. Host Bob Saget regularly extolled the virtues of owning a camcorder, producing regular tips and tricks on how to produce television-ready programming. Despite these efforts, little viewer-generated content constituted the bulk of what was screened on *AFHV*, with as little as seven minutes shown. *AFHV* is viewer-created content post-produced with a strong hand, heavily structured by editors and writers, mere seconds long, remixed with sound tracks and sound effects, and framed by a host in front of a live studio audience. With so little user-generated content, *AFHV* does little to challenge the aesthetic regimes of television. As Ouellette says, "The final product does not present us with an example of participatory television but rather with a ritualistic formula that upholds the power and authority of commercial television" (1995b, 36).

News programs also celebrated the camcorder. *Revolution in a Box* was a 1989 ABC news program in which host Ted Koppel intoned:

> Television used to be the exclusive province of government and enormously wealthy corporations. They decided what you saw and when. Not anymore. Television has fallen into the hands of the people they haven't quite mastered it, but they will. The technology is becoming more affordable and accessible. A form of television democracy is sweeping the world, and like other forms of democracy that have preceded it, its consequences are likely to be beyond our imagination. (Ouellette 1995b)

Despite the political potential suggested by Koppel, and the celebration of video in social movements in the African National Congress and the Solidarity movement in Poland shown in *Revolution in a Box*, Americans were framed as video hobbyists who might accidentally but never intentionally capture important events on video. News departments developed guidelines for accepting this fortuitous footage. The Cable News Network (CNN) established structures for dealing with the video materials. By 1990, "home video was a major part" of CNN who actively sought user-generated content. They established a hotline and traded shirts, mugs, and money for the video material (Ouellette 1995b, 38–39).

When it first began, NBC's *I Witness Video* resisted the alarmist depictions of video-enabled "high-tech snoops." The program claimed to present footage from "the real people behind the news, disasters, criminal activity, family emergencies and an assortment of other incidents by tapping into the vast library created by American home video users" (Ouellette 1995b, 40). In the opening sequence, in front of a wall of televisions depicting speeding cars, shark encounters, and Tiananmen Square protesters in China, host Patrick Van Horn claimed "any revolution puts power in the hands of the people" and continued, "we can all create programming for television" (Ouellette 1995b, 41). Later in the season, he said, "Tonight's stories show that the video revolution is squarely in the hands of the people" (ibid.). To others, this program brazenly disregarded journalistic principles, calling the program a "social planters wart" (ibid.). Journalists for *Newsweek* wrote, "Remember all that talk about a 'video revolution' in which every viewer would become his own producer? Well it's happening but that doesn't mean that networks should abandon the role of gatekeeper" (ibid.).

To its credit, *I Witness Video* did screen a few amateur-produced segments—a family diary on being pregnant, a cross-country drive for a paralyzed boy, and even a segment on video activism in which cruise boat participants document illegal garbage dumping in the sea by the cruise company. Nevertheless, most programming was sensationalistic. In response to the overwhelming negative feedback, NBC relocated the program from its news to its entertainment division. By the middle of the 1993 season, all talk of the revolutionary possibilities of camcorders was dropped, as was the footage from the student movement in China. Now the role of video was not as a tool for raising political consciousness but something more familiar, to "chronicle our lives" and "bring us closer together" (ibid.). In the fall of 1993, NBC made additional changes to *I Witness Video*. The backdrop of the wall of televisions was replaced by a fireplace and library. The youthful Van Horn was replaced by familiar television stalwart, John Forsythe. In this new version, the camcorder was no longer framed as a tool for activism. Camcorders, once dangerous

42   A. FISH

to the status quo in both society and in media production, were now safely domesticated in discourses of accidentalism and sensationalism. Camcorders no longer challenged but rather supported the hegemony.

In the 1970s, video amateurs could revolutionize the system from the inside, regardless of content. In the 1980s, energies shifted to a more pragmatic reformative model that used camcorders and satellites to challenge the aesthetics and content of news. By the early 1990s, a process of cooptation in which the wide distribution of video cameras no longer invited the production of reformist content, but rather video was incorporated into mainstream programming. Early 1990s programs such as *I Witness Video* discuss amateur video in terms of accidental witnessing. Here, agency is gone and with it the political potential of a radical citizen video journalism. Framing amateur video as merely being in the right place at the right time, is an act of "hegemonic containment" that mutes activist potential, making it possible for prime-time television to make sense of amateur camcorder content (Ouellette 1995b, 34).

In the 1980s, the independent television movement in America lost some of its drive. Funding dropped as the novelty of video dissipated for philanthropic art institutes. Independent producers became frustrated and impoverished by the compromises required and the increasing difficulty of reaching large television audiences (Tripp 2012, 10). While producers and funders were becoming disenchanted, mainstream television coopted the handheld, immersive, and intimate style of guerilla television in the making of reality television and mockumentaries. Many guerilla television producers willfully entered the mainstream. By 1987:

> Rather than video politics (video meaning shared precepts, a common politics), video means leisure and industry—video bars, videodrome, video dating, the video column of *Time*, rock video, video movie rental at 'Video Visions' and other equipment, and the circulation of video pornography, the latter a mass subculture, a real paradox. (Mellencamp 1990, 209)

Perhaps it was not an abandonment of social liberal principles but rather a maturing. While the radical potential of 1970s video guerillas may have proven to be an utopian impossibility, and it is certainly true that network television appropriated the style of guerilla television, it is important to remember that the camcorder was produced for mass consumers. Video's activist potential is an unintentional consequence of consumer capitalism. Of the estimated 14 million Americans who owned camcorders by the early 1990s, only a few used

HISTORIES OF VIDEO POWER   43

the tool for activism (Ouellette 1995a, 170). One of the many contradictions of capitalism, video has a simultaneous dual utility as both a tool for activism as well as consumerism. The many applications of video eventually helped the tool leave the hands of the elite and become a tool for resistance.

In the 1980s, video activism transitioned from being demographically dominated by white, educated, middle-class countercultural types to becoming more diverse in terms of gender, race, sexuality, and class (ibid.). In the 1990s, video had transitioned from a revolutionary to a resistance movement:

> Rather than calling this a video revolution, let's simply call it video activism. ... Let's also remember that the camcorder—like the mimeograph machine, the bullhorn, and the photocopier before it—is just one more piece of bourgeois technology that has been pressed into the service of political activism and redefined by its use. Video activists weren't created by the camcorder. They appropriated it. They took it from the entertainment console and turned it into a weapon for change. (ibid.)

Amateurs, hackers, and activists have often been responsible for early innovations of media production and distribution systems. At the same time, they are dependent upon the corporations that produce those very systems. Few people can make a camcorder, magnetic tape for recording, or a satellite. In a theory of resistance instead of revolution, use of these systems and tools does not necessarily denote complicity, but rather the diverse applications of new technologies and the contradictions and slippages within the system of global capitalism.

But while some may consider the 1980s as an era of apathy, cynicism, and cooptation, a closer look at camcorder activism at the end of the decade revealed a progressive moment. Paper Tiger TV and its satellite manifestation Deep Dish TV and their two-season series, the Gulf Crisis TV Project, discussed above, marked one of the most successful projects, bringing amateur and independent video producers to satellite television. The availability of affordable camcorders and the commercial and leasability of satellite time, made the late 1980s open like few other times in American history. And yet, it was not only technology but also human infrastructure—the innovative, frugal, and collaborative energies of many video activists—that made satellites accessible for activists.

The proliferation of video cameras through the 1980s and 1990s meant that no longer were they the tools of an elite, white, counterculture but were being used in diverse communities. Self-representation, a scrappy

44 A. FISH

independent aesthetic, and proto-crowdsourcing of video content, evolved from the widespread use of video cameras. While activists such as the Nicaragua Network, Paper Tiger TV, and Deep Dish TV enjoyed a brief moment of access via satellite to resist the 1991 Persian Gulf War, television networks were also developing ways to corner the market and discourse developing around citizen videographers. While activists struggled to empower amateur and independent camcorder producers to challenge mainstream media and militarization, ABC and NBC in programs like *I Witness Video* and *AFHV* were claiming that camcorders were tools for idiotic jokes, self-surveillance, and other light amusement, not politics.

FLEXIBLE MICROCASTING AND INTERACTIVE TELEVISION IN THE 1990s AND 2000s

Web television in the post-network era appropriated television's tactics for serialization and monetization while using digital distribution to change relationships to production and audiences (Christian 2012, 342). Consider *The Spot*, an internet soap in the television serial format. Much like a text-based *The Real World*, *The Spot* was a series of websites about young adults living together in a beach neighborhood in Los Angeles. Content consisted of photos, texts, and short videos and cost around $100,000 a month after an initial investment of $500,000 from Microsoft and America Online (AOL). Major brands such as Honda, K-Swiss, and Sony flocked to sponsor *The Spot*. Some audience and character interactivity occurred but its serialization made it more a television program than an innovative internet site. It succeeded by being profitable, and its success encouraged others to blend television programming and internet distribution. The rush was on, as broadcasters Paramount, Warner Bros., and Metro-Goldwyn-Mayer (MGM) started interactive divisions, attempting to diversify their offerings into the text-based world of internet entertainment. Far from independent media, Hollywood conglomerates dominated early web television. The internet spurred an historically entrenched fear of uncertainty in the media industries that went back to concerns over competition with radio, cable, and VHS in earlier times. By 1996, there were as many as 60 online soaps. But by 1997, very few existed in this industry of high costs and low returns (Christian 2012, 344–347).

The first lifecasting artist JenniCam (Jennifer Ringley) emerged in 1996, signifying a more adventurous break from television genres. But along with outliers like JenniCam were also moves toward more traditional television-like broadcasting online. The video site Pseudo.com came out in 1998 and featured 50 different programs representing over 200 hours of live entertainment per month. Programs consisted of alternative takes on hip-hop, gaming, music, women's issues, business, and politics. Pseudo.com was founded by Josh Harris, who, along with David Bohrman, was also the CEO. Years later, Harris claimed that Pseudo. com was "the linchpin of a long form piece of conceptual art" (Jardin 2008). Ondi Timenor's (2009) film *We Live in Public* graphically depicts the excesses of Pseudo.com. Political in so far that it addressed the needs of alternative youth; Pseudo.com was also for-profit through innovative product placement and microcasting to specific subcultures.

While Pseudo.com was moderately independent, self-financed by Harris and advertising revenue, others that debuted between 1999 and 2002, like Atom Films, were financed by venture capitalists and Hollywood studios. Most internet networks failed, but comedy and animation had a better chance at success. These successes were bolstered by changes in technology, most importantly Macromedia's Flash software that made it easier to make animation. Heavy.com and Break.com are examples that began in this era and remain competitive today. Comedy works because it could be both advertising-friendly as well as edgy. This enables it to be profitable while securing the desirable young male demographic. "The web has been a great democratizing force in the media landscape, and we figured it was high time somebody put a stop to it," joked Sean Redlitz, head of DotComedy (quoted in Christian 2012, 351). But hits were important and difficult to engineer. When DEN, funded by Dell, Microsoft, and NBC failed in 2000, the netcasting moment too ended. Nevertheless, netcasters continued a tradition that endures today with conservative deviations from television's programmatic strategies mixed with select internet innovation.

The era of streaming video exploded as a viable business option when YouTube became popular in 2005. Internet video was rarely a "complex free-for-all of amateurs, independents, and corporations competing to shape the web into a form of television unrecognized from its network-era past" (Christian 2012, 351). This may describe a period from 2005 to 2009, but soon, through the power of video talent agencies, this era was recolonized by corporate forces so that by today most talent was fully represented by boutique agencies or funded by major software companies

46 A. FISH

and other conglomerates. For internet video entrepreneurs, television was always an object to simultaneously reject and desire.

For example, Oxygen asked their audience to reconsider their television network not as a passive space for consumption but rather as an interactive internet site that democratizes information for everyone. As an internet start-up, Oxygen began in 1998 with venture capital funding of $200 million from Microsoft billionaire Paul Allen and an additional $4.5 from the Markle Foundation, a non-profit "trying to democratize the Internet" (Parks 2004, 145). Through programs like *Oprah Goes Online*, in which Oprah Winfrey and her friend Gail learn to navigate the internet, Oxygen asked viewers to embrace computing through television viewing—not replace it.

In this manner, Oxygen's technological discourse framed consumption as empowering for women. The network hailed women as technology consumers capable of personal as opposed to political transformation. This approach to technological empowerment through consumerism might be described as "corporate feminism: a late capitalist feminism wherein the demand for returns on investments commingles with liberal feminist agendas" (Parks 2004, 146). This approach is generational. Growing up in the late 1960s and 1970s during the days of second-wave feminism and becoming rich in the television industries of the 1980s and 1990s, the discourse of Oxygen executives is a result of "Reagan, Bush, and Clinton administrations' deregulations of the media industries, the growth of family and women's cable television programming, liberal feminist consciousness-raising, nonprofit democratization initiatives, and the emergence of digital technologies" (Parks 2004, 145–147). This mix of social and economic liberalism in the form of digital social entrepreneurialism (Fish and Srinivasan 2012; Sandoval 2013) is indicative of the internet/television convergence companies that follow.

DEN started in 1998 and was one of the first internet video companies. Like Pseudo.com, its 30 interactive episodes focused exclusively on youth. East Los Angeles high school Latinos, punk rockers and their alternative clubs, and science fiction crime-fighting Asians were characters in programs that explored gangs, homosexuality, eating disorders, high school violence such as hate crimes, and other issues not addressed by the major television networks. As can be expected, the short programs were low-resolution, made as they were for low-bandwidth (56 k modem) viewers. A mix of "MTV, a record and video store, QVC, and an entertainment network," as stated by one critic. Or, according to one proud executive, DEN was "capitalism with a social conscience" (Parks 2004, 150–151). Like Oxygen, DEN "combined practices of direct marketing with the language of a digital counterculture to try to turn a profit and make a social impact" (ibid.). While guerilla television producers of the 1970s too mingled countercultural clout with video production for a young audience, they did not integrate concerns for profit into their manifestos. Seamlessly melding social and economic liberalism with digital discourse was a tactic of proponents of the "new economy" from this time.

The internet was central to how DEN saw itself and the service they provided. DEN worked with the presumption that they were serving a digitally savvy generation who preferred the internet to television. Their mission was to be a "hip alternative and replacement to the passive, brain-killing experience of watching network and cable television." Yet this direct marketing to alternative youth was not so much about creating a "countercultural space" as it was about making profit. DEN sold its lucrative though by-and-large non-existent countercultural capital to brands such as Pepsi, Blockbuster, Microsoft, Ford, and Penzoil, whose ads were placed within and between the episodes. Despite these sponsorship deals and a $7 million investment by NBC two months earlier, on May 2000, DEN folded and filed for bankruptcy. The lavish spending on salaries and parties, which were part of the excessive culture of the dotcom era, may have contributed to the lack of solvency. Unlike other dotcom companies, however, DEN had a social mission but not one powerful enough to spend frugally toward their political goal (Parks 2004).

Throughout DEN's brief and extreme history, it identified with the internet and positioned itself against television. This "anti-television rhetoric" ignores the intertwining stylistics and industries of television and internet video (Parks 2004, 151). The way DEN and Oxygen position their video offerings as anti-television, do not show that television and the internet are separate systems, difficult if not impossible to converge, but rather that the terms of convergence itself are contested. Convergence is a struggle over meaning more than a battle over who controls the evolution of technology.

DEN, Oxygen, and Pseudo.com are examples of "flexible microcasting"—niche, individualized, or personalized television that has more to do with making a profit than empowering viewers (Parks 2004, 135). The industries practicing flexible microcasting promise personalization, public participation, and social mobility (Parks 2004, 137). In order to

48 A. FISH

brand and advertise the joys of flexible microcasting in the era of internet convergence, television industries cast television viewers as passive and computer users as active. In this calculation, television is a "feminized and messy form that can be enveloped, reordered, and reactivated by masculine computer technologies" (Parks 2004, 141). Contrast this to the internet and computer user who is masculine, in control, and has authority. "The personalization of TV is ultimately about developing narrowly defined yet infinitely flexible content that commodifies layers of individual identity, desire, taste, and preference" (Parks 2004, 135). Media theorist Lisa Parks developed the theory of flexible microcasting previous to the era of social media, big data, and social analytics. Her critique can be seen as part of a lineage skeptical of claims by data-driven industries that greater data will result in increased "personalization" and customer satisfaction. Instead, Parks and others see personalization as the adaptability of capitalism to transform ever more subtle forms of human creativity into instances of accumulation.

While internet networks promised more personalized television content, software companies like Microsoft promised to improve television through limited interactivity. In 1971, the RAND Corporation issued a report on cable television, clearly skeptical of its potential for interactivity, stating: "as is often the case with emerging technologies … the promise of two-way service on cable has at times been oversold" (Boddy 2004, 114). Regardless of this warning, Time Warner released the failed Qube system in Columbus, Ohio, in 1977. Wedding the interactivity of the internet and the passive spectatorism of television has long been a goal but never an achievement for major media conglomerates. ABC-Disney pumped $100 million into go.com, an online portal for their content, before shutting it down. Microsoft failed to converge MSNBC and AOL as well as develop a successful set-top box for Microsoft's interactive television software. Bill Gates admitted as much, writing, "As we proceeded, there was a slow realization that the costs were higher and the customer benefits lower than we had all assumed they would be. Interactive television wasn't coming together as soon as we expected or in the way we expected" (ibid.). Undeterred, in 1997, Microsoft paid $425 million for WebTV, a start-up founded two years earlier by former Apple employees. Microsoft's WebTV provided customized stock reports, program guides, scheduling alerts, interactive quiz shows, and web links, but the end was near. Despite conveniently offering a service that unified television viewing and internet

HISTORIES OF VIDEO POWER 49

browsing in the same apparatus, subscriptions stalled at one million users. CNET wrote, "WebTV transition has been a sometimes farcical exercise fraught with unclear direction, shameless politics and technological blunders that have already cost both companies untold sums in lost opportunity—if not their assured leadership of the entire interactive TV industry" (Boddy 2004, 115). In March 2001, WebTV was relocated from Silicon Valley to Microsoft Headquarters in Redmond, WA. It was dissolved in what tech journalists called a "decent burial" and its software was merged with a two-tuner personal video recorder that worked within a DirecTV set-top box. This new system, Ultimate TV, was like TiVo, enabling viewers to record, pause, and rewind programming (Boddy 2004, 117). With Ultimate TV, Microsoft again tried the interactive television market.

At an electronics trade fair in January 2001, Bill Gates introduced both Ultimate TV and Xbox. Interactive television, along with handheld computers, cellular phones, and video games consoles were going to be responsible for Microsoft's future growth. In the late 1990s, the personal computing business was slowing down. If Microsoft was to continue its pace of growth, it needed new products to sell. Tech journalists were skeptical, one wrote, "This will be the first indicator of whether this market is real or that there's nothing here and we need to move on. It's a major litmus test for this market genre" (Boddy 2004, 118). Suddenly, during this period of dotcom hysteria, in which the internet was going to replace and revolutionize television, television continued to be an important cultural form toward which internet companies aspired.

Ultimate TV differed from WebTV in substantial ways important for an understanding of what defined participatory versus interactive television. Consider former Microsoft CEO Steve Ballmer's differentiation. For Ballmer, WebTV lets "you get Internet on TV, as opposed to enhancing the TV experience ... Ultimate TV ... is much more about enhancing the way you watch TV, recording shows, pausing. I'm bullish on that" (ibid.). Following Ballmer's bullishness, advertisements for Ultimate TV emphasized the time-shifting functionality, failing to even mention its utility for accessing email or the internet. Ads stressed Ultimate TV as integrated into domestic space: a housewife watching recordings of soap operas, a man pausing a viewing to check a baby, and so on. Like amateur film cameras in the 1950s and camcorders in the 1990s, more politically rewarding applications of participatory media were not accentuated in the Ultimate TV ads.

50 A. FISH

Rather, these tools for media participation were situated as leisure toys for the home. On the one hand, WebTV was designed to appeal to sophisticated computer users who wanted internet participation paired with television viewing. Ultimate TV, on the other hand, provided interactive television time shifting. WebTV invited users into new forms of participatory television, while Ultimate TV provided for a more passive lean-back experience. Ultimate TV attracted but 50,000 subscribers, a small number resulting from the service only being available on DirecTV. Eventually, News Corp. acquired DirecTV and in exchange for being a preferred supplier of interactive TV software for DirecTV, Microsoft would supply News Corp. with $3 billion and transfer Ultimate TV to News Corp.'s satellite service. By 2003, Ultimate TV had been taken off the market despite having cost Microsoft $1.5 billion in its merger with WebTV.

Television has always been a convergent cultural form. First as a hybridization of radio and film, now as a mixing of television and the internet. On the one hand, when the major networks and software companies introduce convergence, they do so in such a manner that they can continue to monopolize the new hybridized form of television. On the other hand, when networks like Oxygen and DEN do so, they discuss convergence as empowering diverse communities such as gender and racial minorities. These networks reveal a fact that convergence, as well as access to the means of production, are unequally distributed. New technologies and newer hybridities of existing technologies can provide creative openings in otherwise closed systems that may fail or eventually give way to more closed, exclusive, and professionalized systems.

Similar hopes and expectations that had played out in earlier times with the development of new capture and broadcast technologies played out with the development of internet video. Internet video matured as broadband speeds increased, storage capacities improved, amateur cameras became cheaper and easier to use, and cultures of consumption, already fragmented by years of cable channel proliferation, increasingly watched online video. A rhetoric similar to that heard in the 1970s and the days of guerilla television developed along with these shifts. As one scholar said, "Many claims for the liberatory power of online video have rivaled the heady utopian predictions made on behalf of the early World Wide Web" (Tripp 2012, 10). Again, a new platform was going to replace television that was dominated by entrenched elites. Both activists and independent video entrepreneurs rushed into the space of the dotcom bubble. A succession of strategies for success emerged: text-based soaps, netcasting, internet-based networks, and streaming video. Web television such as lonelygirl16, Atom Films, Break.com, and Pseudo.com emphasized their grounding in digital media while maintaining continuity with television. But despite appropriating some elements from the internet, sites like DEN, Pseudo.com, and *The Spot*, repurposed much of the aesthetic, serialization, and profit-producing strategies from television. Emphasizing diverse programming for niche audiences, flexible microcasting looked like social liberal activism. But in the form of economic liberalism it was about personalization for profit. Despite technological discursive claims about empowering a new breed of small business, video entrepreneurship in this era was dominated by key software companies who attempted to corner this new market.

TOWARD TERMINAL VIDEO

Not only were the media towers going to topple and the individuals going to have their say, but the realms of art and society were to lose their boundaries—everyone would be a producer; everyone would control information flows. Video's arrival came to symbolize this potential redefinition of the system. It has inevitably disappointed those expectations. (Sturken 1990)

When film cameras were first available to consumers in the 1950s, they were marketed in a manner that differentiated lower classes as amateur and upper classes as aspirational professionals. The lower-income group was encouraged to purchase the lower-fidelity 8mm film cameras with less professional features and the upper classes were invited to buy the higher-fidelity 16mm cameras with faux-professional features. Upper-class 16mm users were subject to a type of predigital digital discourse wherein new technologies were going to empower users with the capacity to ascend to professional ranks. This was a ruse, however, as neither lower nor upper classes were encouraged to really engage with potential film production, as the standard for professional television and cinema directors was 35mm film stock, with projector-ready aspect ratios. In this way, a generation of amateur filmmakers did not consider the political potentials of film production. While economic liberalism existed in the freedom to consume, social liberalism had not yet awoken to the political powers of moving image production to document injustice.

In the 1970s, moving image production shifted from being a hobby to being an art and political intervention. The reasons for this shift are both

52 A. FISH

technological and cultural. The arrival of video technology meant users now had a format that was less expensive and a more consumer-friendly means of moving image production. Video can be reused and viewed immediately, film cannot be recycled and requires costly processing. Video is a tool for immediate reflection, revisiting, and feedback. These technical possibilities were linked to new cultural values. With internal resistance in the form of domestic social justice movements and external conflicts in Southeast Asia, a new generation called upon leaders to look critically at a nation's history of racism, sexism, environmental plunder, and wars of aggression. Critical examination was not relegated to external forces but turned inward with the values placed on self-realization and tactics associated with Eastern mysticism, psychedelic spirituality, and hedonism. The artist hippies of this period adopted the video camera as both a technology to document their world and as a tool with which to reflexively work on their consciousness. If the reason amateur film in the 1950s is theoretically significant is because of how access to production delineates on lines of class, then video production of the 1960s is marked by the origination of the media democratization discourse. In the 1950s, the upper classes were empowered by a technological discourse that said that with the new 16mm cameras they should aspire to professional productivity despite such offers being technically unfeasible. In the 1960s, the technological discourse claimed that with video technology, all viewers could become producers and overturn the hegemonic domination of television by elite cultures of media production.

In the early 1990s, two narratives unfolded, one of citizen video activists producing political content and renting satellite space/time in order to distribute it and resist the Iraq War. The second story follows mainstream television networks as they frame and incorporate citizen-produced video into their programming and in the process enact a form of "hegemonic containment" (Ouellette 1995b). These divergent pathways taken by video in the early 1990s encapsulate the tensions that appear throughout the history of video. At the onset, new technologies create a moment of openness that invigorates social liberal activism while simultaneously (and temporarily) disrupting entrenched media business models. The technology discourse of empowerment is strong in this early phase. As made evident in the previous section on the 1970s, restabilization occurs and traditional business concerns dominate both as activists move on to other projects and the subaltern practices and content are incorporated into the hegemony.

What media theorist Marita Sturken writes above could have been uttered in 1970, 1995, or 2005 at the beginning of Web 2.0. The idea will likely not lose its potency in the future. Accompanying technological change is often breathless euphoria about utopian potential.

"The computer actually is much closer to what *Radical Software* was about than what's become of the video medium," said *Radical Software* editor Beryl Korot (Tripp 2012, 10). While the guerilla television producers prophesied the internet in the pages of their journal *Radical Software* and in their ideals surrounding the political potential of alternative distribution platforms, they failed to recognize how the processes of monopolization and the power of entrenched elites within the television delivery industries would stifle the transformative impacts of guerilla television. While Shamberg writing in 1971 prophetically saw YouTube, as a "national knowledge grid system" for "grassroots television producers," 25 years before its purchase by Google in 2006, he failed to see how this system might begin in good faith for the public sphere but soon transform into a system managed to reap profits from that "video data bank." The commodification of guerilla television in the 1970s is similar to the monopolization of the internet in the 2000s.

However, while it is not radical nor a political economic approach, Shamberg's perspective on guerilla television does emphasize the formal infrastructure of television. A closer analysis, however, shows how power is deployed at numerous layers of the architecture of the internet. While grassroots television producers might be free to produce most forms of content and upload it to various sites, to upload that content often requires users to relinquish intellectual property rights to those who own the physical (servers) and code (user interface frontend and algorithmic backend). YouTube is the quintessential case, regularly implementing measures to root out copyright infringement, censoring videos, and abiding by "false flagging" operations.

Cable, satellite, and the internet each provided brief windows of access for activist and independent television producers. While the problem used to be gaining the means of video production, affordable and user-friendly video camcorders emerged in the 1970s. Then the problem was access to platforms like television where people could see the work, and then satellite and public access television of the 1980s lessened that dilemma. In the 2000s, the internet and YouTube further solved the problem of access to the means of publicity. Today, in this era of data opulence the problem is being discovered. "The hubs are the strongest argument against the

54 A. FISH

utopian vision of an egalitarian cyberspace. Yes, we all have the right to put anything we wish on the web. But will anybody notice?" asks network theorist Albert-László Barabási (2002, 58). Or, as the 1970s guerilla video producer Skip Blumberg said, "Back in the day the issue was, 'How do I get on?' But once you got on, people would know about you because there were only three or four channels, or in New York you had six. ... Now it's easy to get your work on. Now you get on every day. And how do you generate an audience?" (Tripp 2012, 14). So while the internet has made available platforms for potential visibility, it has not guaranteed an audience. Despite the hopes of user-generated content and independent producers, major corporate news sites attract disproportionate traffic to the neglect of smaller and independent producers. In a Raindance Corporation reunion in 2010, Paul Ryan admitted that their early optimism required them to ignore the contradictions of using corporate devices for activist gain: "Our experience with video was irresponsible in a certain way because we exploited the newness of it, which is typically American ... I don't think the enthusiasm over new media is going to carry the day ... They [corporate interests] are milking it for everything it's worth without understanding the consequences" (Coffman 2012, 71).

Subsequent chapters look at those television networks that are "milking it" in an attempt to bring together the audience potential of cable and satellite broadcasting and the production democratizing affordances of internet video.

REFERENCES

Barabási, A.-L. 2002. *Linked: The New Science of Networks*. New York: Basic Books.
Boddy, W. 2004. Interactive Television and Advertising Form in Contemporary US Television. In *Television after TV: Essays on a Medium in Transition*, ed. Lynn Spigel and Jan Olsson, 113–132. Durham: Duke University Press.
Boyle, D. 1992. *Subject to Change: Guerrilla Television Revisited*. New York: Oxford University Press.
Chapman, S. 2012. Guerrilla Television in the Digital Archive. *Journal of Film and Video* 63(1–2): 42–50.
———. 2015. Email to Author.
Christian, A.J. 2012. The Web as Television Reimagined? Online Networks and the Pursuit of Legacy Media. *Journal of Communication Inquiry* 36(4): 340–356.
Coffman, E. 2012. 'VT Is Not TV': The Raindance Reunion in the Digital Age. *Journal of Film and Video* 63(1–2): 65–71.

Fish, A. 2007. Television, Ecotourism, and the Videocamera: Performative Non-Fiction and Auto-Cinematography. *Flow Journal* 5: 5. Accessed December 15, 2015. http://flowtv.org/2007/01/television-ecotourism-and-the-videocamera-performative-non-fiction-and-auto-cinematography/

Fish, A., and R. Srinivasan. 2012. Digital Labor Is the New Killer App. *New Media and Society.* 14(1): 135–150.

Gaines, J.M. 1999. Political Mimesis. In *Collecting Visible Evidence*, ed. Jane M. Gaines and Michael Renov. Minneapolis: University of Minnesota Press.

Halleck, D.D. 2002. *Hand Held Visions: The Impossible Possibilities of Community Media.* New York: Fordham University Press.

Hill, C. 2012. Dialogue Across Decades: BLW and People's Communication Network: Exercises in Remembering and Forgetting. *Journal of Film and Video* 63(1–2): 17–29.

Korot, B., and P. Gershuny. 1970. *Radical Software*, 2.

Jardin, X. 2008. Josh Harris: 'Pseudo Was a Fake Company.' *Boing Boing.* Accessed December 5, 2015. http://boingboing.net/2008/06/26/josh-harris-pseudo-w.html

Lucas, M., and M. Wallner. 1993. Resistance by Satellite: The Gulf Crisis Project and the Deep Dish Satellite TV Network. In *Channels of Resistance: Global Television and Local Empowerment*, ed. Tony Dowmunt, 176–194. London: BFI Publishing.

Mellencamp, P. 1990. Video Politics. *Discourse* 10: 2.

Merrin, W. 2012. Still Fighting 'The Beast': Guerrilla Television, and the Limits of YouTube. *Cultural Politics* 8(1): 97–119.

Ouellette, L. 1995a. Will the Revolution Be Televised? Camcorders, Activism, and Alternative Television in the 1990s. In *Transmission: Towards a Post-Television Culture*, ed. Peter d'Agostino and David Tafler. London: Sage.

———. 1995b. Camcorder Dos and Don'ts: Popular Discourse on Amateur Video and Participatory Television. *Velvet Light Trap* 36(Fall): 34–44.

Parks, L. 2004. Flexible Microcasting: Gender, Generation, and Television—Internet Convergence. In *Television After TV: Essays on a Medium in Transition*, ed. Lynn Spigel and Jan Olson. Durham, NC: Duke University Press.

Pierce, S. 2003. DBS and the Public Interest Opportunity in Satellite Television. In *Public Broadcasting and the Public Interest*, ed. Michael P. McCauley, Eric E. Peterson, B. Lee Artz, and DeeDee Halleck. Armouk, NY: M.E. Sharpe.

Rushkoff, D. 1996. *Media Virus!* New York: Balantine Books.

Ryan, P. 1970. Cybernetic Guerrilla Warfare. *Radical Software* 12.

Sandoval, M. 2013. Corporate Social (Ir)Responsibility in Media and Communication Industries. *Javnost* 20(3): 5–23.

Shamberg, M. 1971. *Guerrilla Television.* New York: Holt Rinehart and Winston.

Solanas, F., and O. Getino. 1969. Towards a Third Cinema. In *Movies and Methods. An Anthology*, ed. Bill Nichols, 44–64. Berkeley: University of California Press.

56   A. FISH

Sturken, M. 1990. Paradox in the Evolution of an Art Form: Great Expectations and the Making of a History. In *Illuminating Video: An Essential Guide to Video Art*, ed. Doug Hall and Sally Jo Fifer. New York: Aperture.

Tripp, S. 2012. From TVTV to YouTube: A Genealogy of Participatory Practices in Video. *Journal of Film and Video* 63(1–2): 5–16.

Turner, F. 2006. *From Counterculture to Cyberculture: Stewart Brand, the Whole Earth Network, and the Rise of Digital Utopianism*. Chicago: University of Chicago Press.

Zimmerman, P. 1988. Trading Up: Amateur Film Technology in the 1950's. *Screen*, 17–29.

CHAPTER 3

Liberalism and Broadcast Politics

THE MODELS OF VIDEO PRODUCERS

The video producers I investigate collectively challenge the socio-technical means of their professional livelihood through guerilla technological practices and policy oppositional models. They are not just broadcasters, pundits, television hosts, or behind-the-scenes waged producers. They are not just activists, seeking social justice for others. They are both broadcasters and media reformers who reform the technological and political conditions for their broadcasts. They dialogue on their future in meetings, panels, and in semi-private conversations. Their mission is how to achieve public goals such as improved democratic dialogue on private media systems while making a living. Throughout their history, video producers have modified their broadcasting approaches, how they addressed the public, and what reformist model they drew from in these pursuits.

Ostensibly, video producers seek to make the conditions for the hegemonic public sphere more inclusive. Their broadcasting practices oscillate among different broadcasting models: (1) the public sphere model, which makes listeners into producers and co-owners; (2) the guardianship model, which is designed to produce enlightened citizens; and (3) the commercial model, which sees audiences as passive markets. Current and Free Speech TV (FSTV) variously have exhibited these models through the course of their historical development. Their broadcasting models oscillate through time from public sphere and guardianship to commercial broadcasting models as they address the public as participants, informed

© The Author(s) 2017
A. Fish, *Technoliberalism and the End of Participatory Culture in the United States*, DOI 10.1007/978-3-319-31256-9_3

57

58   A. FISH

citizens, or consumers. Their reformist models include free speech, anti-monopoly, access, public resource, emergent technology, and democracy models. These broadcast models are most prevalent for FSTV. At Current, the dominant discourses are centered on how television and the internet can best be mobilized to increase democratic participation. As part of this techno-democratic modeling, the agents at Current also dialogue in utopian fashion on the positive role of technology in contemporary life more generally. The major point is that video producers' models, frames and discourses are mobilized to articulate approaches to accessing and contributing to the hegemonic public sphere.

Introduced below, these broadcast and reform models will assist us in categorizing the historically situated practices exhibited by Current and FSTV.

Corporate Liberalism and the Guardianship Model

The guardianship model (McCauley et al. 2003) is recognizable by its impetus to produce enlightened and informed citizen-viewers. It is an application of the ideals of social liberals John Dewey and Walter Lippmann, who believed that the "public needed education, leadership, socialization" (Artz 2000, 5). The guardianship model sees the "audience-as-public" (Ang 1991, 28) and sees itself as a trustee of the public media resource (Avery and Stavitsky 2000). The best examples of this model are state-supported television such as the BBC (British Broadcasting Company) and a less potent but noteworthy example, the American Corporation for Public Broadcasting. The intelligent, informed, and usually photogenic television news talking head is the icon of the guardianship model. These guardians of media see the public as an aggregation of diverse social, ethnic, and classed communities that need to have access to informative programming. The guardianship model recognizes that the consumer model fails to provide comprehensive information about issues important to the lives of the diverse communities that constitute a nation.

The guardianship model does not emphasize citizen participation. The primary quality that distinguishes the guardianship from the public sphere model, as you will read below, is this absence. As such, the guardianship model is "aid-without-development ... [that] ... creates dependencies" on these enlightened public intellectuals capable of guiding the public (Artz 2000, 6). The guardianship model is similar to "libertarian paternalism," as proposed by Richard Thaler and Cass Sunstein (2008), administrator

LIBERALISM AND BROADCAST POLITICS 59

of the White House Office of Information and Regulatory Affairs. "Libertarian paternalism" suggests governments should "nudge" their citizens through better design of the "choice environments in which they act" (Couldry 2010, 65). The idea of guardianship is that elected officials are equipped to direct public information for public good. This statist paternalism should be worrisome to scholars of governmentality (Ang 1991; Ferguson and Gupta 2002; Foucault 1991), who are suspicious of the sophisticated and subtle ways governments construct ideal citizens in the images of markets. This is in line with the suspicions of the cultural industry critics as well (Adorno and Horkheimer 1977). The guardianship model recognizes the media resource as something necessary for the functioning of a non-market "public." Considering how entrenched market logic is in American society, this existence of a guardianship model concerned with nudging citizens toward information can be considered an example of corporations doing the work of the state, *à la* corporate liberalism, or, more ominously, as acts of discreet corporate propaganda.

The guardianship model is identical to the "informed citizen model" (Avery and Stavitsky 2000, 57) that frames the public as in need of carefully selected information not just to become better consumers but also to become better citizens in a representative democracy. The perspective is of "audience-as-public consists not of consumers, but of citizens who must be reformed, educated, informed as well as entertained—in short, 'served'—presumably to enable them to better perform their democratic rights and duties" (Ang 1991, 28–29).

The guardianship model is evident in the present case studies in a different way. As I will describe below, throughout its history, Current was the result of the guardianship model as well as the two other distinct forms of broadcasting practice: the commercial model, which conceptualizes the public as a market of consumers, and the public sphere model, which recognizes and includes the public's multiplicity of voices. FSTV also exhibits a variety of broadcasting models. In FSTV's case, its technological and policy competencies are paired with its guardianship model in facilitating FSTV's expansion on public television.

Television news, with its signature talking heads and cascade of elite pundits, is a prime example of the guardianship model. Examples of progressive guardianship programming include FSTV's *Democracy Now!* and Current's *Young Turks*. In both instances, the audience is positioned as passive recipients of information from well-meaning and more informed newscasters, Amy Goodman and Cenk Uygur. Occasionally, regular

60   A. FISH

citizens will gain access to the televised tables of these newscasters, more affirming than challenging the singular authority of the host, but these instances are rare, and the citizen participants have gained that access through a precise and opaque vetting process on which the public had no input. It is the public sphere model that challenges this approach.

NEOLIBERALISM AND THE COMMERCIAL MODEL

Ang contrasts the guardianship model with "audiences-as-markets," which envisions audiences not as self-governing publics but as consumers (Ang 1991, 29). This model equates the interests of the public with the financial security of the industry under regulation (Avery and Stavitsky 2000, 53). In this model, the profitability of the media companies serving the "audience-as-market" (Ang 1991) is a marker of the correct use of the media license.

An example of the commercial model comes from textual scholarship into the Federal Communications Commission (FCC). Scholars Robert K. Avery and Alan G. Stavitsky (2000) investigated the written language of the FCC. The assumption that drove their research was that the "shared value system of corporate liberalism can be found in the decisions and practices of our policy-makers" (Avery and Stavitsky 2000, 53). They discovered that the model of the FCC is to see the public neither as citizens needing information nor as participants in a vibrant public sphere but as consumers that the FCC needed to bring to corporations. They called this consumer model the "instrumental view," which privileges the concept of "consumer" over "citizen" (Avery and Stavitsky 2000, 53, 57). Avery and Stavitsky's analysis revealed that the FCC is "overwhelmingly tied to such market-orientated concepts as maximizing competition, enhancing market power, promoting investment incentives, insuring competitive rate structures, removing barriers to entry, and encouraging new service providers" (Avery and Stavitsky 2000, 57). Thus, the FCC does not frame the public in terms of participation or becoming an informed citizenry. As a federal commission tasked with managing the media resources in the public interest, not only the corporate interest, this tendency toward a commercial model reveals the FCC's alignment with neoliberal deregulation for corporate gain. This claim remains powerfully true today. My reading of FCC Chairman Julius Genachowski's letter to Senator Upton in 2011 negating the FCC's commitment to the Fairness Doctrine and dedication to competition is a key example of the continuing legacy of the FCC,

LIBERALISM AND BROADCAST POLITICS 61

which sees its duty as providing consumers to corporations, not citizens to polls and public spheres (Genachowski 2011).

The first example of scholarly writing defending the commercial model comes from former FCC Chariman Mark Fowler & Daniel Brenner (1982). Their thesis is that "broadcasters as community trustees should be replaced by a view of broadcasters as marketplace participants. ... The first step in a marketplace approach to broadcast regulation, then, is to focus on broadcasters not as fiduciaries of the public ... but as marketplace competitors" (Fowler and Brenner 1982, 3–4). In this thesis, the market must instrumentalize all resources. The media should not be held in trust for a purpose other than capitalism but should be subject to the logic of capitalism and the rigor of the marketplace. Media studies scholar Nick Couldry identifies the commercial model as a result of "market populism ... which claims markets as the privileged site of popular voice" (2010, 12).

Current is embedded within the commercial model. Though its content and mission could have been appropriate for public broadcasting and the public sphere model, as you will see below, it decided to approach broadcasting from a commercial perspective. Current bought the cable network NewsWorld International on the open market, licensed its content to cable and satellite companies like Comcast in the USA and Sky in the UK, and solicited advertising with the hopes of producing surplus capital. Yet, its mission from 2005 to 2009 was to invigorate the mediated conditions of an American public sphere, and from 2009 to the network's end, Current had become aligned with the guardianship model. Thus, Current throughout its history has used each of the three approaches. While Current has been engaged in issues of democracy through both its commercialized guardianship and public sphere models, these have been economical routes to democracy.

FSTV, on the other hand, has always had a tenuous but necessary relationship with the commercial model. Like Current, FSTV fluctuates between the guardianship and the public sphere model, with guardianship-like news programming as well as participatory media initiatives. It explores these two approaches from its distribution strategy that draws from the satellite set-asides of the public service approach, but its economics are not based on state-supported initiatives but rather on the generosity of viewers and foundations that situate FSTV within the public sphere model. While FSTV is restricted in exploring commercial options on television, it can explore commercial options online. Finally, as a reactive discourse, the commercial model influences how FSTV defines itself. FSTV brands

62   A. FISH

itself as against the commercial model, which it sees as responsible for the lack of independence and the prevalence of consolidation in broadcasting and the erosion of democratic media. While the public service and public sphere models exist variously in the cultural logics of the networks, the commercial model pervades many aspects of the various approaches advanced by both television networks.

Social Liberalism and the Public Sphere Model

The public sphere model frames the public as co-participants in the production of media and co-owners of the media resource. The public sphere model does not see the public as mere consumers of media products, or as citizens needing to passively receive information from informed experts; rather, the public sphere model frames the public as users and producers of media whose citizenry is performed in acts of creation. The public sphere model is the most demanding and potentially rewarding for the public and for individuals. The public sphere model is also the most constrained by the dominant market logic of neoliberalism.

The public sphere approach to broadcasting is characterized by participatory culture, citizen journalism, dialogue among communities or social movements, democratic decision-making, and social ownership of the means of media production and distribution. These efforts are designed to transform consumers into citizens and return public discourse from the public relations managers to those citizens. The public sphere model values dialogue and negotiation in the self-governance of society (McCauley et al. 2003, xxiv). As an attempt to achieve empowerment and equality, the public sphere model aligns with the ideals of social liberalism.

An example of the public sphere approach is the not-for-profit and progressive Pacifica Radio network, which includes KPFK in Los Angeles, KPFA in Berkeley, and 137 affiliate networks around the country. Scholars Michael P. McCauley et al. (2003, xxiv) state that Pacifica uses "the airways to promote community dialogue and to present audio evidence in support of movements for progressive social change. They seek to democratize non-commercial radio in the U.S." Pacifica, unlike National Public Radio (NPR) or PBS, is not just listener-supported but listener-directed. It has local community boards, community programming, and a national board consisting of producers and listeners (Artz 2000, 9). Current and FSTV have engaged viewers to become producers, thereby enacting the public sphere model, but they never engage the viewers as managers, nor do they socialize the ownership of the network in the tradition of the Pacifica network. While being economically situated in the commercial approach, Current was founded on the belief that what American democracy sorely lacked was a television network that served as a public sphere. Current's citizen journalism project, VC2, was the keystone operation to achieve a democratized and participatory destination embodying the public sphere model. It sought to provide vocal support for numerous ethnic, class, gender, and political mini-publics around the world. Current's public sphere approach did not, however, include social ownership of the means of production nor democratic decision-making internal to the corporation. Current did not allow public participants to retain the broadcast rights to their video contributions. Instead it retained traditional corporate ownership practices over media content. Additionally, public participants and communities working within the Current-supported public sphere had no capacity to democratically contribute to the management of the media corporation. These compromises are inherent in an organization that retains important elements of the commercial model while experimenting with the public sphere model. As we discovered across a range of instances in which organizations attempt to "seed" a public, such compromises are more prevalent than anomalous (Fish et al. 2011). These compromises become even more evident through ethnographic and historical analyses of commercial organizations experimenting with the public sphere model.

The technological sophistication of broadcast television requires there to be personnel who mediate the presentation of the participatory public to the public sphere. Direct democratic governance by a public over the media organization is not possible. Representatives of that media company need to perform the technical tasks of mediating even the most participatory project. This mediation by intermediaries includes fundraising, engineering, and even on-camera hosting. FSTV has long considered itself as expressing the public sphere model. It was doing citizen journalism before the internet popularized the practice. It gave voice to social movements, beginning with the WTO protests in 1999, and later with media reform activist groups to whom FSTV "opened up" its airwaves throughout 2011. FSTV even experimented with internal direct democratic self-governance but found it too difficult to make decisions. Yet, throughout the application of its public sphere model it has not been socially owned nor democratically driven, and the access it has given to citizen journalists and social movements has been vetted by professionals and mediated by technicians. The task of creating the multiplatform media conditions for the American public sphere is compromised by technological pressure, competency requirements, commercial imperatives, and pragmatic self-governance necessities. FSTV's primary approach to broadcasting mixes approaches from both commercial and guardianship models. When there are economic difficulties, experiments with the commercial model online become increasingly attractive. Likewise, the guardianship model is becoming a dominant approach for FSTV. Thus, throughout the history of a television network, all three models emerge and mix with the other models.

What distinguishes these two networks are the criteria for entry into the network's public sphere and the degree of participation required. Both networks require vetting by professionals with regard to content, aesthetics, technicality, length, copyright issues, and so on. Current's VC2 program, focused on short and personal documentaries, was a more accessible format for citizen participation than FSTV's format of long-form documentary. What further distinguishes these two networks is how live programming interacted with the public sphere. Current very rarely did live programming, and, when it did, it was for professional, not amateur, coverage of the 2008 US presidential election or *Countdown with Keith Olbermann*. Live programming for FSTV, on the other hand, is an opportunity for citizens and social movements to directly address an audience with little moderation other than an interviewer and several broadcast technicians, as I observed at four activist conferences. This use of live video is a distinct quality of FSTV's public sphere model.

So far I have introduced three models of broadcasting. The models inform practical ways that these television networks envision and implement their responsibilities to publics and consumers. It is likely that most television news producers and programmers recognize that their work has impacts beyond profit. The television news networks I investigate are explicitly attempting to balance their commercial with their guardianship and public sphere models. Because of this, these television news networks can be identified as also being involved in the movement to reform media regulation to make it more responsive to the needs of the public and less beholden to corporations.

Corporations and agencies that control the use of public media resources utilize models to help them guide their practices. Any one media firm or regulatory body uses one or a mix of several of these models throughout their history. For example, in its short existence,

Current used all three. First, it used the public sphere model when framing its approach to broadcasting around democratizing media production. Second, it used the guardianship model to frame its practice of using professional news hosts to broadcast progressive media to the public. Throughout, while Current has used the public sphere and guardianship models, it has simultaneously framed the public, internally at least, as consumers of the advertising that forms the lucrative interstitial materials between broadcasts. During live broadcasts, FSTV "opens up" its airwaves to activist organizations, thereby deploying the public sphere model. On the same day it may also broadcast *Democracy Now!*, which addresses the public in guardianship style as an informed citizenry. Internally, FSTV's identity is formed in opposition to the commercial model of conglomerated media companies like Fox News. Thus, these categories of broadcasting models can be multiple, simultaneous, and transitional through time. These shared traits may simply designate the nimble agencies of media corporations in the information economy or prove to signify an interpellation of public interest broadcasting by the commercial model.

The subjects of this research are television producers, firmly grounded in the conditions of the cultural industries. They are also media reformers, attempting to improve the conditions for the American public sphere by providing access and diversity on American television. In both their production and reformer manifestations, they are politically progressive, focusing on providing progressive commentary or access to progressive content. However, more analysis is required to explain the media reform models of video producers. To do this, I will explore the numerous models of media reform, many of which articulate precisely with the ideals of networks like FSTV and Current.

Video Producers and Their Models

The subjects of this book are media producers and also reformers. Their professional lives consist of a struggle for the recognition of the human right to self-representation and communication justice. To them, information is a right and a resource firmly connected to humanity and citizenship. Their arguments for media justice include access, democracy, and free speech, among other issues. As progressive reformers, they oppose oligarchy. As media makers they resist the negative human impacts of *corporatism*— the merger of states and companies, with corporations having the upper hand, as opposed to fascism, in which the state controls the corporation. As activist media makers, video producers oppose the federal sanctioning of media consolidation. These media justice activists and producers are advocates for access to the means of production and diversely progressive content on radio, television, and the internet. Throughout their histories, FSTV and Current have deployed a number of different methods to increase access, diversity, and free speech on television. These methods range from deeply participatory, citizen-engaged journalism in Current's VC2 program, to the progressively unique television broadcast in FSTV's live coverage of activist conferences, to complicit commercial broadcasting that retains a critique of corporate media in Current's *Countdown with Keith Olbermann*.

The practice of media reform dates back to 1894, when trade unionists and civil reformers focused on ensuring that domestic telephony was a universal service owned by the cities (Schiller 1999). Media reformer and professor Robert McChesney (1993) follows media reform into the 1930s, when reformers fought against the corporatization and capitalization of media. In 1966, the United Church of Christ (UCC) complained that Southern television stations were not reporting on the civil rights movement or African-American issues. It petitioned the FCC to take away the broadcasting license of WBLT in Jackson, Mississippi. The case eventually made it to the US Court of Appeals, which found that the UCC was not serving the public interest (Jansen 2011, 9). This was the beginning of the contemporary media reform movement.

The issues that motivate media justice activists to engage in media reform actions include the fight for anti-monopoly, public interest, free speech, access, democratic representation, rights to the spectrum, and right-of-way givebacks. They resist the idea that new communication technologies, namely the internet, have democratized access and made media reform unnecessary. Communication rights are human rights that include but trump other arguments for access.

THE ANTI-MONOPOLY MODEL

The US media reform movement begins at the start of debates regarding who should be empowered by the emergent technology of radio. The spectrum of radio waves was considered a public resource and fell under the authority of the federal government to regulate. Because of this, the public interest had a right to impact federal proceedings. One of the media reform movement's first arguments was against corporate consolidation of radio spectrum. In the 1920s, a group of media reform activists worked to insert an anti-monopoly clause into the Radio Act of 1927, and they succeeded in including sections 13 and 15, which prohibit monopolies. This was a continuation of the Sherman Act and reappeared in the Communications Act of 1934. Anti-monopoly advocates argued that monopoly is both against democracy and competition (Bagdikian 1983; Halleck 2002). The model of anti-monopoly mobilized the language of capitalism ("competition") to intervene in the realms of increasing corporate power.

The anti-monopoly model was a convincing and effective media reform model because it resonated with the fundamental beliefs of American capitalism. American ideology favors competition—in elections, sports, and business. Anti-monopoly activists use this to their advantage by identifying the un-American trust activities of major media corporations. Nevertheless, in the process they perpetuate the concept that public media resources are within the sphere of capitalist "competition."

Thus, a limitation of the anti-monopoly model is its failure to critique and challenge a profit-driven media system and its deleterious impact on democracy. The anti-monopoly model uses the language of capitalism to reform capitalist enterprises. This might not be possible. Reforming capitalism while using capitalism's model is difficult if not impossible and may signify the presence of Althusserian interpellation (Fish 2005).

In my field research, I encountered the anti-monopoly model obliquely as part of a discourse antagonistic to vertical integration and conglomeration. Current and FSTV both designated the conglomeration of television news networks as a problem for American democracy. The anti-conglomeration model is a version of the anti-monopoly model updated for the late twentieth-century's media mega-corporation when companies attempted to dominate the global media production and distribution chain.

FSTV's core media reform model is best expressed in its resistance to corporate conglomeration and conservative partisan news channel Fox News, a subsidiary of News Corp. Below, FSTV's Executive Director Don Rojas speaks against the 2011 merger of Comcast and NBCUniversal. Vertical integration and a partisan and conservative media system are the objects against which these video producers react.

As one of the key components of progressive political theory, media reform was an issue that FSTV knew its audience cared about. Media

68   A. FISH

reform also impacted FSTV's growth and survival. During my fieldwork, FSTV attempted to expand its carriage onto the Comcast system. Comcast, during this time, was in the process of acquiring FCC approval to purchase NBCUniversal. This merger of a telecommunications company, Comcast, which distributes content, and a studio, NBCUniversal, which produces content, is considered by many in the media justice movement to be a violation of anti-trust laws. Comcast, a major content distributor, could favor the distribution of that content, giving its subsidiary, NBCUniversal, and itself undue advantage over its competitors. The FCC was adjudicating this issue throughout 2010–2011, and it was a major issue at the 2011 National Conference for Media Reform.

On November 8, 2010, I interviewed Rojas and we discussed what the Comcast-NBCUniversal merger might mean for FSTV.

[It is] still being considered by the FCC, a lot of lobbying is going on as we speak. There is some public pressure built up over the last few months. There has been public pressure on Comcast to open up the airwaves to more programming, for more independent television, for what we do. So we are hoping we can get a serious meeting going partly because of the public pressure. There are a lot of groups, media justice groups, Media Matters [for example], that have been putting a lot of pressure on them to democratize more. The fear of course is that Comcast, with the acquisition of NBC, will become this juggernaut, this monopolistic giant, kind of what Fox has become. Hopefully we can get a meeting with them and see what happens. (interviewed November 8, 2010)

This interview segment introduces how FSTV frames its opposition and how that opposition provides opportunities for the network. This transformation of an opposition into an opportunity is part of the flexible reactive discourse of media reform.

THE PUBLIC INTEREST MODEL

"It is inconceivable that we should allow so great a possibility for service to be drowned in advertising chatter." President Herbert Hoover, 1924, discussing radio. (Streeter 1996, 44, fn. 32)

In the public interest model, a public exists and has interests not addressed by capitalism and consumerism. The government needs to protect this public interest from corporate colonization. Unlike the anti-monopoly model, the public interest model is not grounded in the language of capitalism. Rather, the foundation for the public interest model is located in a notion of public resources not unlike how in the USA we conceive of public lands as managed by the US Bureau of Land Management or the US Forest Service. However, while it avoids the language of capitalism in print, the public interest model is not free from the constraints of capitalism. Supporting the public interest means enacting regulation that favors corporate media. Communications professor Thomas Streeter (1996) illustrates this argument by examining President Herbert Hoover, who, in the early 1930s, derided the "advertising chatter" polluting the public interests on radio while also handing over broadcast contract to corporations. This duplicity illustrates how the model of public interest is the other side of the broadcasting commercial model. It is also a primary example of the strategy of corporate liberalism: a corporate agenda masked as a state project. Streeter says of public interest:

> The dominant legal uses of the term suggest a functionalist, systemic vision of social relations, and are easily subsumed into a technocratic interpretation, as a general term for the extra-market social engineering imagined to be necessary to the smooth integration of the corporate system, which stands in a paternalistic relation to a consuming public. (Streeter 1996, 186)

In other words, public interest is the sacrifice made in the act of privatizing the public resources of media. The public and their interests, if not conflated with corporate interests, are linked in a language of compromise in which private corporations receive the benefits.

Despite, or perhaps because of, how the public interest argument cohered to corporate interests, the model held some early successes for media reform and continues to be a model with utility for media justice. In 1941, with radio and, in 1952, with television, the FCC used the public interest model to reserve one or two channels for public use on each networked communication technology.

Both the model and the practice of public interest broadcasting assume the existence of experts, legislators, and broadcasters to produce the technological and policy conditions for a population. This is distinct from the public sphere model and the model of free speech, as I will explore below, both of which attempt to empower the creative voice of citizens, not just their listening ears.

70   A. FISH

The model of the public interest is linked to the guardianship model, which posits that non-market information necessary for citizenship will not be delivered collectively by peers but be meted out by expert news broadcasters, politicians, and sanctioned technologists.

Current approached its problem of access not as a public interest but as a commercial property. FSTV uses the public interest model in a public media policy context to successfully create opportunities on emergent networked communication systems such as satellite and cable television.

THE FREE SPEECH MODEL

Everyone has the right to freedom of opinion and expression; this right includes freedom to hold opinions without interference and to seek, receive and impart information and ideas through any media and regardless of frontiers. (United Nations Universal Declaration of Human Rights, Article 19)

Congress shall make no law respecting an establishment of religion, or prohibiting the free exercise thereof; or abridging the freedom of speech, or of the press; or the right of the people peaceably to assemble, and to petition the Government for a redress of grievances. (U.S. Constitution, First Amendment)

Originally the free speech model relied upon the First Amendment of the US Constitution to advocate for the right to give voice to opinion without fear of censorship or retaliation. A further extension of this argument is that the freedom of speech requires the freedom to access modes of speech amplification and distribution on public media resources. Toward this end, the federal agencies tasked with managing the media resource and upholding the First Amendment need not create an unnecessary economic burden in the articulating and distribution of speech. Legislators advocated for both public interest and free speech while drafting the 1927 Radio Act.

Free speech is "an essential right to information exchange," said video activist and author DeeDee Halleck (2002, 101), who is also a television producer and FSTV board member. "If the First Amendment protects free speech in an age of face-to-face argument and print media, these rights are extended into more complex forms of technology as they are developed," Halleck continued (2002, 101). As the quote above makes clear, the UN stated that communication, including broadcast communication, is a human right. Every citizen has the right to free speech, not just certain eloquent people. This fact illustrates the distinctions between the public sphere and the guardianship models. The model of free speech is linked to the practice of public sphere broadcasting, which seeks to empower everyone's free speech through the application of technology and policy. In an improbable twist of fate, during the history of telecommunication law and policy, the free speech clause of the First Amendment has not only been signaled in the course of protecting individual human rights to free speech but also corporate rights to free speech and personhood. The free speech clause now protects media corporations' capacities to deny citizens access to media broadcasting and protects media corporations from being forced by government to broadcast opinions with which they do not agree. Corporate free speech is now the freedom not to be regulated, in opposition to public interest or pro-citizen free speech regulation. Corporate free speech means the constitutionally defended right to produce profit without concern for citizens' free speech. Free speech "functions to structure industry relations and insulate them from political accountability" (Streeter 1996, 193). This is an example of corporate liberalism, the subversion of social justice in action claimed to be pro-democratic in the overwhelmingly powerful context of corporate-government collaboration.

Morris Ernst of the American Civil Liberties Union (ACLU) railed against the equation that money equals speech as early as the 1920s. Speaking against the corporate liberalism in the 1927 Radio Act, he said,

> "[w]e are deeply concerned in the bill in so far as it relates to the question of censorship and freedom of speech. Even the term 'free speech' is more or less of a misnomer when you have to pay $400 an hour in one of the good New York stations and are lucky if you can get on at all … the whole bill is predicated on money. (quoted in Streeter 1996, 191)

Ernst and the ACLU went on to provide solutions that included preferring non-profit media organizations in the licensing process, a cap on station ownership, and transparency in the licensing system. The public sphere free speech model articulated by the ACLU in the days preceding the 1927 Radio Act failed to persuade a strong defense of free speech for individuals and non-profit media organizations. The ACLU changed its approach from defending individual free speech to defending private institutions, usually businesses, from political interference (Streeter 1996, 192). Since these times, the media justice movement's model of free speech has not been a powerful force of persuasion.

72   A. FISH

The model of free speech, as I have articulated it here, strangely enough, does not describe FSTV's broadcasting model, which is more like the guardianship model of free speech for certain professional journalists and experts. Current also experimented with free speech broadcasting in the VC2 phase, which focused on democratizing media production only to enact the practices of guardianship broadcasting in the following Hollywood phase through the monologues by television hosts, Eliot Spitzer and Cenk Uygur.

THE ACCESS MODEL

The model of access manifests in at least five policy practices that influence guardianship and public sphere broadcasting: (1) the "equal time" doctrine; (2) the Fairness Doctrine; (3) cable public, education, and government (PEG) channel access; (4) leased access; and (5) direct broadcast satellites (DBS) public set-asides. I will briefly discuss each below.

In order to prevent monopoly control over television content, the Cable Communications Act of 1984 (Public Law 98-549) required cable operators to make available several channels for "leased access." In 1961, former US President John F. Kennedy made a statement regarding access to DBS saying, "public interest objectives would be given the highest priority" (quoted in Pierce 2000, 110). The 1994 Cable Communications Act requires that DBS systems such as DirecTV and DISH, being the most prominent after the acquisition of Echostar, by law must set aside 4–7% of their spectrum to PEG channels. In 1996, a federal circuit court reviewed this requirement, and the FCC enforced the provisions. A DBS-like DirecTV with 175 channels was forced to offer 7–12 channels of PEG programming, opening the way for non-profit content creators like FSTV. Another Act that encouraged access is Section 315 of the 1934 Communications Act, which requires political candidates to be given "equal time" in the purchasing of advertisements. Like other social justice elements in US communication policy, the "equal access" ruling was quickly diluted.

While these two Acts have provided routes to expanded audiences for FSTV, the models themselves affirm corporate liberalism, as Streeter says, "[a]ntimonopoly, the public interest, free speech, and access are, in practice, corporate liberal terms" (Streeter 1996, 196). However, the model of access appears to be more effective than the free speech model in achieving the impacts wanted by media reformers.

LIBERALISM AND BROADCAST POLITICS 73

PEG cable access and satellite set-asides are both examples of relatively successful public access granted by the FCC to force the hand of the cable and satellite companies. FSTV would likely not exist without these opportunities. The Fairness Doctrine, which required broadcasters to provide contrasting information on controversial issues, is another example of the access model. The history of the Fairness Doctrine began in 1949 when the FCC interpreted broadcast licensees as public trustees of a limited public resource, the radio spectrum. A closer look at the history of the Fairness Doctrine illustrates how cultural formations attempt to intervene in policy debates. Eventually, the FCC sided with corporate liberalism.

FSTV Communications Director Linda Mamoun wrote an article, "Wielding weapons of mass persuasion: The anti-war TV movement," in 2003. In it she interweaves a history of access to television distribution with a history of the agents of independent media. The article begins with the Communications Act of 1934 that "stipulates that the airways are public property" (Mamoun 2003). Mamoun highlights that "the main condition for use of the broadcast spectrum requires broadcasters to serve the public interest, convenience, and necessity" (Mamoun 2003). In 1949, the FCC established the criteria for the Fairness Doctrine. Broadcasters were regulated to insure that they spent time covering public issues and opposing perspectives. They were also required to allow citizens time to reply to the issues that concerned them. In 1967, specific provisions of the Fairness Doctrine were incorporated into the FCC's regulations. For the next few decades, from 1949 through 1987, independent media had a legal grounding as public interest advocates succeeded in enforcing the Fairness Doctrine that required broadcast licensees to provide balanced coverage of issues.

The application of the Fairness Doctrine by the FCC was a relaxed operation. In 1974, the FCC recognized that Congress gave it the authority to demand "access" for groups or people interested in voicing opinions on challenging issues of public importance. The FCC claimed it did not need to enforce the Fairness Doctrine because the broadcasters were voluntarily following the spirit of the doctrine. Through the years, the media and technological landscape changed. Courts ruled that new technology, such as teletext, an early television interactivity system, was not applicable to the enforcement of the Fairness Doctrine. Instead of just three networks, there were many more, and along with this multiplication came a greater diversity of voices. Through the 1970s, the Fairness Doctrine remained valid.

74   A. FISH

In 1981, the FCC revisited the Fairness Doctrine and eventually ruled against it in 1987, stating that "it reduced the quality and quantity of public affairs programming, did not serve the public interest, and defied the First Amendment" (Mamoun 2003). The FCC had repealed the Fairness Doctrine on "both public interest and constitutional grounds" (Mamoun 2003).

On June 24, 2011, FCC Chairman Genachowski confirmed to Senator Fred Upton, Chairman of the Energy and Commerce Committee, that, "The Fairness Doctrine is not enforced by the Commission and has not been applied for more than 20 years" (Genachowski 2011). On August 22, 2011, the FCC repealed reference to the Fairness Doctrine. Free Press, the media reform organization I investigate along with my work with FSTV, states that the problems with the lack of broadcast diversity is not a result of the revoking of the Fairness Doctrine but rather "the result of multiple structural problems in the US regulatory system, particularly the complete breakdown of the public trustee concepts of broadcast, the elimination of clear public interest requirements for broadcasting, and the relaxation of ownership rules including the requirement of local participation in management" (Halpin et al. 2007, 2). Former US President Barack Obama apparently agreed with Free Press that improvements needed to be made to the policy resources of the public sphere, but these improvements do not have to start with revamping the Fairness Doctrine. Obama's Press Secretary, Michael Ortiz, wrote that the former President

> does not support reimposing the Fairness Doctrine on broadcasters ... [and] considers this debate to be a distraction from the conversation we should be having about opening up the airwaves and modern communications to as many diverse viewpoints as possible. That is why Senator Obama supports media-ownership caps, network neutrality, public broadcasting as well as increasing minority ownership of broadcasting and print outlets. (Eggerton 2008)

The access model is within the logic of corporate liberalism. The model positions the public as the recipient of corporate aid; it must ask for access to broadcasting capacities from corporations (Streeter 1996, 195). "The granting of access is thus easily interpreted as one of the technocratic corporate liberal adjustments useful for maintaining smooth relations between corporations and the consuming public" (Streeter 1996, 195). Like the free speech model before it, the access model can be reversed

THE DIVERSITY MODEL

to seem like a regulation that chills the free speech not of people but of business. In this regard, it affirms broadcasting as centrally located within corporate liberalism.

THE DIVERSITY MODEL

Diversity of opinions is a necessary component of a vibrant public sphere. The internet, in contrast to television, is a networked communication device with a low barrier to entry. Unlike television, production on the internet is seemingly "democratized." Nevertheless, scholars of the internet often fail to recognize that the capacity for content to enter into the public debate needs to be findable. To be findable, the content needs a type of manual or algorithmic promotion. This requires capital. In this regard, internet producers and television producers both face the same challenges: inclusion within a public sphere that requires forms of power beyond having quality content. Producers can manufacture content, but if it is not going to be seen, it is not debatable and is therefore not engaged within a public sphere. In this context, those with less political or economic power have less potential to be included in the public sphere.

One way of thinking about diversity is to address the multiplicity of the political spectrum. Arguments abound about whether producers of political content on the internet are predominantly liberal or conservative. I tend to agree with Communications scholar Matthew Hindman that "[l]iberals seem to dominate the audience for politics online. Across a wide range of politically relevant activities, from gathering news online to visiting government Web sites, liberals outpace conservatives by a wide margin" (Hindman 2008, 23). Journalist Eric Alterman (2003) disagrees, stating that the internet is a hotbed for conservative conspiracies.

Regardless, Fox News, inarguably a bastion of conservative political ideology, dominates the top ten news programs every night in the USA. The social results of this popularity are devastating. In a study (Public Mind Poll 2011), it was discovered that Fox News viewers are less informed about politics than those who watch no news. This conservatism in the American public sphere is not balanced within the media ecology by independent or progressive voices emerging either in cable television or online because these communities lack the resources to scale to the level of impact had by the conservative television broadcasters financed by Rupert Murdoch.

76   A. FISH

Ideally, diverse and competitive opinions would have an equal footing within the American public sphere. Ideally, the more democratic capacities of the internet would somehow balance the more professional opinions commonly voiced in television news. However, this is not the case. Conservative voices dominate cable television news ratings, where progressive and independent voices are marginalized. Independent voices are innumerable online, where progressive voices receive more readers than conservative online voices, but the impact of these independent and conservative online voices is difficult to ascertain. These power inequalities based on the affordances of different technologies and cultures of production and consumption result in a skewed or unbalanced public sphere.

Both Current and FSTV see their role as independent and progressive non-fiction television networks as increasing diversity within the American public sphere. They believe that the offerings of news on television neglect progressive voices. Throughout my fieldwork with FSTV and Current, the mantra of increasing diversity through the inclusion of marginalized voices was heard. For example, Current's co-founder Joel Hyatt and FSTV's Rojas are both quoted as saying they want to be the "anti-Fox" news channel (Dana 2012; Ostrow 2011). Nevertheless, it is not only about being a liberal broadcasting network to complement Fox News. Consistent and progressive programming is necessary for a richly diverse American public sphere. Hyatt criticizes MSNBC, another liberal television news network, saying "[i]t's liberal at night, conservative in the morning, and in the middle it's nothing at all because it needs to fit in under its NBC parent" (Clark 2012). FSTV and Current are attempting to provide ballast, with balance being a key component of the diversity model.

THE PUBLIC RESOURCE MODEL

The writers of the 1927 Radio Act understood the problem that the radio spectrum was a limited public resource being doled out to media corporations. They understood it well enough to mitigate the giveaway but not to stop it. To triage the negative impact of including the media spectrum within the theory of corporate liberalism, the FCC required licensees to consider and make small provisions for the "public interest." The pay-back-for-scarce-public-resource model is founded on the defensible notion that the commons is public domain. In corporate liberalism, the media spectrum is a public resource managed by the state in order to be capitalized by media corporations. Nevertheless, the state also has a waning obligation to the public. The enactment of this public obligation by the state requires considerable mobilization on the part of the public advocating for access to their resource.

A year after former US President Kennedy introduced satellite technology in 1961, NASA and AT&T partnered to create the Communication Satellite Corporation (Comsat), which was a private company tasked with privatizing the new communication technology. The public resource model as regards satellite television developed from an argument that satellite technology developed out of public federal investments and that investment is now being exploited by the private sector, so they are responsible for paying back this government investment (Halleck 2002, 101–102). Radio, the internet, and satellite were all publicly financed industries presently enriching private industries. These corporations are now limiting or potentially limiting public sphere broadcasting. The core of our private and public communication infrastructure "owe their research and development to the enormous public expenditures by the U.S. space and military programs. A few corporations have become very wealthy by using that research as the basis for their business" (Halleck 2002, 102). The public resource model believes that because of these public sacrifices, these enriched private license holders need to substantially provide for ways the public can produce for and access these media systems.

Like satellite, cable television also has a payback component. Cable companies require right of way through the municipalities they hope to serve with entertaining content. This right of way is through the public city lands, and therefore the public and the city council have a right to ask for a payback to use it. This model has been used to acquire public access channels throughout the nation. The payback model is within the frame of corporate liberalism that presupposes the corporation as the primary licensee of the public media resource that kindly returns a small portion of the treasure to the state and public. Payback is but one of the minimal "technocratic corporate liberal adjustments" (Streeter 1996, 195) necessary to secure their licensee rights to the public resource. In this calculation, the public needs to ask corportions and the governent for access.

I was unable to observe actions or overhear discussions while I was within the ranks of FSTV or Current directly performing the public resource model. FSTV is a direct recipient of successes in the public resource model in the form of satellite (DBS) and public television (PEG) set-asides.

78   A. FISH

However, the notion that media systems and spectrum are primarily public resources is a fundamental component of the media reform movement and was a dominant issue in the conferences I attended with FSTV.

THE TECHNOLOGY MODEL

The technology model posits that technology alone will not achieve the goals of media reform without vigilant activism. Video producers resist the temptation to believe that the internet or the next networked communication system is going to democratize media production and distribution and thereby dethrone the incumbent media system and its elites. Each networked communication system emerged with these utopian promises, and each networked communication system becomes owned and operated by the elite. Cable television was first championed as providing unlimited capacities for public interest broadcasters and commercial broadcasters alike. As law expert Tim Wu (2010) notes, what tends to result is each emergent communication system is colonized by commercial companies. Thus it is an irrelevant argument that the internet, for instance, as an inexpensive publishing system, has made media reform issues irrelevant. Media reformers argue against the notion that the one infinite "long tail" (Anderson 2006) of shelf space provided by the internet has created a new media world in which state and federal regulation, and finance are unnecessary. Powerful economic forces soon transform democratized communication systems into commercial entities. New technologies are not enough; public funding is necessary if the conditions for the public sphere are to be met on any present or future networked communication system (McChesney and Nichols 2010).

McChesney criticizes the "conventional wisdom" that says: "[w]ith the rise of multicultural television, with the rise of the Internet, with the 'end of scarcity,' there's no more need for public service broadcast. After all, even the minutest need can be met on the Internet, if not on cable television with 500 channels. So apparently the justification for public service broadcasting is gone" (McChesney 2003, 11). McChesney is baiting the reader with the concept that the internet is improving democratic mediations. With the exception of select scholars (Morozov 2011), it is accepted that the internet facilitates democratic practice from the days of the internet bubble in 2000 to the social media-assisted revolutions in Iran, Tunisia, and Egypt; the hacktivism of Anonymous; and the online mobilizations of the Occupy Movement. McChesney (2003) argues that the problem is not the way we use the technology but how we finance the use of the technology for private economic and not for social gain. He does not think that the opulence of technology should justify the lack of response to the democratic communication problem. Infrastructure is not enough. What is needed is an opening-up of the media to public and federal investment in journalism and communications. At the National Conference for Media Reform, which I attended with FSTV, I met with Bill Nichols, *Nation* writer, who stood by his and McChesney's theory that what is needed is a refocus on public media and its public funding, not new technology (McChesney and Nichols 2010).

Case in point, Current and FSTV are endeavoring to undergo the difficult, years-long operation of acquiring a cable and satellite television license instead of focusing singularly on internet broadcasting. Despite evidence in support of techno-utopianism at Current, former Vice President Al Gore knew that neither the internet nor any technology alone is enough to create the conditions for an American public sphere. Each network needs to use all available technologies in addition to grassroots organizing and fundraising to create a pro-democracy movement.

THE DEMOCRACY MODEL

The democracy model states that democracies should promote democracy-facilitating practices such as investigative journalism and its distribution. This means that the state should manage media resources first for the promotion of democracy. This would mean an emphasis on public sphere and guardianship models and a minimization of the impact of the commercial model. The media reform movement has been arguing for the democracy model since before the 1934 Communications Act that gave broadcasting licenses to the telecommunications companies.

Trumping the public resource model and inclusive of the technology model, the democracy model argues that the state should advocate for pro-democracy practices. Media reform

> has nothing to do with scarcity of resources or an abundance of technology. It is much more fundamental than that. The founders of public service broadcasting ... said that democracy needs a healthy nonprofit, noncommercial media sector. That's the core issue involved here. You can't have a democracy without having a healthy, democratic media system. ... That scarcity stuff was something lawyers and politicians cooked up later, to sell public broadcasting to legislators, judges, and bureaucrats. You can't get people off their butts on the scarcity thing. You organize a movement on the

80   A. FISH

vision of democratic media, not all this talk about gigabytes in the spectrum. (McChesney 2003, 16)

McChesney makes a clear argument that the central point of media reform is improving the vibrancy of national democracy. I quote this passage at length because it is a definitive statement from a partner with FSTV. McChesney and Gore are in agreement on these points regarding culture, technology, and power (Gore 2007). The democratic model for which he argues here is shared by FSTV, Current, and the social justice media organizations with which they associate.

Gore draws from the democracy model:

> The remedy for what ails our democracy is not simply better education (as important as that is) or civic education (as important as that can be), but the reestablishment of a genuine democratic discourse in which individuals can participate in a meaningful way—a conversation of democracy in which meritorious ideas and opinions from individuals do, in fact, evoke a meaningful response. (Gore 2007, 254)

Gore argues that the for-profit motivation in today's television news networks creates conditions that singularly elevates profit over public service. This process is making the viewer less reasonable, less logical, and less based on facts. Gore asks, "Why has America's public discourse become less focused and clear, less *reasoned?*" (Gore 2007, 2). He argues that consolidated media results in an emphasis on entertainment and a degradation of the news, which leads to less reasonable, more distracted, and less capable citizens. This tendency has a deleterious impact on democracy. This democracy model frames the necessities of media reform in terms of democracy itself. As such, the democracy model is the most principled of the media reform models.

In this chapter I have briefly introduced the numerous models used by broadcasters and media reformers to articulate, motivate, and justify their media reform activism and broadcasting activities. Broadcasters' models are arrayed across the public sphere, the guardianship, and the commercial models. Guardianship and commercial broadcasting models are represented aesthetically with traditional news broadcasting featuring wizened television journalists. The public sphere model, requiring transformation of the audience into media producers and shareholders, is a less prevalent yet more radical broadcasting model. Any single broadcaster, Current and

FSTV included, may move through these models or use a number of them simultaneously. This practice reveals how broadcast models are cultural inventions, flexible in their application into realms of hegemonic power. Most media reformers want serious reform and believe that the media are public resources that have been given to commercial interests. Their project is to mobilize a suite of models to challenge the privatization of public media resources and defend public control over the scant examples that remain of public interest media. A range of models are used by media reformers with entry points beginning in anti-monopoly, public interest, free speech, access, public resources, emergent technology, and democracy.

These models are used in concert to defend or regain access to public media. The broadcast models as well as the media reform models are both cultural interventions into the American public sphere. Current and FSTV syncretize various models throughout their tenure to motivate specific results. This flexible use of media reform models reveals the mobility of cultural interventions but may also symbolize the resourceful deployment of mission and market admixtures necessary to generate profit.

REFERENCES

Adorno, T.W., and M. Horkheimer. 1977. The Culture Industry: Enlightenment as Mass Deception. In *Mass Communication and Society*, ed. J. Curran, M. Gurevitch, and J. Woollacott, 349–383. London: The Open University Press.

Alterman, E. 2003. *What Liberal Media? The Truth about Bias and the News*. New York: Basic Books.

Anderson, C. 2006. *The Long Tail: Why the Future of Business Is Selling Less of More*. New York: Hyperion.

Ang, I. 1991. *Desperately Seeking the Audience*. London: Routledge.

Artz, B.L. 2000. Introduction. In *Public Broadcasting and the Public Interest*, ed. Michael P. McCauley, Eric E. Peterson, B. Lee Artz, and DeeDee Halleck. Armouk, NY: M.E. Sharpe.

Bagdikian, B. 1983. *The Media Monopoly*. New York: Beacon Press.

Clark, A. 2012. Can Current TV Establish Itself as a Real Competitor in Political Broadcasting Without Keith Olbermann? *Alternet*. Accessed December 5, 2015. http://www.alternet.org/news/154135/can_current_tv_establish_itself_as_a_real_competitor_in_political_broadcast–with_or_without_keith_olbermann

82   A. FISH

Couldry, N. 2010. *Why Voice Matters: Culture and Politics After Neoliberalism.* London: Sage.

Dana, R. 2012. Gore's Desperate Bid to Keep Keith Olbermann—And Save Current TV. *The DailyBeast/Newsweek.* Accessed March 20, 2012. http://www.thedailybeast.com/newsweek/2012/02/05/iskeith-olbermann-the-last-hope-for-gore-s-current-tv.html

Eggerton, J. 2008. Obama Does Not Support Return of Fairness Doctrine. *Broadcasting & Cable.* Accessed March 20, 2012. http://www.broadcasting-cable.com/article/114322-Obama_Does_Not_Support_Return_of_Fairness_Doctrine.php

Ferguson, J., and A. Gupta. 2002. Spatializing States: Towards an Ethnography of Neoliberal Governmentality. *American Ethnologist* 29(4): 981–1002.

Fish, A. 2005. Native American Places and the Language of Capitalism. *Future Anteriors: The Journal of Historic Preservation, History, Theory, and Criticism* 2(1): 40–49.

Fish, A., L.F.R. Murillo, L. Nguyen, A. Panofsky, and C. Kelty. 2011. Birds of the Internet: A Field Guide to Understanding Action, Organization, and the Governance of Participation. *The Journal of Cultural Economy* 4(2): 157–187.

Foucault, M. 1991. Governmentality. In *The Foucault Effect: Studies in Governmentality,* ed. Graham Burchell, Colin Gordon, and Peter Miller. Chicago: University of Chicago Press.

Fowler, M., and D. Brener. 1982. A Marketplace Approach to Broadcast Regulation. *Texas Law Review* 60(2): 207–257.

Genachowski, J. 2011. Chairman Genachowski's Response to Rep. Upton and Rep. Walden. 24 June. Accessed March 20, 2012. http://hraunfoss.fcc.gov/edocs_public/attachmatch/DOC-308274A1.pdf

Gore, A. 2007. *The Assault on Reason.* London: Penguin Press.

Halleck, D.D. 2002. *Hand Held Visions: The Impossible Possibilities of Community Media.* New York: Fordham University Press.

Halpin, J., J. Heidbreder, M. Lloyd, P. Woodhull, B. Scott, J. Silver, and S. Derek Turner. 2007. The Structural Imbalance of Political Talk Radio. *Center for American Progress.* Accessed March 20, 2012. http://www.americanprogress.org/issues/2007/06/talk_radio.html

Jansen, S.C. 2011. Media, Democracy, Human Rights, and Social Justice. In *Media and Social Justice,* ed. Sue Currey Jansen, Jefferson Pooley, and Lora-Taub Pervizpour. New York: Palgrave Macmillan.

Mamoun, L. 2003. Wielding Weapons of Mass Persuasion: The Anti-war TV Movement. *Z Magazine.* Accessed March 20, 2012. http://www.zcommunications.org/wielding-weapons-of-mass-persuasionby-linda-mamoun

McCauley, M.P., E.E. Peterson, B.L. Artz, and D.D. Halleck. 2003. Introduction. In *Public Broadcasting and the Public Interest,* ed. M.P. McCauley, E.E. Peterson, B.L. Artz, and D.D. Halleck. Armouk, NY: M.E. Sharpe.

McChesney, R. 2003. Public Broadcasting: Past, Present, and Future. In *Public Broadcasting and the Public Interest*, ed. M.P. McCauley, E.E. Peterson, B.L. Artz, and D.D. Halleck. Armouk, NY: M.E. Sharpe.

McChesney, R., and J. Nichols. 2010. *The Death and Life of American Journalism: The Media Revolution That Will Begin the World Again*. New York: Nation Books.

Morozov, E. 2011. *The Net Delusion: The Dark Side of Internet Freedom*. Jackson, TN: Public Affairs Books.

Ostrow, J. 2011. 'Anti-Fox' Free Speech TV Wants a Spot on Comcast. *Denver Post*. Accessed March 20, 2012. http://www.denverpost.com/ci_17993536?source=bb

Public Mind Poll. 2011. Some News Leaves People Knowing Less. *Public Mind Poll*. Accessed March 20, 2012. http://publicmind.fdu.edu/2011/knowless/

Schiller, D. 1999. Social Movement in Telecommunications: Rethinking the Public Service History of U.S. Telecommunications, 1804–1919. In *Communication, Citizenship, and Social Policy*, ed. A. Calabrese and J.C. Burgelman, 137–155. Lanham, MD: Rowman & Littlefield.

Streeter, T. 1996. *Selling the Air: A Critique of the Policy of Commercial Broadcasting in the United States*. Chicago: University of Chicago Press.

Wu, T. 2010. *The Master Switch: The Rise and Fall of Information Empires*. New York: Knopf.

CHAPTER 4

Corporate Liberalism and Video Producers

PROFORMATIONS

Proformation is a portmanteau of *pro* duction/re *formation*—technological and political action for public access to the means of production on information infrastructures, be they satellite television systems or the internet. Proformers produce information for those reformed infrastructures, be it television programming or internet content. Proformations are also political. The term addresses the hybrid culture of information reform and information production at the interface of infrastructural praxis and communications rights. Proformers believe that the ability to access information infrastructures is a human right (Sithigh 2012). It is a project for "media democratization" (Hackett and Carroll 2006; Klinenberg 2007; MacKinnon 2012). In the logic of proformation, information infrastructures are commons, public resources that should be allocated to prodemocracy projects (Exoo 2009). Broadly speaking, proformers tend to be social liberals or "progressives" advocating for civil liberties, multiculturalism, universal health care, unions, free speech, free press, a strong central state, and federal funding for education and environmental protection, and public media (Coleman and Golub 2009). Progressive proformers are for citizen media production access, the use of scarce public media resources for the advancement of democratic dialogue, the use of emergent technology for democratic aims, and the importance of public media for a working democracy. While social liberalism is neither in direct conflict with the corporate form nor markets, it challenges the privatization central

© The Author(s) 2017
A. Fish, *Technoliberalism and the End of Participatory Culture in the United States*, DOI 10.1007/978-3-319-31256-9_4

86 A. FISH

to most corporate liberal practices. The contradiction is that toward their goals of progressive media production/reform, proformations are enabled by corporate liberal regulations that require some public access to private information infrastructures.

This is a practice theory-based approach to media production that defines both the agencies for media production/reform and the policies that enable or structure practices, such as corporate liberalism (Bourdieu 1990; Ortner 2013). Corporate liberalism is a form of governmentality, or the art of government (Foucault 1991), by which corporate agendas are masked as social policies creating consenting subjects. Corporate liberal policies provision limited public media resources—airwaves, spectrum, right-of-way, and extra-terrestrial space—to corporations that are required to provide a select few channels for public use (Streeter 1996). In corporate liberalism, the state performs a paltry duty to the "public interest." Scant pro-public interventions into media monopolies are allowed under corporate liberalism, such as the small amounts of public media "set-asides" enjoyed by public television stations (Sterne 1999, 507). In this process, proformers become embedded within the capitalist world system that the socially liberal content they produce often critiques.

The theory of proformation developed from an analysis of material collected from FSTV, a small, USA-based, public interest satellite, cable, and internet news network founded in 1995. FSTV is a not-for-profit organization that finances its operations through viewer support and foundation grants. From offices in Denver, Colorado, FSTV broadcasts to potentially 30 million viewers on the Dish and DirecTV satellites, access to which they received because of corporate liberal policies. The network's roster included Al Jazeera and *Democracy Now!*, the award-winning independent and progressive television and radio news program. The workers at FSTV are not exclusively television pundits or behind-the-scenes waged producers. They are also reformers who adapt to changes in corporate liberal media policy and lobby their organized public in media reform. FSTV's production and reform practices include shooting, logging, hosting, and editing live and taped video; online community management, audience interactivity, and internet content sharing; citizen video aggregating and satellite uplinking; partnering, networking, and conference collaborating; lobbying regulatory bodies and piecing together emergent video-internet-satellite technologies. They are both *pro* ducers and media re *formers*—proformers—who reform the technological and political conditions for

CORPORATE LIBERALISM AND VIDEO PRODUCERS   87

their broadcasts and mobilize an organized public to open up information infrastructures and thereby diversify the public sphere. FSTV produces live television coverage from political events such as Netroots Nation, the National Conference for Media Reform, and Take Back the Dream—all multiday US progressive political conferences I attended with FSTV in 2011 as an observer and volunteering television producer. Between 2010 and 2012 as part of a two-year research project investigating the synergies between media reform, internet video, and television production, I interviewed over 80 television and internet video producers, produced 16 television documentaries, and spent over a month in the offices of television and internet video production companies in Los Angeles, San Francisco, New York City, and Denver. Following the research of ethnographers of television (Dornfeld 1998), my research included working in FSTV's offices where I also interviewed the majority of its personnel. In these experiences, I saw and heard evidence revealing FSTV as a proformation attempting to gain access through corporate liberal policy and technological interventions to information infrastructures.

Proformations attempt to reform and produce content for privatized information infrastructures. Information infrastructures refer to the material technologies that carry networked communication—cables, satellites, antennas, broadband networks, television studios, Wi-Fi routers, mesh networks, servers, cloud storage facilities, and so on. Information infrastructures also include the less tangible but still materially impacting elements such as applications, programs, and protocols, as well as the laws and regulations which are difficult to differentiate from programming language (Lessig 2000). Information infrastructures are also cultural and include "the set of organizational practices, technical infrastructure and social norms" (Edwards et al. 2007, 6). While some scholars discuss information infrastructures in terms of their openness (Hanseth 2010), other focus on how they are regulated (Borgman 2000). Information infrastructures are built from non-private media resources such as radio frequency spectrum, public lands for cable television right of ways, and extra-terrestrial space for communication satellite orbits. Information infrastructures are expensive to build and operate, and they trade in scarce resources. Their finitude and the centrality of communication for deliberation in democracy have explicitly politicized information infrastructures.

To better grasp the practices of proformers, it is instructional to elaborate upon the differences between hegemonic, counterhegemonic, and

88 A. FISH

anti-hegemonic practices. Because of their costs and political importance, hegemonic political and economic forces such as governments and corporations seek to control information infrastructures. Counterhegemonic practices are reformative, seeking a *transition* of hegemonic information infrastructures (Carroll 2006). Anti-hegemonic practices are radical, seeking a *transformation* of hegemonic information infrastructures. Proformers are counterhegemonic actors who do not transform but rather transition pre-existing information infrastructures into more progressive formulations. For example, proformers can work to bridge the "digital divide" or bring the internet to rural parts of the world. They focus on "open" technology, information technologies for development (ICT4D), and community-owned infrastructures. Proformers build and expand access to public Wi-Fi networks (Powell 2008), low-power FM radio (Dunbar-Hester 2012), and satellite television (Halleck 2002). They may critique hegemonic information infrastructures and the political economies that support them, but their presence also extends these hegemonic information infrastructures to new regions. FSTV's public media "set-asides" allowed by corporate liberalism permits its counterhegemonic content to exist without threatening the integrity of the hegemonic and privatized information infrastructure. One might say counterhegemonies expand the capitalist hegemony into new markets. In the conclusion, I will briefly consider whether anti-hegemonic information infrastructures are possible.

The central problem faced in this chapter is the perception shared by many progressive media activists that they are anti-hegemonic, actively working against the brutality of capitalism and the corporate liberal state. Several proformers with whom I spoke expressed socialist aspirations. My primary confidant, FSTV's General Manager Don Rojas was the press secretary for the Marxist Prime Minister of Grenada, Maurice Bishop, when US Marines invaded the island in 1983. During the invasion he was flown to Moscow where he met Fidel Castro and other Marxist political leaders. However, FSTV is far from an anti-hegemonic force. While FSTV's content may defend the values of social liberalism, proformations are counterhegemonies whose presence justifies hegemonies. By materializing as conscience-clearing tokens of social liberal practices within these hegemonic systems, they enable governments to allow media corporations to privatize the information infrastructures. In this way they consent to and are complicit in their own subjugation. This is a form of "symbolic violence" or "violence which is exercised upon a social agent with his or her complicity" (Bourdieu and Wacquant 1992, 167). However, while

CORPORATE LIBERALISM AND VIDEO PRODUCERS 89

capitalism is a violent system, this violence does not explicitly exist in the domestic workworlds of proformers who tend to be underpaid, overworked, and have precarious job security—unsurprising for work in the non-profit creative industries. Without this workworld violence, however, the likelihood of anti-hegemonic forces arising decreases, and a more sustained form of domination is achieved. The case study that follows charts a historical analysis of FSTV as a proformer: a political reformer, a technological innovator, and a producer of political content.

As described in greater detail below, FSTV engineered and used access points provided by corporate liberal policy to expand its audience across a number of information infrastructures. First, in the form of The 90s Channel, it was on seven cable networks (1989–1995) before being ejected by an anti-public interest telecommunication conglomerate CEO, John Malone. For the next five years (1995–2000), FSTV was a "program service," packaging content that it "bicycled" to public interest networks that would air the content. During this period, FSTV petitioned the US Congress and adapted itself to new policies regulating emergent information infrastructures. For example, the Cable Communications Act of 1984 required terrestrial cable networks to provide channels for "leased access" to public service stations. The Cable Television Consumer Protection and Competition Act of 1992 and its November 1998 FCC guidelines required direct-broadcast satellites to provide 4–7% of their channels for public access. FSTV's co-founder John Schwartz, an aloof and wealthy progressive, personally wrote letters to Congress to support this bill. In this way the satellite firm DISH came under pressure to provide for public access and gave FSTV a deal on an out-of-the-way channel, and the network was on its first satellite. Through the same process, a decade later, FSTV was on its second satellite, DirecTV.

FSTV's programmatic choices express its political identity. It reported on important political events, such as the protests in 1999 against the World Trade Organization, the 2003 Iraq War, and the upheaval of the Arab Spring and the Occupy Movements in 2011. FSTV's technological skill was evidenced in the way it used amateur technologies in professional ways, such as being pioneers in the use of video online in the mid-1990s, and using MPEG2 video compression and a T1 delivery line for a daily television news production. They were also innovators in citizen video journalism, beginning with the 1999 WTO protests and the 2000 Democratic National Convention.

90   A. FISH

During the 2008 global financial crisis, after a change of management, rebranding itself, shaking up its use of internet video and social media, FSTV started in-house and live production, and took on new partnerships with progressive media groups. The period of my fieldwork (2010–2012) represented a culmination of these efforts as I observed a new campaign consisting of new studio news and live political event programming paired with attempts to capture audience engagement through social media.

In the case study that follows I describe these points in detail articulating FSTV as a policy-driven, technologically innovative, media-producing *proformation* constrained by corporate liberal media policy.

CASE STUDY: FREE SPEECH TV

"What is the role of independent media in sustaining free speech and equal access in a privatized and regulated world? FSTV, the non-corporate independent television and internet video network, is at the National Conference for Media Reform to give our audiences an intimate look at the debate and to open our airwaves to activists in the fight for free speech, independent media, and equal access to the internet."

An experience that I had in the field that reveals FSTV deliberating their approach to accessing private information infrastructures was our co-authoring the umbrella statement above, a public explanation used on television to describe who FSTV was and why we were going to the 2011 National Conference for Media Reform. While FSTV prepared for this conference, they were also preparing for meetings with Comcast, the largest telecommunication company in the USA, with the hopes that they could gain one public interest station. While we were writing this statement, I naïvely asked my informants about their perspective on media regulation, whether FSTV was for or against it. FSTV Marketing and Development Director Giselle Diaz Campagna said,

> There is good regulation and bad regulation. ... There used to be a time when monopolies were an outright no. Now we see them everywhere. If Comcast ends up owning, or some other carrier, more and more of the pipeline, can we survive that? We know what Comcast is, it is a very conservative [company], and can FSTV gain a PI [public interest channel] there? Why wouldn't they give it to the evangelicals? Can we survive in a privatized and regulated world?

Campagna, an educated woman and mother of Puerto Rican descent with a mohawk, does not simply support regulation but "good" regulation that moderates conglomerates in line with corporate liberal policies requiring Comcast to provide public interest stations. These forms of regulation also impact FSTV's "survival," as another employee said, because without "good regulation," FSTV will not exist. Other examples of "good regulation" are the policies that forced satellite corporations DISH and DirecTV to provide public access channels to FSTV. With this regulation comes a chance for FSTV to survive but with it also comes a "responsibility" to the public good, as another worker said in writing the umbrella statement. This social liberal "responsibility" to use their allocated public resource to "survive" and diversify content within the American public sphere came into conflict with the political values of the private owners of the information infrastructures that FSTV was attempting to access.

FSTV employees discussed how their name, motto, and mission—"Free Speech"—was a liability for their "survival," as Comcast might see it as a moniker of left-wing free speech maximalism. Comcast is instructed by FCC law to relinquish a small percentage of its television spectrum to public interest networks, but it retains the right to select which networks acquire the channel. As Campagna said, "Why wouldn't they give it to the evangelicals?" FSTV fears that it would be marginalized because its content and social liberal mission are often antagonistic toward capitalism, media conglomeration, and conservative politics. The challenges of social liberal "responsibility" and "surviving" as a non-profit television network are internalized in the work practices and externalized in the institutional history of FSTV. These tensions of "good regulation and bad regulation" are also mediated by corporate liberalism. As of publication, FSTV has failed to acquire a public interest station on Comcast, but the history of how they have acquired public interest stations on other private information infrastructures shows how corporate liberalism works to secure with specific limited critique the privatization of public media resources.

Media reform has a long history in the USA. Throughout the twentieth century, as each new network communication technology emerged—broadcast television, cable television, satellite television, and the internet—movements fomented to challenge corporate liberalism and advocate for the social liberal values of pro-public media (McChesney 2008; Pickard 2011). The advent of each new information infrastructure brings with it new needs for proformative action. For example, when cable television entrepreneurs in the 1950s wanted to entertain audiences, they had to lobby city commissioners for access, or right-of-way, to lay cable through cities. In corporate liberal fashion, city officials requested small concessions for the public,

92 A. FISH

including public access channels and television production equipment and facilities. "If the city negotiated well, they got good access, if not, they got bad," said FSTV co-founder John Schwartz (Farabee 2007, 4). This was the origin of the PEG (Public, Education, and Government) channels on which FSTV broadcasts to 200 such stations. In a corporate liberal era increasingly critical of public concessions, PEG channels have been routinely challenged as a social responsibility imposed upon the free speech of corporate media. But these channels remain, despite their underfunding and unknown audience metrics (Aufderheide and Clark 2010, 7–8).

FSTV's employees see themselves, their work, and their progressive programming as central to dominant national issues within what they consider to be a single, national American public sphere, constituted by American television, print, and internet news. They are not interested in producing the conditions for a revolutionary "subaltern counterpublic" (Fraser 1990, 67). They want to be a player on a national level with the likes of Fox News, MSNBC, and other major US television news outlets and thus to contribute diverse voices to an American public sphere (Habermas 1992, 427). Their programs, such as *Democracy Now!*, represent "critical media" (Fuchs 2010), counterhegemonic content that seeks to change hegemonic society, not oppose it by anti-hegemonic practice. Counterhegemonic positionality strangely situates FSTV in a *complementary* role to corporate liberalism, in which an organization critical of media corporations helps media corporations abide by federal regulations and retain their monopoly control.

FSTV's first cultural intervention as a proformation was to gain access on Tele-Communications Inc. (TCI), the largest cable company in 1989. In order to prevent monopoly control over television content, the Cable Communications Act of 1984 (Public Law 98-549) required cable operators like TCI to make available several channels for less expensive "leased access" by public media producers. The Act was a "virtual dead letter" to non-profit television organizations because the cable operators set the price and terms (Aufderheide 1992, 56). However, "leased access" worked for FSTV, as they were able to pay for access and survive under this policy for six years (1989–1995). To do so, The 90s Channel, the precursor of FSTV, needed to hack together early cable video technology while exploiting the corporate liberal "leased access" regulations.

The content on The 90s Channel was progressive, exposing environmental decay; race, class, gender, and sexual inequality; and loss of personal freedom. The content production practice was recursively participatory as it solicited content from any would-be documentary producers, who also constituted the audience. In this early example from FSTV, the network realized the ends, distributing progressive content, justified the means—complicity with the media monopoly TCI. With their "organized public" providing viewer financial support, The 90s Channel proceeded to exploit the small window of opportunity provided by the "leased access" federal law that required TCI, in typical corporate liberal fashion, to distribute The 90s Channel content at cut rates while at the same time making tremendous profit from the public's resource. By "organized public" I refer to the publics that are seeded with practical or informational resources by a "formal social enterprise" (Fish et al. 2011). The production of an organized public is one of the key practices by which proformations generate audiences.

With a network of professional-amateur producers and active audience members, The 90s Channel produced two hours of content every week. It packaged this content on three-quarters VHS tapes and sent those tapes to the seven American Southwest cities covered by TCI. These tapes would run on a loop all day until the next tapes arrived the following week. This project "utilized the power of television to give a voice to, and build alliances with, social justice organizations, independent media organization, and grassroots activists," according to FSTV co-founder Jon Stout (interviewed March 10, 2011). Thus, The 90s Channel expanded horizontally across the organized public, acquiring content and cobbling together VHS technology and satellite access, while exploiting leased access regulations. In this fashion, The 90s Channel was able to rebroadcast to their organized public, creating a feedback loop of content, user-supported finances, and political activism.

In order for TCI to profit from access to the right-of-way, it had to abide by the corporate liberal elements of the Cable Communications Act of 1984. FSTV acquired access on TCI and facilitated TCI's compliance with "leased access" regulations that legalized TCI's monopolistic business. In this process, FSTV functioned as a necessary component in the privatization of public media resources, in this case, right-of-way through cities in the American Southwest. This form of capital inclusion denotes instances in which actors comply with economic structures that they otherwise reject. As proformers, FSTV politically opposed the privatization of the public media resource. But they accept this particular politic because they would rather distribute progressive television news content than embody a silenced resistance to the privatization of the public media resource. This capitulation forces FSTV into the circuits of capitalization

94 A. FISH

that they reject. Non-compliance would result in denied access to information infrastructures and the finality of the proformation. Survival and responsibility, not mere conflicting interests, merge as FSTV complies with corporate liberal media policy.

These triages are necessary because proformers require access to costly and immense information infrastructures. Communicative capitalism is critical of how reflexivity within networked labor reinforces capitalism (Dean 2010). Marxist communication scholar Jodi Dean (2010) isolates anthropologist Christopher Kelty's (2008) computer and network geeks as exemplars of reflexive communicative capitalism. She says, "The networks of communicative capitalism at the basis of Free Software ... produce inequality, insecurity, and subjection to the conditions and demands of a recalcitrant finance sector" (Dean 2010, 27). Dean's criticism is dependent upon Kelty failing to identify how geeks are structured by hegemonic power. Kelty writes that recursive publics are "structured in response to the historically constituted layering of power and control within the infrastructures of computing and communication" (Kelty 2008, 10). Add to these structures capitalism and regulation and a fuller picture of proformation as a complex apparatus of power and yet at the same time rejecting power becomes clear. While Dean overstates it, her point directs attention to how compliance with forms of corporate liberalism is capitulation to capitalism.

Like geeks, proformers "are capable of speaking to existing forms of power through the production of actually existing alternatives" (Kelty 2008, 4). These alternatives are embedded within a corporate liberal television regulatory system that is complementary to existing hegemonic power. TCI is not directly extracting wealth from FSTV, but rather media corporations are satisfying their corporate liberal responsibilities by providing a channel for FSTV. This process enables them to extract wealth from public media resources that they are usually allowed to exploit free of charge. Likewise, while free software constitutes an alternative to dominant proprietary software, it also complements the development of for-profit proprietary software and is wedded to a highly commercialized internetwork of internet service providers, search companies, cloud storage firms, online advertising schemes, computerized derivatives trading, and the for-profit workworld of geeks. Neither American public television nor free software represents explicit calls for the overthrow of capitalism. Rather, they represent a counterhegemony complementary to the hegemony.

The TCI "leased access" opening was soon to close, however, and FSTV had to direct its policy and technological competencies toward

CORPORATE LIBERALISM AND VIDEO PRODUCERS 95

gaining access on a new commercial information infrastructure—satellite. By August of 1994, The 90s Channel management knew the network was going to be deleted from TCI on Halloween 1995. The loss of the seven full-time cable channels on TCI was no "small setback, I want to stress that we remain[ed] committed—if anything, more strongly—to the task of building a network for progressive television," concluded Schwartz (1995). The year The 90s Channel folded, FSTV was born. It was this capacity to reformulate its technological and political identity that illustrates FSTV's agencies as proformers. When the access closure occurred because of the neoliberal values of TCI CEO John Malone, The 90s Channel mobilized its agencies to create openness in the next networked communication system: satellite television in 2000. Inhabiting a feedback loop with organized publics, enabled by policy, adapting to new technologies, while expressing the liberal values of free speech—these are traits of proformers exhibited by FSTV during this period.

"Program service" describes the way content producers distribute content, with the burden of distribution carried by the producer. When The 90s Channel/FSTV was kicked off TCI's seven stations, it borrowed a page from the Manhattan-based, progressive, non-profit satellite collective, Deep Dish TV. FSTV produced four hours of content and shipped it to 50 PEG stations, which then shipped the tapes to a second and sometimes a third tier of stations. FSTV called this process its "program service." In this way, they could continue to broadcast, develop an audience, remain a brand, and stay in the industry. However, the total audience was smaller for FSTV during this period than in the days of The 90s Channel when Schwartz and Stout had seven dedicated channels. Under the early FSTV plan, it had more channels but less total airtime. The 50 public access channels would air the block of programming not on a schedule but mixed in with the heterogeneity of public access talent. Despite its difficulties and lack of consistency, this "program service" period was strategic for FSTV. Because of Schwartz's long-time dedication to media reform, he was aware that the possibility that the guidelines for satellite set-asides might change to favor FSTV. The "program service" phase helped FSTV prove that it was capable of providing content for a satellite television provider needing to broadcast public interest television on its DBS (direct-broadcast satellites) set-asides.

The Cable Television Consumer Protection and Competition Act of 1992 (and its November 1998 FCC guidelines) required DBS to "set aside" 4–7% of their channels for non-commercial television at reduced rates. The Association for Public Television Stations, a media reform

96 A. FISH

organization, along with the federally funded PBS, supported the set-asides. A DBS like DirecTV with 175 channels was forced to offer 7–12 channels of PEG programming. The DBS corporate liberal set-aside is a compromise by the public to media corporations with the public capable of exercising its communications rights (Sithigh, 2012) on as little as 4–7% of the spectrum allocated to for-profit DBS. Of that total, much is given to Christian television.

The FCC gave the satellite companies discretion about how to do it. Schwartz had long lobbied Congress for these public interest set-asides, and when they came, FSTV was ready. Stout told me: "We were waiting for this day to come" (interviewed March 10, 2011). Stout said that the interim period between The 90s Channel and the FCC's 1998 guidelines, when it was "bicycling" tapes on its "pedestrian network," was difficult, but it was necessary to continue to broadcast. "It was important to develop a library, identity, infrastructure, and audience, so when the time came to apply for a satellite channel, we existed as a network, not just on paper" (interviewed March 20, 2011). By "library, identity, infrastructure, and audience," Stout refers to the assemblage of forces, materials, and people that come to constitute a proformative public.

In January of 2000, Dish provided three channels for educational programming. Two went to Christian stations, and one went to FSTV. Schwartz and Stout were elated and stunned, "we went from being a programming service, a syndicator of content, to a full-blown national television network. We went from coming up with four hours a week to sending out to the country to 24-7 365 to fill," said Stout (interviewed March 10, 2011). This opening for FSTV was engineered over many difficult years by developing an organized public of active viewers and politically progressive producers; putting together emergent recording, distributing, and broadcasting technology; petitioning politicians; and modulating to public media policy. At the same time, however, FSTV had difficulty gaining access on a corporate liberal system tilted to favor pay-to-play for-profit media corporations and non-political religious programming.

FSTV's Dish channel was the result of much policy work. Schwartz "personally, or through supported/commissioned lobbying firms (like Media Access Project, pushed policy agendas, lobbied Congress and petitioned the FCC" (Jon Stout, email, November 6, 2012). For example, a letter written to the FCC by Schwartz in 2002 advocated for satellite distribution companies Echostar and DirecTV to be consolidated, which would allow for a more efficient use of the satellite-available

CORPORATE LIBERALISM AND VIDEO PRODUCERS   97

spectrum and therefore "increase the number of public interest programmers" by converging the public interest channels from both satellite systems (Schwartz 2002). The attempt to sway public interest policy, exploit the openings provided by new technological and corporate mergers, and therefore impact FSTV's distribution footprint, are actions consistent with the political proactive theory of proformation. In these practices, FSTV's attempts to persuade the FCC are not particularly unique. What is novel is how these practices reveal the mitigation of values as Schwartz advocated for something in practice he opposes in theory—conglomeration.

In developing the theory of proformations, it is instructive to again compare the relative structuration of public television producers against computer geeks. Some see Kelty's reading of geeks as "optimistic" in its figuring of geeks as "autonomous and creative individuals" (Meng and Wu 2013, 3) unencumbered by corporate liberal policies. However, recursive publics *are* constrained by policies. For example, geeks are structured by intellectual property regimes such as the Digital Millennium Copyright Act (DMCA) of 1998 that prohibits the circumvention of access controls on proprietary software. Such laws limit geeks' capacity to exercise free speech and to "argue-by-technology" (Kelty 2005, 186). However, while the computer industry and the internet are both highly commercialized and increasingly monopolized (Wu 2010), the internet is relatively unencumbered by federal regulation or centralized corporate control. Granular computer code and internet deregulation make it less difficult for recursive publics to express "radical technological modifiability" (Kelty 2008, 3). Without considerable regulatory assistance, geeks can access their information infrastructures while other proformers such as public television producers cannot. FSTV's access to television systems such as TCI or Dish necessitated their complicity with corporate liberal regulations. FSTV gained access on Dish because it was required to "set-aside" 4–7% of their possible channels for public television. This is an example of the truncated autonomy allowed to proformers working on highly structured information infrastructure, such as television. These processes continued into the twenty-first century.

With the Bush administration beating the drums of war after the tragedy of September 11, 2001, FSTV began programming *World in Crisis*. The series was about the anti-corporate globalization movement, the 2000 US political party conventions, and the upcoming Iraq War. To produce it, FSTV took a crew of five people to rural Cheyenne, Wyoming, where

98   A. FISH

its satellite uplink antenna was located. They would camp out overnight and in the morning set up a makeshift studio with "really flimsy movie lights on a clamp, aluminium foil, duct tape, and old TV monitors spray painted black and stacked up" as the studio backdrop (Stout, interviewed March 10, 2011). From here they would go live from a video camera wired straight to the satellite and report on the events leading up to war in March 2003. This makeshift studio was within the budget, following the politics, technological competency, and aesthetic of public interest television.

In *World in Crisis* FSTV successfully brought their organized public into production. They linked citizen video journalists with a satellite uplink truck and their video-enabled website, an early predecessor of the citizen journalist of the so-called "Web 2.0" era (Gillmor 2006). FSTV broadcast live political reporting and commentary, partnering with *Democracy Now!* to cover the Democratic National Convention in 2000 in Philadelphia. This was "the first ever live satellite-distributed protest coverage under control of a grassroots-based, independent media coalition" (Alston 2002). Citizen video journalism shares a number of characteristics with proformers: lateral collaboration, innovative use of new technologies, collective reworking of the means of production, interventions into information infrastructures, political intentionalities, a collaboration between platform producers and a street team of activists, and an ordering of worth prioritizing content over form.

Democracy Now! has been airing on FSTV since 2000. The show uses a groundbreaking method of distribution using a file transfer protocol (FTP) on a fast T1 internet line to send a compressed MPEG2 video from New York City to Cheyenne, Wyoming, to distribute daily a low-fidelity TV program. No other program is distributed nationally on this scale, let alone on a daily basis. It had not been possible before. "We've piecemealed some existing technologies into a new application," FSTV engineer Chase Pierce explained (Alston 2002). Stout elaborated on how FSTV delivered content to the Dish satellite: "It was very low tech, and you would walk into this ... empty room with three pieces of equipment in it; this was our broadcast head-in. ... There was no precedent for this, but our tech people researched what was the cheapest way to accomplish it. It flew in the face of TV, but it worked" (interviewed March 10, 2011). Pushing the limits of satellite and mobile video technology was an unprecedented example of the socio-technical interventions of proformers in a television context. FSTV accepted the loss of aesthetic fidelity resulting from the flotsam and jetsam *World in Crisis* studio, MPEG2 video compression and T1 delivery, and citizen video journalism from the 1999 WTO protests and the 2000 Democratic National Convention. This was acceptable because the goals justified the means.

During the global financial crisis of 2008, the yield from FSTV's pledge drives fell by 30–40%. Foundation money had dried up. FSTV had to develop socio-technical competencies with the emergent hegemonic information infrastructure, the internet. To do this, they acquired Facebook, Twitter, and YouTube accounts and repurposed their *Democracy Now!* content for an online audience. FSTV's expansion into social media, while comparatively delayed, was an opportunity to expand their organized public. However, corporate liberal media policy did not enable FSTV's expansion online the way it had on cable and satellite. This internet era and its absent regulatory assistance for public media can be more accurately correlated historically not with corporate liberalism but with neoliberalism, which in its market fundamentalism denies statutory obligations to public media.

Despite FSTV functioning online without corporate liberal support, the participatory technical affordances of the internet invigorated new competencies for proformers. The participatory technical affordances of social media correlate with FSTV's practices as an inclusive organized public. FSTV sees few boundaries between the audience, its staff, and its content producers. Campagna was adamant about this point, saying a number of times that she was attempting to "give away" the television network to activists. She challenged large activist organizations to consider "what they would do with a television network" (interviewed February 3, 2011). The interactivity provided by social media was seen by Campagna as a way to incorporate its organized public, embody its mission to galvanize social justice, and diversify the American public sphere, while remaining economically viable despite the absence of regulatory assistance. But in order to exploit the internet, FSTV developed social media practices with which to politically engage their organized public. With platforms producers who are also policy and technologically competent and capable of engineering the means of their production, it is tempting to identify proformation as signifying an emergent agency. I have instead tempered this judgment with emphasis on how economic and political power, as well as access to information infrastructures, systematically structures the agencies of proformers.

Conclusion: From Corporate Liberalism to Neoliberalism

The successful operation that FSTV developed for the One Nation Working Together Rally in October 2010 illustrates their internet convergence strategy. It also exhibits the transition from corporate liberalism in which a modicum of state support is provided to neoliberalism in which the internet is unregulated. During the rally, FSTV would produce live coverage, which it would stream online and broadcast on television. Short clips would be produced from the live video stream. Campagna would give interns and volunteers editorial comments on each video clip. Beforehand they would spend hours online and identify more than 600 social justice blogs, from large blogs such as Crooks and Liars and the DailyKos, to much smaller, personal blogs. Campagna would then contact these partners at 10 minutes before 10:00 a.m., asking each if they would embed FSTV's live feed on their blog. In this way, FSTV's video player would be seen on the webpages of such magazines and organizations as *Mother Jones*, the *Nation*, and the NAACP (National Association for the Advancement of Colored People). If they agreed, Campagna would ask the partner to send her the link so she could verify it. She and the interns would then use social media to "buzz" throughout the days of the live coverage. "My interns would start buzzing online, on Facebook and Twitter, not as employees but as people," she said (interviewed February 3, 2011). "And we would send them [the social media audience] not to FSTV['s website] but to their group, because it is trust in their community that is important. But I gain the eyeballs because that is our player" (interviewed February 3, 2011). FSTV's goal was to spread the political message of the live video coverage online and quantify its breadth through the plug-in that counts the views on the video player. It does this regardless of which website the video player is on. This technological affordance and the quantifiability of internet video encourage "shareability," as Campagna calls the social, economic, technological, and political practice (interviewed February 3, 2011). I say economic because it is the number of views on these video players spread across the internet that becomes a significant talking point for board meetings and pitch sessions to possible funders. It is also technological in that the quantity of viewers contributes to arguments in favor of the television network focusing more resources on the internet as opposed to television, which does not produce quantitative results. As she said,

But what ended up was something amazing, eight people full-time and staff here, and we do it all, from production on, and we were able to beat our satellite viewer numbers by thousands. And clearly that is a new audience, that is a different demographic because we know TV and web audiences are different. So definitely a win, baffling to us that we could do this. (interviewed February 3, 2011)

While Rojas and Campagna saw this transition to internet-based video as positive and inevitable, along with it also came a problem. Access to the internet is "democratized" and not regulated by corporate liberalism. It is relatively inexpensive to access the means of production on this information infrastructure. Therefore, no regulatory assistance is necessary to insure citizen voices can be digitally produced. Power has shifted, however, from access and production to algorithmic search, for this no regulatory mechanisms have been devised (Hindman 2009). Search and its political promotional potential are a wholly privatized facet of digital information infrastructures dominated by multinational information companies Google, Yahoo, and Microsoft. In this, the internet is facilitating the transformation from corporate liberalism to neoliberalism, from some publicly supported media to none. It is unlikely that FSTV and others like it without the regulatory assistance to promote their diverse content in search engines will survive this transition to "informational neoliberalism" (Neubauer 2011), a more rigorous version of "digital capitalism" (Schiller 1999). The convergence or the co-creation of neoliberal and technolibertarian thought reinforces the co-occurrence of the concepts that the state is unnecessary, bureaucracies are troublesome, market forces are natural and just, and successful subjects are mobile, flexible, and above all, networked via the internet (Golumbia 2013). By the end of my fieldwork with FSTV in 2012, some of this faith in digital networks and the networked individual had become prominent but the flourishing of informational neoliberalism was tempered by the strong belief in a regulatory state.

Globally accessible information infrastructures are extremely expensive and no state or corporation is likely to turn away from the surveillance and profitable potentials of big data and its "siren servers" (Lanier 2013). Access to a nation's information infrastructure is central to national defense, as was shown with the allegedly US/Israeli-made Stuxnet virus that likely shut down centrifuges in Iran's Natanze power station (Warrick 2011). Hope for democratic deliberation in a data-driven public sphere is also dependent upon these privately held and corporately networked servers and infrastructures. Public alarm over the corporate violation of personal privacy under the guise of better "personalization" by social media companies and the mass government surveillance by the US National Security Agency (NSA), the British Government Communications Headquarters (GCHQ), and other networked authoritarians (often aided by Silicon Valley companies) will subside and, in its absence, informational neoliberalism will continue unabated.

With the neoliberalization of the internet, what information infrastructures will exist for the public good? Models of robust anti-hegemonic information infrastructures in post-capitalist contexts are few. Considering the prohibitive cost and strong regulation of information infrastructures, such anti-hegemonic information systems will be difficult, if even possible, to develop. Until anti-hegemonic information infrastructures develop, we will have proformers working to transform information infrastructures and hacktivists and networked activists working on those platforms. This is not to say that anti-hegemonic activity is impossible on hegemonic information infrastructures. There are unintended consequences on hegemonic information infrastructures. Magnified within other information infrastructures such as television, internet-based social media does facilitate the street organization for political revolution. But infrastructure is not neutral; its affordances are biased toward particular practices that are path-dependent and structured by dominant political and economic forces that are present at genesis (Starr 2004). Recent information infrastructure disruptions, smart phones and cloud computing, for example, if they had been the product of small-scale entrepreneurs, might have been briefly counterhegemonic for the dominant economic order, before quickly becoming the new hegemony. But dominant forces engineer for the most part these information infrastructures for dominant purposes.

While some information infrastructures—radio, telephone, satellite television—originally first emerged as counterhegemonic before becoming hegemonic forces, they were never anti-hegemonic.

Some ethnographers agree that a "reorientation of knowledge and power" is upon us (Kelty 2008, 8). Citing Kelty, communications scholar Sara Schoonmaker (2012) makes the bold claim that free software challenges "the dominant form of neoliberalism" and is a "virus" capable of "infecting" the "body of capitalism" (2012: 516, 503). From one perspective, FSTV is that virus spreading progressive content on corporate liberal information infrastructures. Platform reformers such as FSTV represent the policy-enabled distribution of counterhegemonic content that

CORPORATE LIBERALISM AND VIDEO PRODUCERS 103

subtly diversifies the hegemonic American public sphere on television. From another perspective, FSTV is complicit with corporate liberalism, allowing major cable and satellite companies like TCI, Dish, and DirecTV to comply with federal regulations while they profit from the privatization of public media resources. This chapter acknowledges that FSTV and its progressive content challenge the hegemony but it is incapable of "infecting" it with any mortal wound. Embedded within the hegemony, FSTV is a counterhegemonic social form that affirms the present configuration of privatized information infrastructures. Without this configuration, however, FSTV would not survive to critique the system it supports.

REFERENCES

Alston, A. 2002. Democracy Now! History in the Making. *The Independent*. Accessed March 20, 2012. http://www.aivf.org/node/5

Aufderheide, P. 1992. Cable Television and the Public Interest. *Journal of Communication* 42(1): 52–65.

Aufderheide, P., and J. Clark. 2010. *GN Docket No. 10–25, FCC Launches Examination of the Future of Media and Information Needs of Communities in a Digital Age*. Report submitted to the FCC. May 6. Accessed March 20, 2012. https://prodnet.www.neca.org/publicationsdocs/wwpdf/5610csm.pdf

Borgman, C. 2000. The Premise and Promise of a Global Information Infrastructure. *First Monday* 5(8).

Bourdieu, P. 1990. *The Logic of Practice*. Cambridge: Polity Press.

Bourdieu, P., and L. Wacquant. 1992. *An Invitation to Reflexive Sociology*. Chicago: University of Chicago Press.

Carroll, W.K. 2006. Hegemony, Counterhegemony, Antihegemony. *Socialist Studies* 2(2): 9–43. Accessed October 16, 2013. http://www.socialiststudies. com/index.php/sss/article/view/27

Dean, J. 2010. *Blog Theory: Feedback and Capture in Circuits of Drive*. Cambridge: Polity.

Dornfeld, B. 1998. *Producing Public Television*. Princeton: Princeton University Press.

Dunbar-Hester, C. 2012. Soldering Towards Media Democracy: Technical Practice as Symbolic Value in Radio Activism. *Journal of Communication Inquiry* 36: 149–169.

Edwards, P., S. Jackson, G. Bowker, and C. Knobel. 2007. *Understanding Infrastructure: Dynamics, Tensions, and Design*. Report of a Workshop on History & Theory of Infrastructure: Lessons for New Scientific Cyberinfrastructures, NSF Grant 0630263 Human and Social Dynamics Computer and Information Science and Engineering Office of Cyberinfrastructure.

104   A. FISH

Exoo, C.F. 2009. *The Pen and the Sword: Press, War, and Terror in the 21st Century.* Thousand Oaks, CA: Sage.

Farabee, M. 2007. Cable TV Tuning Out the Left. *Reclaim the Media.* Accessed November 27, 2012. http://www.reclaimthemedia.org/index.php?q=broadband_cable/cable_tv_tuning_out_the_left=5288

Fish, A., L.F.R. Murillo, L. Nguyen, A. Panofsky, and C. Kelty. 2011. Birds of the Internet: A Field Guide to Understanding Action, Organization, and the Governance of Participation. *The Journal of Cultural Economy* 4(2): 157–187.

Foucault, M. 1991. Governmentality. In *The Foucault Effect: Studies in Governmentality*, ed. Graham Burchell, Colin Gordon, and Peter Miller. Chicago: University of Chicago Press.

Fraser, N. 1990. Rethinking the Public Sphere: A Contribution to the Critique of Actually Existing Democracy. *Social Text* 25(26): 56–80.

Fuchs, C. 2010. Alternative Media as Critical Media. *European Journal of Social Theory* 13: 173–192.

Gillmor, D. 2006. *We the Media: Grassroots Journalism, by the People, for the People.* Sebastapol: O'Reilly.

Golumbia, D. 2013. Cyberlibertarianism: The Extreme Foundations of 'Digital Freedom'. Accessed December 5, 2015. http://www.academia.edu/4429212/Cyberlibertarianism_The_Extremist_Foundations_of_Digital_Freedom

Habermas, J. 1992. Further Reflections on the Public Sphere. In *Habermas and the Public Sphere*, ed. Craig Calhoun. Cambridge: MIT Press.

Hackett, R.A., and W.K. Carroll. 2006. *Remaking Media: The Struggle to Democratize Public Communication.* New York: Routledge.

Halleck, D. 2002. *Hand Held Visions: The Impossible Possibilities of Community Media.* New York: Fordham University Press.

Hanseth, O. 2010. From Systems and Tools to Networks and Infrastructures—From Design to Cultivation: Towards a Design Theory of Information Infrastructures. *Industrial Informatics design, Use and Innovation.* 11: 122–156.

Hindman, M. 2009. *The Myth of the Digital Divide.* Princeton: Princeton University Press.

Kelty, C.M. 2005. Geeks, Internets, and Recursive Publics. *Cultural Anthropology* 20: 2.

———. 2008. *Two Bits: The Cultural Significance of Free Software and the Internet.* Durham: Duke University Press.

Klinenberg, E. 2007. *Fighting for Air: The Battle to Control America's Media.* New York: Metropolitan Books.

Lanier, J. 2013. *Who Owns the Future?* New York: Allen Lane.

Lessig, L. 2000. *Code and Other Laws of Cyberspace.* New York: Basic Books.

MacKinnon, R. 2012. *Consent of the Networked: The Worldwide Struggle for Internet Freedom.* New York: Basic Books.

CORPORATE LIBERALISM AND VIDEO PRODUCERS   105

McChesney, R. 2008. *The Political Economy of Media: Enduring Issues, Emerging Dilemmas*. New York: Monthly Review Press.

Meng, B., and F. Wu. 2013. Commons/Commodity: Peer Production Caught in the Web of the Commercial Market. *Information, Communication, & Society* 16(1): 125–145.

Neubauer, R. 2011. Neoliberalism in the Information Age, or Vice Versa? Global Citizenship, Technology, and Hegemonic Ideology. *TripleC* 9(2): 195–230.

Ortner, S.B. 2013. *Not Hollywood*. Durham, NC: Duke University Press.

Pickard, V. 2011. The Battle over the FCC Blue Book: Determining the Role of Broadcast Media in a Democratic Society, 1945–1948. *Media, Culture & Society* 33(2): 171–191.

Powell, A. 2008. WiFi Publics: Producing Community and Technology. *Information, Communication, and Society*. 11(8): 1068–1088.

Schiller, D. 1999. Social Movement in Telecommunications: Rethinking the Public Service History of U.S. Telecommunications, 1804–1919. In *Communication, Citizenship, and Social Policy*, ed. A. Calabrese and J.C. Burgelman, 137–155. Lanham, MD: Rowman & Littlefield.

Schoonmaker, S. 2012. Hacking the Global: Constructing Markets and Commons Through Free Software. *Information, Communication, and Society* 15(4): 502–518.

Schwartz, J. 1995. Massive Rate Increase by Media Giant TCI Forces the 90's Channel to Shut Down at Midnight November 1. *Coalition for Networked Organization*. Accessed March 20, 2013. http://old.cni.org/hforums/roundtable/1995-04/0090.html

———. 2002. Comments of Public Communicators, Inc. Before the FCC. CS Docket No. 01-348.

Sithigh, D.M. 2012. From Freedom of Speech to the Right to Communicate. In *Routledge Handbook of Media Law*, ed. Monroe Price, Stefan Verhulst, and Libby Morgan. New York: Routledge.

Starr, P. 2004. *The Creation of the Media: Political Origins of Modern Communications*. New York: Basic Books.

Sterne, J. 1999. Television Under Construction: American Television and the Problem of Distribution, 1926–62. *Media, Culture, and Society* 21: 503–530.

Streeter, T. 1996. *Selling the Air: A Critique of the Policy of Commercial Broadcasting in the United States*. Chicago: University of Chicago Press.

Warrick, J. 2011. Iran's Natanz Nuclear Facility Recovered Quickly from Stuxnet Cyberattack. *Washington Post*. February 16.

Wu, T. 2010. *The Master Switch: The Rise and Fall of Information Empires*. New York: Knopf.

CHAPTER 5

Technoliberalism and the Origins of the Internet

POLITICAL RITUALS AND DIGITAL DISCOURSE

During the 2000 and 2012 US Presidential campaign trail, former Vice President Al Gore and former President Barack Obama prominently celebrated how the US government had financed the development of the internet. While Obama defended the role of government against neoliberal anti-statism, Gore defined himself as a politician with visionary acumen. By associating themselves with technology of immense economic, scientific, political, and social significance, the two politicians hoped to elevate themselves to higher political office. And yet, summoning the internet on the campaign trail produced two of the most catastrophic gaffes for both of these politicians as journalists willfully misinterpreted these claims. First, these campaign trail events exhibit the rituals, myths, and fetishes of digital discourse. Second, this rich discursive field helps to define technoliberalism, a term that designates how digital discourses are mobilized to mitigate the contradictions of Democratic Party liberalism.

Social life—which includes politics—has a ritualistic character (Durkheim 1976; Geertz 1973; Turner 1974). Political power is contingent upon struggles of control over symbols (Alexander 2010; Fortes and Evans-Pritchard 1950). The media magnify political rituals by enshrining political power through evocative rituals (Couldry 2003). Live campaign speeches and television interviews during "presidential campaigns have roles decisively similar to that described for mythology and ritual in traditional societies" (McLeod 1999, 363). Elevated talk on technology

© The Author(s) 2017
A. Fish, *Technoliberalism and the End of Participatory Culture in the United States*, DOI 10.1007/978-3-319-31256-9_5

108   A. FISH

is performed in campaign rituals; as such the internet becomes a fetish or myth in a ritual of mediated and political power. In this manner, the internet has become a "key symbol" (Ortner 1973) in contemporary liberalism's emphasis on the liberatory power of technology.

This chapter addresses digital discourse, or the ways the elite speak of technology and around the contradictions of liberalism. In digital discourse, technology talk mitigates incongruities within liberalism (Fisher 2010). Digital discourses are performed within political rituals (McLeod 1998), which include performance props like digital fetishes (Hornborg 2001) and historical narratives like digital myths (Mosco 2004). Gore's case is an example of the digital fetish, how powerful objects such as the internet are embodied by politicians. Obama's case illustrates digital mythologies, or how narratives are told in order to link power to their narrator. In both contexts, the internet is performed in a political ritual as a symbol of economic and technological potency capable of elevating those seeking political power. The digital discourse hails listeners to not see what the politicians are willfully overlooking—internet policies and practices that do not support the liberal agenda of civil rights and a public sphere but of surveillance, monopolization, and crony capitalism.

Journalists commenting on Gore's and Obama's internet remarks enacted their own form of media ritual (Bennett 1981), a degradation ritual designed to take power and status away from the subject (Garfinkel 1956). Degradation rituals "refer to particular practices—forms of ritualization—that work to transform the status and identity of the ritual target into a devalued category" (Thérèse and Martin 2010, 6). Addressing Obama's internet historiography, three journalists draw from liberalism's rich history to enact degradation rituals. These authors amend Obama's statements to emphasize liberalism's components: capitalism (Crovitz 2012), individualism (McCracken 2012), and populism (Johnson 2012a). A fourth journalist reads the former President's remarks through the discourse of progressivism (Manjoo 2012). Technoliberalism designates a specific type of digital discourse, namely, how the Democratic elite dialogue on technology in attempts to mitigate the tensions of liberalism, the simultaneous attractions of capitalism, individualism, populism, and progressivism.

The diverse discourses of liberalism make them both useful and dangerous for politicians hoping to exploit particular interpretations of symbols through political rituals, myths, and fetishes. Adding to the complexity of liberal theory is the digital discourse that attempts to mitigate the contradictions of liberalism through talk on technology. Four examples of digital discourse extend traditional liberal discourses into the networked society. Technocapitalism links networked technologies to capital production. Technoindividualism stresses the power of individual agency in networked production cultures. Technoprogressivism describes how progressive politics are aligned with the structure of networked technologies. Technopopulism emphasizes how collaborative publics cohere to networked structures. The four technoisms are iterations of social liberalism (technopopulism and technoprogressivism) and economic liberalism (technocapitalism and technoindividualism) and constitute discourses of technoliberalism.

Social and economic liberalism's coexistence under the rubric of liberalism is itself a contradiction. Sociologist Immanuel Wallerstein writes, "The self-contradiction of liberal ideology is total. If all humans have equal rights, and all peoples have equal rights, we can't maintain the kind of inegalitarian system that the capitalist world-economy has always been and always will be" (1995, 161). This broad contradiction is refined within the four digital discourses of technoliberalism that as dyads contradict each other and are also internally contradictory. On the economic liberal side, technocapitalism is dependent upon state financing for the creation of the information infrastructures used by corporations that claim to reject state support. Technoindividualism claims the individual is responsible for innovation while social scientists of technology understand that technologies are socially and collaboratively constructed (Bijker 1987; MacKenzie and Wajcman 1985). On the social liberal side, technoprogressivism seeks to work within existing power structures of democratic capitalism failing to acknowledge that social equality and economic freedom cannot coexist. Technopopulism claims to identify a post-capitalist form of value production but flounders in acknowledging how technoliberal elitism perpetuates domination. To discuss these digital discourses of the internet and their contradictions requires an expansive concept like that of the assemblage.

The internet is difficult to historicize and easy to symbolically exploit because of the multiplicity of its parts. Like assemblages, the internet should be recognized by the presence of three components: "heterogeneity of component elements," "exteriority of relations," and the "agency of component parts" (Anderson et al. 2012, 174, 177, 180). Like an assemblage, the internet is a globally distributed network of networks, consisting of exterior, agential, and heterogeneous components:

material technologies, corporations, user publics, codes, and state laws in perpetual change. Paul Baran, the inventor of packet switching technology, describes the internet as an assemblage when he says: "The process of technological development is like building a cathedral. ... Over the course of several hundred years new people come along and each lays down a block on top of the old foundations, each saying, 'I built a cathedral.' ... If you are not careful, you can con yourself into believing that you did the most important part" (Hafner and Lyon 1998, 79–80). Baran emphasizes the "heterogeneous within the ephemeral" and instability "infused with movement and change" (Marcus and Saka 2006, 102). This historically shifting, technologically enabled, and culturally inflected internet of historical contingencies, technologies, institutions, politics, and people looks more like an assemblage than anything described by Gore, Obama, or the journalists below. In political rituals, aspects of this assemblage are emphasized and other denied.

Gore's digital discourse has a long history. As a Tennessee Senator, Gore wrote, "high speed networks must be built that tie together millions of computers, providing capabilities that we cannot even imagine" (Gore 1991, 150). In 1994, then as the US Vice President, Gore gave a speech about convergence to the Television Academy at the University of California, Los Angeles: "Our current information industries—cable, local telephone, long distance telephone, television, film, computers, and others—seem headed for a Big Crunch/Big Bang of their own" (Gore 1994). Three months later, addressing the International Telecommunications Union in Buenos Aires, Gore discussed the potential of this Big Crunch on democracy, "networks of distributed intelligence ... will spread participatory democracy" (quoted in Brooks and Boal 1995, xii). Thus, the unimaginable, technological convergence, and participatory democracy were woven together by a younger Gore into a myth about the role of network communication technologies in helping democracy. This is the power of mythology: the ambiguity of its polysemy can be utilized in different contexts, for differing audiences.

In 2005, Gore started Current, a for-profit television network broadcasting in the USA and throughout the world. With citizen video journalism, Current attempted to convergence the participatory possibilities of internet-based affordances with the broadcasting power of television. "Our aim is to give young people a voice, to democratize television," Gore claimed proudly to *Slate* (Manjoo 2005). In *The New York Times*, Gore called Current "crowd-sourced television" (Itzkoff 2011). In *Fast*

TECHNOLIBERALISM AND THE ORIGINS OF THE INTERNET   111

Company, Gore gleefully admitted, "One of the happy problems we've had is explaining Current TV to investors and distributors. Nobody believes how low our production costs were, or how good the business model was" (McGirt 2007). Because of convergence Current could be both socially and economically liberal. Such attempts at internet and television convergence reveal how myths are mobilized in acts of solving democracy and capitalism. These myths are spoken by technoliberal media executives and imperfectly implemented by media workers who bear the brunt of risk for such Silicon Valley-based and Hollywood-based mythic adventures.

As a left-leaning, independent, and reformative television network espousing populism, celebrating the internet, founded by a Democrat, and seed-funded by Democratic Party leaders and liberal Hollywood insiders, Current is politically progressive in the traditional social liberal sense: valuing civil liberties of free speech and a free press, cultural diversity, gender, and racial equality, a strong government, and "speaking truth to power", as Gore said earlier. Add to this progressivism a belief that the internet provides a new and empowering model for society and what results is "peer progressivism" (Johnson 2012b). Peer progressives champion decentralization, collective wisdom, amateurs, "virtuous" peer-to-peer sharing (Benkler and Nissenbaum 2006), and "organizing without organizations" (Shirky 2008). They are unconvinced by hierarchy, centralization, and professionals. Their key example for a working model for peer progressivism is the internet and within it Wikipedia, fan fiction, and free and open-source software. As I describe below, peer or technoprogressivism is one genre within the digital discourse mobilized by the technoliberal elite to mitigate the contradictions of liberalism.

The technoliberal elite believe that tools trump debate and that capitalism and progressivism, and individualism and populism, can coexist. Discourse on technologies facilitates the confluence of these seemingly contradictory ideals. The term "technoliberal elites" can apply to both Republicans and Democrats but it most aptly describes Democrat technocrats like Gore and Obama, for whom the contradictions seeking mitigation are most extreme. Publicly, Democrats are aligned with social liberal, "left," or progressive values that champion cultural diversity, the expansion of civil liberties, environmentalism, community over the individual, and the state over the corporation. A Democratic state invests in science, infrastructure, innovation, education, and technologies. This is what those aspiring

112 A. FISH

to Democratic political office say in television interviews and in campaign speeches. However, this is a discourse. Gore and Obama both publicly celebrate social liberal values—and yet fail to note the subsequent privatization of the internet infrastructure, its monopolization, its lack of regulation, and increasing commercialization. The technoliberal discourse is particularly useful for Democratic presidential hopefuls because the contradictions between their public social liberal policies and their economic liberal pursuits are particularly hypocritical, requiring complex negotiations.

Gore and Obama are criticized for the factuality of their claims but a more nuanced approach is to focus on how politicians use technology to legitimate themselves and to mitigate other faults in their campaigns. For Gore, it was 1999 and the dotcom boom was in full force, networking businesses and consumers, and creating precarious employment for many and millions of dollars for a wealthy few. Gore wanted the symbolic power of the internet to legitimate his candidacy while mitigating the perception that he was personally "stiff" and not "cool." Obama, faced with a multipronged anti-state attack from right-wing radio, the Tea Party, Fox News, and Governor Mitt Romney, needed to legitimate government through associating himself with the wealth and technological power of the internet. Obama needed to mitigate this assault on the federal government through reminding the public of its positive practices. As factual as it may be that Gore and the US government were responsible for helping to develop the early internet, the reason why the internet was discussed on the campaign was because of its legitimating and mitigating power as a discourse. Talk on technology cannot be easily dismissed. It is material, factual, and inarguably good. To resist technoliberalism is to be non-modern, to reject freedom, and deny progress. The digital discourse creates complicity through making its subjects matter-of-fact and common sense. This ritual becomes ideology when "[c]hoice is overborn by duty" (Turner 1974, 35). The technoliberal discourse is able to obfuscate hypocrisy and engender obedience through discussions of tools. Inclusive of both social and economic liberalism in its focus on the relationships between technology and freedom, technoliberalism is a discourse that attempts to make concentration on contradictions impossible.

Former Vermont Governor, Howard Dean, and his campaign director, Joe Trippi, borrowed discourse from the free and open-source public during the 2004 Democratic primaries by publicly discussing their campaign to journalists as an "open-source campaign." This strategy linked their campaign to the rhetoric of Silicon Valley, decentralization, the new economy, and the rising hype of participatory culture (Kreiss 2011). These fabricated connections enabled journalists to write about the campaign through powerful symbols (Kreiss 2011, 373). Dean is a technoliberal for his strong digital discourse and his campaign's internet iconography. Gore's digital discourse too sought to link his campaign to the new economy of the dotcom era. Obama's digital discourse connected the federal government to the heights of technological innovation. Their digital discourse works "ideologically to elide dynamics of organizational power" (Kreiss 2011, 367). This ideological maneuver is manufactured through transforming the internet into a fetish and a myth.

Digital discourse assumes two forms that can be observed in the Obama and Gore cases, digital fetishism (Hornborg 2001) and digital mythology (Mosco 2004). Gore fetishizes the internet while Obama mythologizes it. For Gore, the internet is a powerfully symbolic thing to be embodied in a political ritual. For Obama, the internet is a character in a narrative, an epic story that celebrates the federal government. In both instances, the technoliberal digital discourse, its fetishistic and mythic proportions, exceed semantic boundaries while obscuring power relations.

THE INTERNET AS FETISH AND MYTH ON THE US PRESIDENTIAL CAMPAIGN TRAIL

During my service in the United States Congress, I took the initiative in creating the internet.
—former Vice President Al Gore March 9, 1999, CNN

Gore's remarks to Wolf Blitzer on CNN were uttered at a time when "the fascination with markets, privatization and deregulation and a correlate antipathy to government regulation—seemed to be on the wane" (Streeter 2003, 655). A new myth was needed and was emerging to galvanize investment, passionate work, political purpose, and citizens to go to the voting booths. The new myth came in the form of the internet with Yahoo, Amazon, and eBay's IPOs in 1996, 1997, and 1998 and with them the dotcom bubble. To link himself to this new technological wonder, Gore needed to make the internet into a fetish, then index himself to it, embodying the internet.

Gore's digital discourse reflects a specific type of symbolic discourse that can be categorized through the concept of the fetish (Taussig 1980;

114   A. FISH

Appadurai 1986; Mauss 1967). Anthropologist Alf Hornborg (2001, 474) defines fetishism as "the mystification of unequal relations of social exchange through the attribution of autonomous agency or productivity to certain kinds of material objects." Through this process "the thing may well be regarded or spoken of as though they were alive with their own autonomous power" (Taussig 1980, 36). Fetishes obscure power relations behind symbols. Assemblages like the internet become fetishes when deployed to valorize specific historical processes and social relations. Gore was attempting to conflate himself and the internet, valorizing his involvement in the development of the internet, while obscuring the multiple assembled elements and trajectories which challenge Gore's simplistic narrative.

In Marxism, capitalism is a fetish whose power is taken for granted. As such, it mystifies unequal power relations. More specifically, the fetish alienates producers as the commodities they produce are taken as givens, as signs without signifiers. Gore was involved in developing what became the internet, while he became alienated from the networked technology he helped create. The subsequent journalist misinterpretation further mystified the internet from its origins. Gore's comment to Blitzer was an attempt at demystification, of empirically seeing the internet as a material and historical assemblage that was partially the result of his federal involvement. But as Gore brought the internet into circuits of political positioning, the internet was remystified as a fetish.

Gore mystifies the internet through a specific variety of fetishism. Fetishism manifests in two important manners: conflations of signifier and signified and ambiguous power relations (Ellen 1988, 2013). Gore conflates himself (signifier) with the internet (signified). Gore/internet becomes an index or an object that is its symbol. Gore attempts to ameliorate producer alienation (himself/federal government) from commodity (the internet) through indexing himself to the internet. He attempts to indexically embody the internet. Signifier and signified are conflated and Gore embodies or personifies the internet. His is a digital discourse uttered by a technoliberal elite seeking public office in a capitalist democracy. Gore utilizes a discourse of technology to ameliorate the contractions within liberalism.

While Gore attempted to manage a political ritual for CNN, his remarks became a gaffe as politically driven pundits exaggerated and misconstrued his statement. These journalists performed a degradation ritual on the pages of their newspapers and across the internet and television.

TECHNOLIBERALISM AND THE ORIGINS OF THE INTERNET 115

The "degradation agents" (Thérèse and Martin 2010) at the technoliberal *Wired* attacked one of their own for being too young to have been involved in the development of the early internet, for focusing on supercomputers instead of networking, for not being involved in the internet's privatization, and for a lack of technical knowledge (Agre 2000, 2). Despite Gore's obvious involvement in what became the internet (Khan and Cerf 2000), the degradation ritual obfuscated the details in a ritual that deleted status and authority. Political rituals are rites performed with fetishes whose powers can be channeled but never fully contained by neither narrator nor degradation agent. The slippages of polysemy are also evident when discussing Obama and the mythic utilities of the digital discourse.

> The internet didn't get invented on its own. Government research created the internet so that all companies could make money off the internet.
> —President Barack Obama July 13, 2012

In a campaign speech at a humid fire station in Roanoke, Virginia, two months after Facebook's IPO, President Obama also exploits the internet-as-symbol. Obama's 2008 and 2012 victories were as much a *result* of dynamic symbol manipulation and ritual as prudent understandings of demographics and grassroots organizing (Alexander 2010). Success was a result of coordinating heroic political rituals in such a way as to optimize the networked news cycle. The difference is that instead of personifying the internet as a fetish in which the signifier and signified are unified, as was Gore's practice, Obama situates the internet as a symbol within a mythic narrative. In cultural anthropology, myths are historical narratives that help individuals transcend or ignore the contradictions of their society and focus on positive future possibilities (Lévi-Strauss 1978). Myths about technology in political rituals request citizen obedience to technoliberal democratic capitalism, while ignoring the contradictions of Western liberal traditions.

Like Gore, Obama wanted citizens to consider government and, by extension, his present administration when it thought of the internet. To present the internet and his administration as ideally as possible, Obama had to ignore the negative impacts of the networked society. "The myths that swirl around digital media convergence—managerial efficiency, experiential immediacy, global interactivity and interpersonal connectedness" media theorists Richard Maxwell and Toby Miller demand us to

116   A. FISH

consider, "must be countered with the histories of the environmental plunder and toxic sweatshops that have made old and new media possible" (2011, 595). Thus, in potting a history of the internet, Obama politicized the internet by depoliticizing it. Communication scholar Vincent Mosco says, "Myths can foreclose politics, can serve to depoliticize speech but they can also open the door to a restoration of politics to a deepening of political understanding" (Mosco 2004, 16). Technoliberal myths on the campaign trail reduce the negative industrial politics of the internet while attaching politicians to the positive social politics of networked communication technologies. Myths are created for specific purposes by the technoliberal elite capable of reaping the benefits of investment and the aggregation of power that comes along with public excitement. By reducing complexity and eliminating contradictions, myths invite listeners to act without the hesitation of contemplation. Either as a material fetish object, as in the case of Gore, or as a story point in a narrative myth about the positive history of federally subsidized innovation as in the case of Obama, the internet is a symbol whose power is exploited in political rituals.

Internet historiographies tend to be either Whiggish, featuring a celebration of the present, or teleological, which "cleanse their neat narratives of contextual factors that are presumed to be extraneous" (Russell 2012, 4). In both politicians' and journalists' internet historiographies, the excellent past is a result of the candidate of the present. Obviously, Obama had not the time nor was it the place for nuance. Campaign speeches need sound bites that are broadcast on television and radio and remixed for online video. Once released, the floating signifier can be remixed by sound bite cultures to the benefit or detriment of the politician (Slayden and Whillock 1999). When it doesn't, it becomes a disaster. The internet-as-symbol on the campaign trail has proven to be a fetish or myth that often exceeds its political intentionality with unintentional consequences. The internet is an assemblage whose semantic power unleashed in political ritual is difficult to contain. As politicians seek to anchor the signifiers to specific signs, their opponents exploit gaps and slippages to construct "gaffes" in degradation rituals such as the rite performed in *The Wall Street Journal.*

FOUR DIGITAL DISCOURSES OF TECHNOLIBERALISM

It's an urban legend that the government launched the Internet.
—L. Gordon Crovitz (2012), *The Wall Street Journal*

TECHNOLIBERALISM AND THE ORIGINS OF THE INTERNET 117

Soon after the injudicious edits of Obama's remarks were broadcast on television screens and internet video sites, four arguments emerged about who *really* made the internet. L. Gordon Crovitz (2012) at *The Wall Street Journal* started the polemic by going against the accepted wisdom and saying that former President Obama was wrong, it was Xerox PARC, and therefore corporations and not the government made the internet. Farhad Manjoo (2012) of *Slate* rebutted that the President was correct, the state did fund and support what became the internet. Harry McCracken (2012) of *Time* added to the debate by bringing back an old idea that never gets old in technology journalism, that it was not the state or corporations, but brilliant individuals like Tim Berners-Lee who created HyperText Markup Language (HTML), who should be thanked for creating the internet. Finally, Steven Johnson (2012a) writing in *The New York Times* said it was not states, corporations, nor smart individuals but *the people*, namely, a public of open-source coders that should be thanked for building the software with which states, corporations, and individuals access the internet. These four liberal historiographies form contradictory dyadic pairs between economic and social liberalism.

Former President Obama may have gaffed, assistant editors at the conservative Fox News network and the US Republican National Committee exploitatively edited the misquote, but it was *Wall Street Journal* writer L. Gordon Crovitz who mistook the misedits as evidence for US executive revisionism. Crovitz, ex-publisher of the *Journal*, ex-executive at Dow Jones, and social media start-up entrepreneur, attacked Obama's statement that the internet was funded and engineered by the federal government. It was not the government but a corporation, Xerox PARC, that invented what became the internet. Crovitz's problem is that the "urban legend" (Crovitz 2012) that the government created the internet has been a given fact for most of internet history (Abbatte 1999; Hafner and Lyon 1998). Crovitz's digital discourse is traditional *laissez-faire* capitalism. "*Laissez-faire*" qualifies the type of capitalism that leaves the workings of capitalists out of the reach of the state. Crovitz is a technocapitalist, who wants to live in a world unshackled and unassisted by central governments.

However, the state did assist in the development of the internet as a form of crony capitalism, a government and corporate alliance, which fundamental Smithian capitalists deplore as not the "invisible hand" at work but rather a tax-funded pampering. Crony capitalism is a lighter form of corporate welfare or corporatism in which corporations are dependent upon

118   A. FISH

economic and material support, tax breaks, and subsidiaries provided by a central government (Thiessen 2011). In his Roanoke statement, Obama was not criticizing the development of the internet as a manifestation of crony capitalism. Instead, he was mythologizing the co-dependent relationship held by corporations and states. Opposed to Obama's progressive reading of internet history, Crovitz's digital discourse is technocapitalism, crony capitalism masked as *laissez-faire* capitalism within a milieu of technology. Drawing from a technoliberal digital discourse and, Crovitz is unfazed by the contradictions of crony capitalism. The oxymoron is that technocapitalism is dependent upon the state to fund the development of information infrastructures used by corporations who reject that very state.

> In tech, no one does anything on his own. ... in the tech industry, it takes a village.
> —Farhad Manjoo (2012), *Slate*

Two days after *The Wall Street Journal* opinion was published, Manjoo (2012) rebutted Crovitz's "almost hysterically false" argument that the internet emerged from Xerox PARC. Aligning with given wisdom, Manjoo stated that the internet was financed and materially supported in its creation by the US government. In reminding the residents of Roanoke of the government's role in the founding of the internet, Obama, according to Manjoo, "argued that wealthy business people owe some of their success to the government's investment in education and basic infrastructure" (Manjoo 2012). This argument is progressive—advocating for responsible taxation and the shared burden of national identification, and is therefore a technoprogressive digital discourse opposed to the Darwinian technocapitalism expounded by Crovitz.

The technoprogressive digital discourse acknowledges the role of the state in funding technology and science while addressing the shared costs and responsibilities of a state-supported networked society. Technoprogressivism "assumes that technoscientific developments can be empowering and emancipatory so long as they are regulated by legitimate democratic and accountable authorities" (Carrico 2006, n.p.). Manjoo, and Obama before him, express technoprogressivism by claiming that it is the democratic and regulatory mechanisms, not to mention the US federal funding, that made the internet possible.

TECHNOLIBERALISM AND THE ORIGINS OF THE INTERNET 119

Technoprogressivism advocates for regulatory mechanisms to make it impossible for media corporations to control the entire production, storage, search, hardware, software, advertising, and distribution chain. To solve the "corrupting effects of vertically integrated power," Law scholar Tim Wu proposes the "separations principle" or the regulatory "creation of a salutary distance between each of the major functions or layers in the information economy" (Wu 2010, 304). His concern with information monopolies is progressive as is his comfort with applying regulation to solve what he perceives as problems. While Obama's and Manjoo's arguments attempt to situate the internet's origins firmly within the government, Wu attempts to pivot that ontogenesis into regulation and reform. The paradox is that technoprogressivism is a reform movement that works within the existing system of democratic capitalism failing to recognize that economic freedom and social equality cannot coexist.

[I]n the end, everything is invented by individuals.
—Harry McCracken (2012), *Time*

Time magazine tech writer Harry McCracken (2012) added that the technoliberal digital discourse that both Manjoo and Crovitz missed was the role of "gifted individuals" in the development of the internet, the World Wide Web, and web browsers. McCracken (2012) begins by calling DARPA (Defense Advanced Research Projects Agency) director Robert Taylor a "visionary." He then populates his text with the great men of internet history: Vint Cerf as the maker of the internet protocol TCP/IP, Douglas Engelbart as the creator of the mouse and hypertext, Ted Nelson, the father of the term "hyperlink," and Marc Andreessen and Eric Bina, the inventors of Mosaic, the first graphical browser. These "visionary" and "gifted" "individuals" who invent "everything" work within both state-funded and private-financed institutions and are the real builders of the internet (McCracken 2012). McCracken's great-white-men-theory-of-history was first popularized by nineteenth-century Scottish author Thomas Carlyle and debunked by anthropologists and their precursors, but its persistence in these instances of Whiggish internet historiographical revisionism illustrates how liberal discourses of individualism continue to articulate with origin stories of networked technology.

What McCracken expresses is what I call technoindividualism, a negative liberal theory of self-actualization galvanized by networked technol-

120   A. FISH

ogy, triumphant despite the attempted oppressions of state regulation, consumers with poor taste, and the ignorance of bottom-line-feeding CEOs. Individualism is central to the "*technoliberal* disposition" which embodies "personal freedom and ... liberal faith in the aggregate effects of individual actions" (Malaby 2009, 361). Technoindividualism meshes with technocapitalism in that each concept emerges from a belief in technological entrepreneurial exceptionalism. The theory goes: some people just have the preternatural gift of understanding the supernatural internet and consumers get the honor of relishing their work. In technoindividualism, entrepreneurial triumphalism and exceptionalism are aligned with the pro-selfishness of Randian Objectivism, Smithian self-interest, and the Nietzschean *Übermensch*.

Technoindividualism is often perpetuated by deadline-pressured technology journalists working with few informants, ambitious venture capitalists (VCs), pre-VC entrepreneurs, and corporate boards hoping to create hype and investment bubbles around their genius producers and sublime products. The list of hagiographical books titled after these individuals include: *Steve Jobs* (Isaacson 2011) and *Bill Gates* (Gatlin 1999). Gore's self-indexing fetish is also an example of technoindividualism. Narratologically, the individual is a convenient subject for a linear history, from birth to death creating a teleological flow of events and time. First introduced by Max Weber (1968), Talcott Parsons (1937, 43–51), and Friedrich von Hayek (1944), methodological individualism posits that society can more accurately be explained through recourse to individuals, their actions, and states of mind. Some technoliberals add an ethical egoism, that individuals have a moral obligation toward self-interested pursuits. Others speak of the romantic or utilitarian technoindividual, one using technology for "self-transformation" and the other for "anticipatory pleasures" and short-run hedonism (Streeter 2003, 660). Technoindividualism is a digital discourse that attempts to secure the symbolic power of these triumphant individualisms. It obscures how individualism conflicts with its dyadic other within liberalism, populism. The inconsistency is that technoindividualism claims that the individual is the singular source of innovation while technologies understood as being socially constructed (Mackenzie and Wajcman 1985).

> The internet was the creation of: "networks of peers ... decentralized groups of scientists and programmers and hobbyists (and more than a few

TECHNOLIBERALISM AND THE ORIGINS OF THE INTERNET   121

entrepreneurs) freely sharing the fruits of their intellectual labor with the entire world"
—Steven Johnson (2012a), *New York Times*

It was not the state, corporations, or genius inventor-entrepreneurs who made the internet, Steven Johnson (2012a) claimed in *The New York Times*, but populist citizens in peer networks who built the internet. It was the much-celebrated free and open-source volunteers who built the internet, which is like "the people" only with a lot more coding competency and free time than most "people." To support this claim, Johnson has to veer away from the specific technologies of the internet (packet switching, TCP/IP, HTML) to discuss the open-source origins of the Linux operating system, UNIX kernel, and Apache software—systems on which governments and corporate work now depends.

Johnson invites us to consider the open-source "success stories that prove convincingly that you don't need bureaucracies to facilitate public collaboration, and you don't need the private sector to innovate" (2012a). In Johnson's argument, decentralized peer-to-peer networks have qualities particularly conditioned for the fast-paced and disruptive evolution of consumer technology. "Peer networks," he says, "don't suffer from the sclerosis of government bureaucracies" (Johnson 2012a). Following Benkler (2006), Johnson claims that a new form of social organizing has emerged of which peer-production is the leading edge. This is technopopulism.

Populism "pits a virtuous and homogeneous people against a set of elites" (Albertazzi and McDonnell 2008, 3). This traditional view of populism sees the people as a legitimate source of authority and creativity (Laclau 2005). Scholarship on open-source software tends toward technopopulist digital discourse. Schoonmaker makes the arguement that free software challenges "the dominant form of neoliberal" (Schoonmaker 2012, 516). In Dean's (2010) calculation, open-source software is not a "reorientation of knowledge and power" (Kelty 2008, 8) toward populism but a securing of that power within technocapitalism (Dean 2010). Johnson disagrees, stating that open-source publics are central to the historical development of the internet. The paradox is that they are both correct. As technopopulism celebrates post-capitalist values, it fails to acknowledge how those values are subsumed by the technoliberal elite into forms of capitalist value creation.

Because of their multiple components, assemblages can be selectively articulated and politically manipulated. Technoliberalism because of its

122 A. FISH

multiplicities contains contradictory discourses that can be selectively developed for political gains. Taken as a digital discourse, technoliberalism attempts to ameliorate these contradictions through an emphasis on tools. The contradictions of capitalism and progressivism, individualism and populism, however, cannot be eliminated through discourse when media workers are also citizens and their workworlds and civic values do not coordinate. Progressivism and capitalism, one a system for maximizing social equality and another a system resulting in economic inequality, cannot coordinate on a structural level. Individualism and populism, one a practice of isolationism, another a practice of collectivism, cannot coordinate structurally. Compounding the paradox, each digital discourse has its own internal contradictions. Fetishes and myths are needed to divert attention from these contradictions and instead create allegiance to the precarious liberal system through exploiting faith in technology.

THE TRIUMPH OF TECHNOCAPITALISM

Gore and Obama are technoliberal Democrats who express both social and economic liberalism through their digital discourses. The four journalists expressed the contradictory dyads within social and economic liberalism. But this is not to imply that digital discourses of technoliberalism have equal resources and equal impacts. One digital discourse, technocapitalism, is better resourced to exploit the polysemy of the internet as well as its material capacities to achieve its goals. The reconstitution of AT&T, federal US anti-trust prosecutions failing to limit Google's online advertising, and under-regulated financial trading are but a few examples of the technoliberal monopolization of the internet. Considering the ascent and present domination of technocapitalism in the last two decades, to read Crovitz is to hear the gloating of a victor. News Corp. owns *The Wall Street Journal* in which Crovitz gave his technocapitalist historiography that falls directly in line with the neoliberal principles which governs News Corp. in its longtime relationship with governments and other media corporations. With the 2008 US Supreme Court ruling, *Citizens United v the Federal Election Commission*, enabling unlimited economic contributions by corporations to political campaigns, on the premise that money is speech, the centrality of economic liberalism in US representational democracy is secured.

Like their Republican opponents, Democrats are also a party of big business willing to triage the environment, civil liberties, the social safety net, the state, and public investments in science and technology to placate corporations and acquire campaign finance contributions and lobbying power. The Democratic Party is economic liberalism masked as social liberalism. Evidence of the Democrats' shift to economic liberalism is evident in Gore's and Obama's digital discourse on the origins of the internet. Both publicly celebrate how the government supported the development of the internet, framing the internet as a social liberal gift of the state to the people. However, in their internet policies, these two policymakers oversaw the widespread privatization of the infrastructure and commercialization of its services. In what was written to be a flattering defense of Gore's remarks, internet pioneers Robert Khan and Vint Cerf (2000, no page number) claimed: "Gore provided much needed political support for the speedy privatization of the Internet when the time arrived for it to become a commercially-driven operation." Obama appointed two pro-privatization chairmen to the FCC, oversaw the US National Security Administration collaborate with Silicon Valley in citizen surveillance programs, and pursued internet-based whistleblowers Chelsea Manning and Edward Snowden. Both see the internet as a decentralized tool that needs centralization to increase public safety, stop terrorism, boost financial efficiency, and further consolidate US information imperialism. The internet's positive impact for democracy is in organizing volunteers and donations for political campaigns and in assisting the formation of public spheres elsewhere, in Egypt and Tunisia, as former Secretary of State Hillary Clinton's "Internet Freedom" speech declared. In the USA, the internet is a tool for technocapitalism, networked authoritarianism, and vertically and horizontally integrated corporations. It is a symbol to fetishize and mythologize in the pursuit of higher office and centralized power.

Wallerstein (1995, 161) writes that if the contradictions of liberalism are "openly admitted, then the capitalist world-economy will have no legitimation in the eyes of the dangerous (that is, the dispossessed) classes. And if a system has no legitimation, it will not survive." The privatization of information infrastructures and personal data on convergent information infrastructures challenges the social equality for all and also the economic freedom celebrated by technocapitalism. Corporate consolidation limits not only media democratization and equal protections advocated by technoprogressives but also the money-is-free-speech and pro-competition

124   A. FISH

rhetoric of technocapitalists. The contradiction of personal weekend technoprogressive values and privatized weekday technocapitalist actions can be a *negotiated* compromise.

In a technoliberal politics in which both the left and the right manipulate political rituals for hegemonic gain, an anti-hegemonic technological myth needs to be written for structural change to occur. It too will exploit the polysemy of dominant technological assemblages and thus will be manipulative. A cast of mythic characters and characteristics are emerging from anti-hegemonic internet production cultures. These include the hacker collective Anonymous, the espionage escapades of Julian Assange, the interventions of the Pirate Party, the "social movement media cultures" of the Occupy Movement (Costanza-Chock 2012), the "concrete utopias" of free software (Broca 2012), and the trials of Edward Snowden. What contradictions will we be willing to accept in participating in future digital myths and political rituals? Will the contradictions be able to be mitigated through discourse or will the contradictions destroy these movements and moments? Chapter 6 examines these questions.

REFERENCES

Abbatte, J. 1999. *Inventing the Internet*. Cambridge: MIT Press.

Agre, P. 2000. Who Invented 'Invented'?: Tracing the Real Story of the 'Al Gore Invented the Internet' Hoax. Accessed December 5, 2015. http://lists.essential.org/pipermail/random-bits/2000-October/000443.html

Albertazzi, D., and D. McDonnell. 2008. *Twenty-First Century Populism: The Spectre of Western European Democracy*. New York and London: Palgrave Macmillan.

Alexander, J.C. 2010. *The Performance of Politics: Obama's Victory and the Democratic Struggle for Power*. New York: Oxford University Press.

Anderson, B., M. Kearnes, C. McFarlane, and D. Swanton. 2012. On Assemblages and Geography. *Human Geography* 2(2): 171–189.

Appadurai, A. 1986. *The Social Life of Things: Commodities in Cultural Perspective*. New York: Cambridge University Press.

Benkler, Y. 2006. *The Wealth of Networks: How Social Production Transforms Markets and Freedom*. New Haven, CT: Yale University Press.

Benkler, Y., and H. Nissenbaum. 2006. Commons-Based Peer Production and Virtue. *Journal of Political Philosophy* 14(4): 394–419.

Bennett, L.W. 1981. Assessing Presidential Character: Degradation Rituals in Political Campaigns. *Quarterly Journal of Speech* 67: 310–321.

TECHNOLIBERALISM AND THE ORIGINS OF THE INTERNET 125

Bijker, W. 1987. *The Social Construction of Technological Systems*. Cambridge: MIT Press.

Broca, S. 2012. *L'utopie du logiciel libre: La construction de projets de transformation sociale en lien avec le mouvement du free software*. Paris: Université Panthéon Sorbonne—Paris I.

Brooks, J., and I.A. Boal. 1995. Introduction. In *Resisting the Virtual Life: The Culture and Politics of Information*, ed. J. Brook and I.A. Boal. San Francisco: City Lights.

Carrico, D. 2006. Technoprogressivism: Beyond Technophilia and Technophobia. Accessed December 5, 2015. http://technoprogressive.blogspot.co.uk/2006/08/technoprogressivism-beyond.html

Costanza-Chock, S. 2012. Mic Check! Media Cultures and Occupy Movement. *Social Movement Studies* 11(3–4): 275–385.

Couldry, N. 2003. *Media Rituals: A Critical Approach*. New York: Routledge.

Crovitz, G. 2012. Who Really Invented the Internet? *Wall Street Journal*. Accessed December 5, 2015. http://online.wsj.com/article/SB10000872396390444464304577539063008406518.html

Dean, J. 2010. *Blog Theory: Feedback and Capture in Circuits of Drive*. Cambridge: Polity.

Durkheim, E. 1976. *Elementary Forms of Religious Life*. London: George Allen & Unwin.

Ellen, R.F. 1988. Fetishism. *Man* 23: 213–235.

Fisher, E. 2010. Contemporary Technology Discourse and the Legitimation of Capitalism. *European Journal of Social Theory* 13(2): 229–252.

Fortes, M., and E.E. Evans-Pritchard. 1950. *African Political Systems*. London and New York: International African Institute.

Garfinkel, H. 1956. Condition of Successful Degradation Ceremonies. In *Sociological Theory: A Book of Readings*, ed. Lewis A. Coser and Bernard Rosenberg, 455–462. Long Grove, IL: Waveland Press, Inc.

Gatlin, J. 1999. *Bill Gates*. New York: Harper-Collins.

Geertz, C. 1973. *The Interpretation of Cultures: Selected Essays*. New York: Basic.

Gore, A. 1991. Infrastructure for the Global Village. *Scientific American*, 152. Accessed December 5, 2015. http://www.scientificamerican.com/article/infrastructure-for-the-global-villa/

———. 1994. Speech Delivered at the Information Superhighway Summit at UCLA January 11, 1994. Accessed March 22, 2012. http://www.uibk.ac.at/voeb/texte/vor9401.html

Hafner, K., and M. Lyons. 1998. *Where Wizards Stay Up Late: The Origins of the Internet*. New York: Simon and Schuster.

Hayek, F. 1944. *The Road to Serfdom*. Chicago: University of Chicago.

Hornborg, A. 2001. Symbolic Technologies: Machines and the Marxian Notion of the Fetish. *Anthropological Theory* 1: 473–496.

126   A. FISH

Isaacson, W. 2011. *Jobs*. New York: Simon and Schuster.
Itzkoff, D. 2011. Plot Twist? If Viewers Say So, Let It Be. *New York Times*. Accessed December 5, 2015. http://www.nytimes.com/2011/02/11/arts/television/11karma.html?_r=0
Johnson, S. 2012a. The Internet? We Built That. *New York Times*. Accessed January 6, 2013. http://www.nytimes.com/2012/09/23/magazine/the-internet-we-built-that.html?pagewanted=all
———. 2012b. *Future Perfect: The Case for Progress in a Networked Age*. New York: Allen Lane.
Kelty, C.M. 2008. *Two Bits: The Cultural Significance of Free Software and the Internet*. Durham: Duke University Press.
Khan, R., and V. Cerf. 2000. Al Gore and the Internet. *Politech: Politics and Technology*. Accessed December 5, 2015. http://www.politechbot.com/p-01394.html
Kreiss, D. 2011. Open Source as Practice and Ideology: The Origin of Howard Dean's Innovations in Electoral Politics. *Journal of Information Technology & Politics* 8(3): 367–382.
Laclau, E. 2005. *On Populist Reason*. London: Verso.
Levi-Strauss, C. 1978. *Myth and Meaning*. New York: Routledge & Kegan Paul, U.K, Taylor & Francis Group.
MacKenzie, D., and J. Wajcman. 1985. *The Social Shaping of Technology*. Buckingham: Open University Press.
Malaby, T. 2009. *Making Virtual Worlds: Linden Lab and Second Life*. Ithaca: Cornell University Press.
Manjoo, F. 2005. The Television Will Be Revolutionized. *Slate*. Accessed December 5, 2015. http://www.salon.com/2005/07/11/goretv/
———. 2012. Obama Was Right: The Government Invented the Internet. *Slate*. Accessed January 2013. http://www.slate.com/articles/technology/technology/2012/07/who_invented_the_internet_the_outrageous_conservative_claim_that_every_tech_innovation_came_from_private_enterprise_.html
Marcus, G.E., and E. Saka. 2006. Assemblage. *Theory, Culture & Society* 23(2–3): 101–109.
Mauss, M. 1967. *The Gift: Forms and Functions of Exchange in Archaic Societies*. Norton, MA: Norton Library.
Maxwell, R., and T. Miller. 2011. Old, New and Middle-Aged Media Convergence. *Cultural Studies* 25(4–5): 585–603.
McCracken, H. 2012. How Government Did (and Didn't) Invent the Internet. *Time*. Accessed January 5, 2013. http://techland.time.com/2012/07/25/how-government-did-and-didnt-invent-the-internet/
McGirt, E. 2007. Al Gore's $100 Million Makeover. *Fast Company*. Accessed December 5, 2015. http://www.fastcompany.com/60067/al-gores-100-million-makeover

McLeod, J.R. 1999. The Sociodrama of Presidential Politics: Rhetoric, Ritual, and Power in the Era of Teledemocracy. *American Anthropologist* 101(2): 359–373.

Ortner, S.B. 1973. On Key Symbols. *American Anthropologist* 75(5): 1338–1346.

Parsons, T. 1937. *The Structure of Social Action.* New York: McCraw-Hill.

Russell, A.L. 2012. *Histories of Networking vs. the History of the Internet.* Paper presented at the 2012 *SIGCIS* Workshop, October 7.

Schoonmaker, S. 2012. Hacking the Global: Constructing Markets and Commons Through Free Software. *Information, Communication, and Society* 15(4): 502–518.

Shirky, C. 2008. *Here Comes Everybody: The Power of Organizing Without Organizations.* New York: Penguin Press.

Slayden, D., and R.K. Whillock. 1999. *Soundbite Culture: The Death of Discourse in a Wired World.* London: Sage.

Streeter, T. 2003. The Romantic Self and the Politics of Internet Commercialization. *Cultural Studies* 17(5): 648–668.

Taussig, M.T. 1980. *The Devil and Commodity Fetishism in South America.* Chapel Hill: University of North Carolina Press.

Thérèse, S., and B. Martin. 2010. Shame, Scientist! Degradation Rituals in Science. *Prometheus* 28(2): 97–110.

Thiessen, M.A. 2011. Crony Capitalism Explained. *The Washington Post.*

Turner, V. 1974. *Dramas, Fields, and Metaphors: Symbolic Action in Human Society.* London: Cornell University Press.

Wallerstein, I. 1995. *After Liberalism.* New York: New Press.

Weber, M. 1968. In *Economy and Society,* ed. Guenther Roth and Claus Wittich. Berkeley: University of California Press.

Wu, T. 2010. *The Master Switch: The Rise and Fall of Information Empires.* New York: Knopf.

CHAPTER 6

Technoliberalism and the Convergence Myth

MORAL TECHNICAL IMAGINARIES

I was in a rented car on my way to my hotel in Nicosia, Cyprus, when I looked out the window and saw a tent encampment under olive trees and a large and tattered Iraqi flag. I immediately asked the driver to stop, and got out with my video camera, ran across the street, and was suddenly in the United Nations (UN) "green zone" that separates the Greek Cyprus from the Turkish Cyprus. UN security towers hovered over me, the deflated tents, broken chairs, and four Iraqi men. I introduced myself and they told me their story. They had smuggled themselves here from Iraq and were camping out, protesting for asylum or a work visa. I spent days collecting the stories of these secular scientists, teachers, artists, and military personnel who were being harassed by the religious fundamentalists of an Iraq recently liberated from the chaos of the US occupation.

I was nervous carrying this footage to the USA but made it through customs and back to Los Angeles. I had about 15 interviews and five hours of b-roll footage for the short documentary *Divided Cyprus* (Fish 2008), about the divided city of Nicosia between the Greek South and the Turkish North, and four interviews and an hour of b-roll for *Secular Iraqi Refugees* (Fish 2007). I edited these footage into two 5–7-minute short documentaries and uploaded them onto current.tv. Current used their online video site to solicit, display, vote on, and decide to purchase short documentaries from VC2 producers. The response to

© The Author(s) 2017

A. Fish, *Technoliberalism and the End of Participatory Culture in the United States,* DOI 10.1007/978-3-319-31256-9_6

129

130   A. FISH

my short documentaries within the online VC2 community was positive and soon the manager of the Collective Journalism (CJ) department was requesting a phone call. He wanted the short documentaries and was willing to pay $750 for each. The vision I had of myself as a rogue cosmopolitan journalist was happening; not only had I been to one warzone and recorded the stories from another, I would be bringing these stories to television. These stories would provoke dialogue among viewers about the negative human impacts of war and partitions, I hoped.

Two of the Iraqi refugees, Jawad and Ammar, saw the pod short documentary online and left comments on the video post, updating the audience about their situation. Among other things, Ammar wrote that they "came here seeking refuge into this country to escape death in our country."' The Current executive, upon seeing these Iraqi refugees' comment on my pod, made a video himself and uploaded it. He discussed the refugees' comments and how this was Current's fifth pod on Iraqi refugees from all over the world, including Kurdistan, Jordan, Syria, Sweden, and now Cyprus. This video and my pod were shown together on television. This recursive loop, inclusive of a VC2 producer, a diverse and engaged audience, a Current employee, and Iraqi refugees, shows the power of a multiplatform and interactive approach to television journalism. We had produced a small public sphere on the issue of war diaspora, and it felt good.

As I wrote earlier, Current is a for-profit television network founded in 2005 by former US Vice President Al Gore and lawyer entrepreneur Joel Hyatt with the expressed goal of "democratizing television." With citizen video journalism and collaborations with Twitter to bring social media to a US Presidential debate, Current attempted to converge the participatory possibilities of the internet with the broadcasting power of television. Such attempts at internet and television convergence reveal how myths are mobilized in acts of technological solutionism, the myth that technologies can solve problems social in nature. These myths are corporately directed. They are spoken by media executives and imperfectly implemented by media workers who bear the risk for such Silicon Valley-based and Hollywood-based mythic adventures. These myths are examples of digital discourses that attempt to mitigate the contradictions of liberalism.

I come to this project on participatory culture as a participant observer. Beginning in 2006, I worked for Current as a contract-by-contract, freelance citizen video journalist, or what Current called a VC2 producer until they ceased the VC2 program in 2009. Based on these years as a television producer for Current, textual analysis of journalistic reports, and over 30 interviews with executives, producers, designers, marketers, and engineers, this chapter documents how television producers imagine the internet as a tool in the service of diversifying the American public sphere. Like anthropologist Barry Dornfeld (1998) before me, I produced media with and for my project participants, namely 16 television documentaries from such globally distributed sites as India, Palestine, Cyprus, Native America as a place, and Los Angeles. Making these documentaries afforded me a number of opportunities to see, hear, and experience the convergence myth. I continued to monitor Current's historical development through the trade presses and by watching the network until it was purchased by Al Jazeera in early January 2013.

As a technoliberal elite, Gore has long spoken of the convergence myth; "giving ordinary Americans network access had excited Senator Al Gore since the late 1970s" (Campbell-Kelly and Aspray 1996). Networks and participatory democracy were woven together by Gore into an early myth about the role of network communication technologies in helping democracy into the early 1990s. Depending on the context, the audience got a different formulation of the convergence myth. This is the power of mythology: the ambiguity of its polysemy can be utilized in different contexts, for differing audiences. After the 2000 US election debacle, Gore began to conceive of a media outlet that would benefit citizens. He approached people capable of helping with this vision. Hyatt, a Democratic Party contributor who had made millions through providing inexpensive legal advice, became a co-founder and CEO. Joanna Earl, with broadband and personalized video as well as strategic planning experience for entertainment conglomerates, joined Gore and Hyatt. Gotham Chopra, son of the New Age guru Deepak Chopra, a well-connected television journalist, and representative of the target demographic of 18–35-year-old upwardly mobile men, was brought on board. Michael Rosenblum, a bombastic teacher of citizen video journalism with a New York accent, also joined the team. These individuals were all active believers in the power of the internet to diversify

132 A. FISH

the hegemonic public sphere. Should they propagate this myth they may reap the economic and social capital rewards that come with being associated with a visionary technological project. As early as those first meetings, the differing moral technical imaginaries of television and the internet came into conflict. Chopra said they were consistently asking themselves, "Which one, the internet or TV, is the real platform and which is the complement? It was a debate. Joanna [Earl] was adamant. She thought that online was the portal" (interviewed September 13, 2010). Even within this small think tank, opinions differed. Chopra, with experience in television at Channel One, carried more of the television vision. Rosenblum was a fierce advocate of the solutionistic idea that inexpensive video gear and the internet would revolutionize television. Gore wanted it both ways by emphasizing technological convergence—the two-way communication of the internet paired with the wide audience of television. Each original member of Current brought a different mix that further developed the concepts that would become the foundation of the myth that an ideal balance of technological convergence would result in a solution to the problem of the participatory deficit in democracy.

In May of 2004, Gore and Hyatt made a surprise appearance at the National Cable & Telecommunications Association convention where they announced that they had acquired the news and information network News World International (NWI) from Vivendi Universal for $70.9 million and renamed it INdTV. With a television network they could proceed along a number of paths toward producing content that would satisfy their lofty moralities of diversifying the hegemonic public sphere. They could make a liberal television network, but that already existed in the non-profit progressive network FSTV. What content could they produce or acquire for this new network that would satisfy their moral obligation to diversifying the American public sphere, align with their internet-centrism, and be affordable? The answer to all three questions was found in user-generated content, Silicon Valley's newest buzz from circa 2005. As internet-centrists do, Current took a model from the internet—crowdsourcing of video content—as the signature project to democratize television. Current rebranded user-generated content as Viewer-Created Content or VC2.

At his ultra-chic cliff home perched over the Hollywood Hills, Current's President of Programming David Neuman explained to me the concept of VC2, an internet-centric solution to Gore's perceived problem that the American public sphere was being despoiled by the elite control and professionalization of news by industrially converged corporations. In VC2, "the selections of stories would be democratized, and the sourcing of the stories would be democratized" (interviewed April 19, 2010). The participatory affordances of the internet would make this possible. Thus the internet-centric solution to industrial convergence was the use of technological convergence to empower users.

Neuman had previously been the President of DEN which was the earlier dot-com answer to internet and television convergence. In 2004, Neumann was the Chief Programming Officer for CNN when he got a call from Hyatt and later Gore. He suggested to Gore that he take a model from the internet and crowdsource content production, not from a few well-trained professionals, but from thousands of less-trained and globally distributed media workers. VC2 was an example of internet-centrism deployed to solve the problem of the lack of diverse voices in the American public sphere. Its additional benefit was that it resulted in inexpensive content.

Speaking to VC2, Earl, who became Current's Chief Operation Officer (COO), figured that if you gave this talent pool enough "structure, assets, assignments, training, support financially, inspiration-mentoring, then the end result would be good enough to put on TV" (interviewed September 3, 2010). This is an internet-centric viewpoint that if you build the right kind of internet site, suddenly content "good enough" would magically appear. Neuman and Earl knew that if this new approach to diversifying the hegemonic public sphere was going to take hold, it needed to be reproducible through education and align its structure with the perceived structure of the internet. The problem was that the VC2 content did not appear in the quantity or quality needed. Good enough VC2 producers did not want to give Current unlimited rights to their work. On varying issues and of differing lengths, VC2 proved difficult to schedule. By the end, it was necessary to employ full-time professionals and traditional television programming, confounding Current's internet-centrism and democratization efforts.

Neuman confided in me that he would prefer to have no employees and crowdsource the entire production operation to freelance VC2 producers. I challenged this assertion by stating: "But it doesn't create a living wage for 200 people." Irked by my comment he quickly stung back,

> No it doesn't ... I didn't think that was really what the company was about, the company was about facilitating the democratic dialogue, the company wasn't about how many full-time jobs we can create with benefits in San Francisco for an elite cadre of young creators. In fact, we never intended it to be that. In fact, I wanted to have no full-time employees, really. To me, the ideal would have been eBay ... my desire was, let's have 30,000 people making content for Current TV. That would be beautiful. (interviewed April 19, 2010)

Neuman here was borrowing a labor model from internet-centrism. A living wage was not a part of the morality Neuman needed to fulfill in his focus on diversifying the hegemonic public sphere. Labor justice and traditional long-term employment were not criteria in this age of networked abundance and labor precarity.

VC2 reached toward new experiments and on September 26, 2008, then Senator Obama and Senator McCain debated live on national television. Current licensed a broadcast of this feed and "hacked it." For members of the public with a Twitter account, they could send 140-character messages to Twitter which would route the hashtagged thread to a caffeinated battery of Current employees, who would vet and broadcast messages from the debate-viewing public on live Current. The tweets would first appear on the bottom of the screen and slowly percolate up over the bodies of the Senators before dissolving and breaking apart. By doing this "Current is helping Twitter amplify the opinions, news, and trends that matter right now. Together, we're influencing more than media— we're evolving conversation," Twitter co-founder Biz Stone concluded (McCarthy 2008). "We chose the name 'Hack the Debate' for this interactive TV experiment because our young adult audience often uses 'hack' to mean cleverly modifying something by adding access or features that otherwise aren't available," said Chloe Sladden, Vice President of special programming at Current, who now works at Twitter (Harper 2008). These moral technical imaginaries of hacking-facilitated "conversation" are examples of internet-centric tech fixes of televised debates. This period in Current's history is marked by an emphasis on the technical imaginary of the internet—hacking, social media, an IPO, and an attempt to buy the social media site Digg (Lacy 2008). These aesthetically jarring experiments in social media/television obscure their more pressing goal, perform competency for investors for the IPO, for possible purchasers of the network such as Google, or for Kevin Rose, the founder of Digg,

TECHNOLIBERALISM AND THE CONVERGENCE MYTH 135

which Current hoped to acquire. Hack the Debate also illustrates how Current transitioned around late 2008 from explicit media democratization through citizen-produced television to implicit participation through short internet-based commentary like tweeting. As Current tried each iteration of technological convergence (citizen video journalism with VC2 and socially networked television with Hack the Debate), the threshold for participation decreased and with it its political potential. The myth remained that technological convergence would solve the participatory deficit but the application of the myth migrated to different platforms and projects. In each instance, the precarity of the media worker was neglected.

The years of experiments with outreaching to citizens to encourage videographical participation in the hegemonic public sphere left the company bloated with young personnel. A week after Obama won the 2008 US Presidential election—having won Hack the Debate—Current fired 30 employees and relocated another 30 to other departments. Exactly a year later Current fired another 80 people, collectively cutting almost a quarter of its staff. Tech blogs were calling it a "major bloodbath" (Rao 2009). The convergence myth had taken 140 casualties. As Current implemented its technological convergence as a solution to the problem of the lack of participation in democracy, their core myth about the power of technology was revealed to be incompetent in ameliorating the labor problems associated with user-generated content as well as the once disgruntled—and now unemployed—convergence workers.

"We've also got this TV property. That is not such a bad thing."
—*Vanguard* Vice President Adam Yamaguchi. (interviewed April 20, 2011)

According to Current's press release addressing the "blood bath," the network was shifting away from its trademark short-form video packages and "towards proven 30–60 minute formats" (Rao 2009). Current hired a new CEO, Mark Rosenthal, ex-president and COO of MTV Networks, a network that had also exchanged its short-form for long-form content. COO Earl soberly admitted that, "We have learned that short-form content is not the best to drive audiences and engage large audiences on television" (interviewed September 3, 2010). Later Earl told me regarding the VC2 phase, "We are acknowledging that we did not do a great job on the cable television front" (interviewed September 3, 2010). Under Rosenthal, Current will "start operat-

136   A. FISH

ing like a more traditional network" (Schneider 2009). This includes program development, licensing and acquisitions, and talent management—as in traditional television. As internet-centrism was replaced by television, Current's solutionism matured. Television alone was going to solve the democratic deficit. It would not be citizen voices but rather politically progressive professional voices that Current would contribute to the American public sphere. Current hired liberal newscaster Keith Olbermann and Democratic politicians Gavin Newsom and Eliot Spitzer. With citizen participation thoroughly evacuated from the mission of Current, so too was its internet-centrism. *Vanguard* Vice President Adam Yamaguchi explained:

> For a while we were so bullish about the internet changing everything, we didn't know where it was going and we didn't know what it was going to do and we jumped on it, whatever that meant. It turned out not to be the right move. We took a few steps back. We came to the realization that we have to embrace this somehow. We've also got this TV property. That is not such a bad thing. (interviewed April 20, 2011)

Vanguard producer Jeff Plunkett asked, "How much can you stand aside and say we are not a part of the TV world? And I think Current for a long time said, 'we are not a part of that ugliness'" (interviewed September 1, 2010). Yamaguchi and Plunkett, as *Vanguard* producers, were understandably supportive of a shift away from the internet and toward television. *Vanguard* was the most television-ready of Current's programs at 28-minute episodes, the most well-regarded, and the most independent from the internet, and therefore the least likely to be cut. These television professionals were marginalized at the earlier peak of Current's internet-centrism. Now it was their time to enact their version of solutionism, this time with television and professional voices. From a certain perspective internal to the corporation, this is a success story. The people who had been arguing for "proven" models of television as illustrated by Plunkett and Yamaguchi finally won out over those "bullish" about the internet imaginaries who could only gesture toward the future.

> "Convergence is nothing more than an over-hyped illusion."
> —A. Michael Noll, Professor Emeritus, University of Southern California.
> (Noll 2002, 12)

Current was a "pioneer in not one but three emergent media trends: the use of user-generated content, web video, and social media" (Holmes 2013). But in their timely pursuit of each, they failed in both television and the internet. Current's "neurotic" or "sinusoidal" imaginary of television versus the internet provided it a repertoire of ways to envision itself, on the one hand, as a digital, social media entrepreneur interested in diversifying the hegemonic public sphere with televised social media, on the other, as a for-profit television network. This nimbleness might be good for trend-setting but it creates an unstable workworld for employees and freelance user-generated content producers, as well as a difficult viewing experience for audiences. As Current experimented and failed and the network retired its brand in early 2013 as a rather mundane progressive television network, not a convergence groundbreaker or a political earthmover, it also lost some of its internet-centrism as it moved toward its television property.

This chapter has articulated the myth that the coming together of television and the internet will provide for the public participatory and grassroots ways of overcoming the corporate domination of the media. As myths do, this one provides to its believers an overarching worldview that galvanizes action in precarious worlds. This convergence myth is supported by the argument for internet-centrism, the belief that productive models for society should be based on the internet's structure. These facets of the convergence myth and internet-centrism are examples of digital discourse—a solutionistic and obfuscating mitigation of the contradictions of liberalism through talk on technology.

But like all digital discourse, the convergence myth reveals as much as it conceals about the actual workings of a social system. Using interviews and observations I documented the "moral technical imaginaries" of those tasked with solving the problem of democratic participation with technological convergence. The workers' consternated reactions to the task of solving democratic problems with technological convergence proves that the convergence myth does what myths do, revealing a realm of utopian possibility while negating the pragmatic work to get there. In the process, Current workers experienced and rejected the mitigations of the digital discourse.

Convergence is not merely industrial hype mobilized to galvanize profitable use of social media by a public reticent about divulging private information into corporatized public space. Convergence is not essentially a way of ideologically obscuring the non-democratic manifestations

138 A. FISH

of industrial conglomeration, namely, the minimizing of pluralism and diversity through vertical integration. With convergence will not come democratization of closed communications systems and an opening of the American public sphere to diverse voices. Like "platform" before it, convergence is a working word that signifies both political and economic potentials (Gillespie 2010). It can be mobilized by corporations, regulators, and activists. Its polysemy is its power but with it comes a dizzying effect that obscures more than it reveals. This is mitigation through obfuscation and it is the goal of digital discourse.

How can we discuss networked communication technologies and peripheral systems without recourse to myth and metaphor-laden language? Language constitutes a metaphor-exploiting system. Without metaphors, there would be no myth but also no language. To speak and to write is to use symbols that do not resemble their referents. Thus a highly complex system unifying some aspects of television and the internet cannot be described in one word: "convergence." Such systems require a phrase that contains a polysemantic universe capable of inspiring and triggering imaginations.

"Convergence is a myth and not a mantra to be followed."
—A. Michael Noll, Professor Emeritus, University of Southern California.
(Noll 2002, 13)

Convergence was first discussed as the "convergence of modes" and the "blurring of the lines between media" (Pool 1984). This "blurring" of internet video and television, for instance, is occurring because both media are increasingly delivered in the same format (as binary code) and on the same network (packet-switching networks), a result not only of technology but also of regulatory and corporate practices. "[C]onvergence discourses" form a "dominant ideology" which affects "the way people think about the unfolding media and communication industries" (Dwyer 2010, 3, 9, 10). In this digital discourse, convergences result in "unquestionable benefits," business "synergies," and emerge within "discursive frameworks of neoliberalism and technological determinism" (Dwyer 2010, 3). This "technological determinism" is a result of internet-centrism or the tendency to replicate a model taken from the internet as the solution to world problems (Morozov 2011, 2013). I align media studies scholar Tim Dwyer's digital discourse with communication professor Vincent Mosco's mythology (2004)—the ways stories about technology both open and close possibilities. The obscuring or occultic power of mythology resonates with the traditional notion of ideology as "false consciousness" or the carrying of a misplaced belief. But instead of being either true or false, digital discourse attempts to mitigate the paradoxes of liberalism. The spoken "discursive frameworks" of Current workers I refer to as "moral technical imaginaries" (Kelty 2008)—the way media workers negotiate the political and technical contradictions of their craft. Current's existence as a peer-progressive network results from three convergences: industrial, technological, and critical utopian.

Industrial convergence refers to vertical and horizontal integration of corporations across a number of media sectors. It is an attempt to minimize risks and maximize returns for large media companies within a disintermediating digital economy. Noll notes: "Such industrial convergence is really consolidation in the name of convergence" (2002, 13). Gore agrees and identifies how industrial convergence appropriated new divisions into profitable conglomerates. He writes: "[The] journalism profession morphed into the news business, which became the media industry and [is] now owned almost completely by conglomerates" (2007, 18).

Regulatory convergence refers to how politicians facilitate industrial convergence. The Telecommunication Act of 1996 was pushed through the US Congress by the Bill Clinton and Gore administration and led to a "merger mania." This is an example of corporate liberalism with regulators assisting industrial convergence by lifting how many and what types of media properties companies can own. Current self-defines as an independent television network in reaction to industrial convergence.

In her ethnographic research on independent film producers, anthropologist Sherry Ortner explains the discourse of independence as a "reactive discourse" that opposes the hegemony of Hollywood (Ortner 2013). In a reactionary online video shot in the basement of Current's headquarters in San Francisco in late 2011, Cenk Uygur, founder of *The Young Turks,* affirms why he is bringing his most subscribed YouTube news program to Current. Gore welcomes Uygur to Current, saying, "We want you to keep speaking truth to power, without fear or favor; you are on a truly independent network now." Uygur responds, "I love it. I want to be independent, progressive, *and progressive.* And I know you are not going to mind that." Gore chuckles, "Not a bit. We encourage it" (Current 2011). The oppositional nature of this discourse is an example of a reactive discourse that constructs an independent identity against an industrially converged entity.

140   A. FISH

Technological convergence explains how various media services can be provided by fewer delivery mechanisms. Gore says "We are moving … [as a] world … into a converged platform where everything is a stream of digital bits" (2007, 269). Current attempted to be first to market in television/internet convergence. However, technological convergence is not a "natural" inevitability but rather a result of social processes historically situated and inflected by discourse (MacKenzie and Wajcman 1999). Technological convergence is happening but becomes mythologized when wedded to politics. This results in solutionism and emerges from an internet-centrism about the positive political potential of appropriating models for society from the internet. This complex of myths leads to a type of "critical utopianism" (Jenkins 2006, 2011).

Critical utopian convergence (Jenkins 2011) posits that producer-user communities and media industries are in a state of co-constitution as a result of technological convergence. Critical utopianism invites individuals to "imagine alternative structures that might better meet human needs" (Jenkins 2011). Current exploited the actualities of technological convergence and the agencies given to citizens by digital cameras and prosumer editing suites; it was created to democratize access to media audiences where regulatory and industrial convergence had minimized public media access points; and it is an example of critical utopian convergence in its strategic and ultimately unsuccessful bids to reflexively implement and "*imagine* alternative structures" (Jenkins 2011, my italics).

Current attempted "to build a peer network to solve the problem" of the lack of participation within news production through citizen video journalism and socially mediated television. In their emphasis on peer networks as models for society, peer progressives can be considered "internet centrists" (Morozov 2013). Like "critical utopians" (Jenkins 2006), who celebrate how technological convergence empowers grassroots actors, internet-centrism de-emphasizes the impact of political and economic power. Embodying the peer-progressive hype that the internet is a model with which to overcome the deficiency of participation in democracy, Current failed to pay due attention to the operation of making technological convergence economically feasible, viewable for audiences, and sustainable for user-generated and below-the-line labor. The convergence myth alone was not enough to overcome the economic collapse that was to befall the media workers at Current.

Revealing the many experiments with internet convergence—from citizen video journalism to Twitter-on-television—this project reveals what media scholar Evgeny Morozov (2013) called "solutionism"—Silicon Valley-based attempts to engineer technological fixes for political problems. In this case the political problem that they attempted to solve was the participation deficit in democracy. Gore wanted to use the internet along with television to diversify the voices in the hegemonic public sphere. This solutionism is a more extreme form of "critical utopianism" (Jenkins 2006) or what Morozov calls "digital utopianism" which includes "irrational exuberance ... quasi-religious belief in the power of the Internet to do supernatural things ... [such as] Opening up closed societies and flushing them with democracy juice" (Morozov 2011, 19). Solutionism is an embodiment of the convergence mythology. As Mosco says, "[m]yths can foreclose politics, can serve to depoliticize speech but they can also open the door to a restoration of politics to a deepening of political understanding" (Mosco 2004, 16). In the case of Current, the myth was that the convergence of television and the internet would result in a solution to the problem of the lack of participation in democracy. But digital discourses in general, and digital myths in particular, also foreclose important issues such as user-generated and below-the-line labor. They relegate the difficult and pragmatic work to other people or networked computers, believing that technology alone will fix problems that are social in origin.

At Current, the "myths that swirl around digital media convergence" (Maxwell and Miller 2011, 595) also include the promise of "experiential immediacy, global interactivity and interpersonal connectedness" (ibid.). And like the no-collar "sweatshops" of hardware production, the white-collar sweatshops of user-generated and precarious labor are a misunderstood externality of convergence. Convergence is a much more problematic and difficult operation for the workers tasked with solving it.

Myths are examples of digital discourse which are created for specific purposes by individuals capable of reaping the benefits of investment and the aggregation of power that comes along with public excitement. Myths exploit metaphors and metaphors exploit polysemy. Geographer Mark Graham (2013) discusses the problems of the spatial metaphor—cyberspace, for instance—in digital discourse, explaining how this metaphor allows politicians purchase to understand and importantly control the internet. Another example of digital discourse comes from the technoliberal elites at YouTube, which ambiguously uses "platform" to describe their service. "Platform" is a digital discourse because it replaces precision with a "comforting sense of technical neutrality and progressive openness" (Gillespie 2010, 360). Likewise, Current's use of the idea of

142   A. FISH

convergence sounds good to investors and Silicon Valley employees looking for politically important, technologically satisfying, and profitable work. In Current's case, convergence is also an example of a solutionist's digital discourse as convergence is articulated as capable of improving American democracy by "flushing it with democracy juice" (Morozov 2011) in the form of citizen participation capable of overturning the elitist control of television.

Observe the diverse interpretations and performances attached to the concept of convergence by Current upper and middle management. Current Programming President David Neuman used the concept of internet and television convergence to sell the idea of Current to would-be citizen video journalists as the "HBO of user-generated content" (Darling 2008). In reference to interest from commercial sponsors, Current CEO Joel Hyatt discussed Current as "the first truly two-screen experience" (Peterson 2007). To attract sponsors, investors, or content producers, the myth of convergence is an ambiguous digital discourse mobilized to convince diverse audiences of the political, artistic, and professional possibilities of the young television network.

However, technological convergence is not inevitable; industrial convergence is not apolitical; and user/producer convergence is not so "utopian" for those implementing it. Rather, convergence is a social process of difficult negotiation and challenging practices. The convergence myth is also a digital discourse in that it attempts to mitigate the contradictions of liberalism through talk on technology.

These discourses on convergence are what anthropologist Christopher Kelty calls "moral technical imaginaries" (2008, 170). Speaking about open source software and the internet as both technical and moral systems, Kelty says, "By moral, I mean imaginations of the proper order of collective political and commercial action; referring to much more than simply how individuals should act, moral signifies a vision of how economy and society should be *ordered* collectively" (2008, 140, my italics). Both the "technical" and the "moral" are interwoven and constitute imaginaries—the intellectual work performed just prior and during practices. Talk about convergence reflects personal and corporate moralities—the way the world ought to be *ordered* socially and politically—but also the way the world is—impossible to consistently contain in circuits of political and economic productivity.

An example of moral technical imaginaries comes from hacker culture. On one level, hackers' moral technical imaginaries begin with technical discussions of computers, networks, protocols, and their distaste for proprietary software. On another level, hackers' talk reveals moralities regarding free speech, meritocracy, privacy, and individualism. Hacker "morality" (Coleman and Golub 2008, 267) is experienced in the context of networked participation and resistance and thus offers a revision of selfhood, property, privacy, labor, and creativity for the digital age. For an example of moral technical imaginary, read the experiences of Current marketing executive Joe Brilliant who says,

> The defining story of Current TV is the constant cultural and business conflict between the goals and objectives of the TV and filmic based components and the web-centric elements of Current; how those two things were both at the table; how they were reconciled and how they were not in some cases; the challenge of being a new media company where you are trying to draw from both pools and satisfy different distribution platforms and customers and consumers. (interviewed May 26, 2010)

Such moral technical imaginaries form the subjective epistemology of media work (Perin 2006; Postill 2008). Technical talk is always already moralistic. Anthropologist Mark Allen Peterson says, "[t]he organization of productive roles is never a simple technological distribution but always also a profoundly moral one" (2003, 194). Brilliant's narrative is about the difficulties of convergence but it is also about the challenges of creating inclusion in the hegemonic public sphere with existing technologies, communications policies, market constraints, and talent pools.

With a sound engineering metaphor, developer Dan Linder describes Current's history, "We are in this sine wave thing. Before we let ourselves dip way up high or way down low again, let's get a band pass filter in there and keep it bouncing around in the middle, rather than today we are a web company, tomorrow a TV company, tomorrow a web company" (interviewed October 11, 2010). This technical imaginary of fluctuating allegiances also reflects the fluctuations of the moral commitment to diversity within the hegemonic public sphere. Others are less delicate than Linder. "Current is a neurotic company. I define neurosis as actions you return to time and time again even though they don't work," said Current producer Jimmy Goldblum about Current's fluctuating commitments to television or the internet (interview February 6, 2011). This neurosis is a problem Current workers tried to solve through imagining the proper use

144   A. FISH

of broadband and broadcast technologies to solve the participatory deficit in media democracy.

Digital Discourse and the Convergence Myth

For VC2 producers like myself as well as full time employees, internet and television convergence was supposed to be personally, politically, and professionally empowering. This digital discourse celebrates the post-Fordist workplace as flexible, mobile, creative, less bureaucratic, and more collaborative. This digital discourse is the internet version of the "new spirit of capitalism" which incorporates the "artistic critique" that capitalism has become less alienating (Boltanski and Chiapello 2005). Political purpose and meaningful work coalesce around digital technologies. The potential contradictions that might arise at the subjective confluence of politics/labor are mitigated by the presence of digital technologies. Digital discourse is an attempt by technoliberal elites not to ideologically obscure but rather to mitigate the difficult moralities of work, business, and politics within technocapitalism (Fisher 2010).

Current's digital discourse was driven by cosmopolitanism, political passion, creativity zeal, and the pleasures of collaboration. Current employees worked long hours, sometimes 60 hours a week, and the freelance user-generated video producers like myself, also worked flexibly and in precarious locations to create the inexpensive and political content that filled Current's programming. (A terrifying example of corporeal precarity is what happened to Current reporters Laura Ling and Euna Lee who were captured in North Korea while producing a documentary, jailed, and freed after a visit by Bill Clinton in 2009, vaulting Current to global infamy). VC2 producers like myself were paid to cover the costs of production ($500 to $2000, depending upon seniority and project) and described as a media "Peace Corps" by an early consultant. We felt that we were part of an insurgent political media movement led by Gore and driven by the inevitable democratizing power of internet and television convergence. We were democratizing the otherwise exclusive television platform and a lucrative IPO was about to make everyone wealthy. We would proceed to an impactful future in Silicon Valley, Hollywood, or Washington, DC.

This digital discourse assumes a unique form within Current as a myth that internet and television convergence will assist in the transcendence of the elite control of political dialogue. Myths are historical narratives that assist subjects in transcending the contradictions of their society (Lévi-Strauss 1978). Mosco (2004) claims that myths about technologies both open and close realms of political possibility. Myths are non-intentional obfuscations that gesture toward a potentiality. This accidental deception is what makes the convergence myth a digital discourse instead of an ideology, which is an intentional deceit (Flichy 2007). By Current's demise, a cynical ideology had triumphed but not before a conceit of discursive optimism. The myth of convergence is an ambiguous digital discourse mobilized to convince diverse audiences of the political, artistic, and professional possibilities of the young television network.

Current is important for what it reveals about the fate of pro-democratic projects that are constrained by the profit imperative and the affordances of specific media systems. The case shows what can and cannot be done for democracy with networked technologies and displays the conflicts between elite discourses and professional and user-generated content practices. Current tried everything a media company could to bring diversity to television: user-generated content, television/internet convergence, social media, popular left-wing television pundits like Keith Olbermann, and a global footprint as an independent broadcaster in monopolized media ecologies like Italy, the USA, and the UK. They failed quite dramatically because the capacity for media systems to assist in the dialogue on democracy is limited not only by the affordances of networked technologies but also by the commercial imperative of those very media systems. Current may seem like a small case but it was a historic experiment that many entrepreneurs, politicians, and entrepreneurial politicians paid close attention to at a crucial moment in the radically changing landscape of global media conglomeration. Current can be used to speak directly to core contradictions of Western liberal society, namely, the euphemism "capitalist democracy."

The convergence myth attempted to conceal labor, legal, economic, and aesthetic difficulties. This point is made through an analysis of seven cases: (1) Current's onscreen studio and non-programmatic "shuffle" programming; (2) rivalry between Current's television-centric Hollywood and internet-focused Silicon Valley offices; (3) Current's appropriation of intellectual property rights strategies from television for a digital platform; (4) the diaspora of Current employees; (5) the commercialization of user-generated content; (6) Current's failed IPO; and (7) the network's eventual sale to Al Jazeera. As Current was profitably sold in December 2012 and many former Current employees proceeded to become economically

146   A. FISH

successful in other businesses from Twitter to YouTube in transforming the internet into a profitable television-like platform, the concept of digital discourse shifts from an idealistic mitigating myth to a blinding for-profit ideology.

THE INTERNET ON TELEVISION: SHUFFLE PROGRAMMING

Several Current employees thought that they were instructed to bring to television the parts of the internet that do not work on television. From 2005 to 2009, Current did away with the practice of scheduling specific shows at particular hours and replaced it with the "shuffle format," where short VC2 or user-generated content was randomly presented throughout the day like an Apple iPod on shuffle. VC2 producer Josh Wolf described the experience of viewing Current: "The combination of serious journalism with Current Hottie left people with 'what the fuck is this?' We had sex trafficking, base-jumping, and male model sexography all on the same day, in the same 10 minutes. On launch day all three were on there. They fractured the audience in this idea that they thought all 18- to 34-year-olds were a weird mix of people" (interviewed September 3, 2010). YouTube had a similar approach to viewing and had recently been sold to Google in 2006 for $2.65 billion. Current also had these aspirations toward scalability and profitability and tried YouTube's non-programmatic approach to programming—short, random, shuffled, amateur, user-generated content. But the internet on television did not work for audiences or producers, according to Current employees. Brilliant said, "It doesn't work on TV, so they picked the wrong battles" (interviewed May 26, 2010). The strategy did not work in generating an audience or in creating a vibrant public sphere. Journalist Jeff Howe (2008) called Current.com in the summer of 2007 a "ghost town." While the shuffle modeled the rich diversity of voices necessary to produce a public sphere, it did so at the expense of the prolonged debate, analysis, and timeliness of (some) television news. Current purchased and commissioned from VC2 producers like myself and Wolf what they called "pods," or 3–5-minute short documentaries, that were "evergreen"—not tethered to contemporary issues and therefore could be programmed indefinitely into the future. Evergreen content is better for the profitability of a proprietary video library but does not make for newsworthy television. Political pods were rarely "evergreen" because politics tends to be temporally contextual.

Current employees imagined a better network, one that resisted the temptation to adopt some aspects of the internet video and retained other traditional television tactics. Plunkett was frustrated: "Of all the accepted practices of TV, we plucked that one—we needed pretty people and a pretty set—instead of picking we needed routines and block programming" (interviewed September 1, 2010). Several thought that Current needed to "work within the structures of TV, namely the block programming [and] build routines around big personalities and high concept shows" (interviewed September 1, 2010). In the prelaunch era, Chopra thought a celebrity might draw audiences, but Gore was against it. Gore did not want to be the star on Current, despite being one in 2007 and 2008 when he won an Emmy, an Oscar, and a Nobel Peace Prize. Current rejected some traditional expressions of television, such as scheduled long-form, block, or star-driven programming, while appropriating the legacy of hosts and a studio set. It combined this with the internet's user-generated content and shuffled viewing practices. It was this mixture of practices that Current hoped would become popular, and diversify the hegemonic public sphere while making investors wealthy.

The odd hybridity led to or fueled Current's identity crisis. Plunkett asked, "Are we a news station? Should we send people to cover Katrina? … Who are we competing with? CNN? Are we trying to be a younger, more authentic news gathering agency? Or are we trying to be 'current' in a trendy way, the purveyors of cool. … We wanted to have it all" (interviewed September 1, 2010). Plunkett's remarks resonate with statements by another Current producer, who said that Current was a "neurotic" company. For Current elites who were focused on both mimicking successful internet video strategies as well as bringing as much citizen-produced content to television, the shuffle programming strategy was an ideal solution. On the other hand, for Current workers with the difficult directive to graft the internet shuffle format to television, it was a mistake. The digital discourse that the internet would produce a more satisfying work environment and the convergence myth that internet and television convergence would improve democracy were each illusions.

INTELLECTUAL PROPERTY RIGHTS

Current's creative executives wanted to buy VC2 producer Mary Matthew's pod *My First Girlfriend* about her coming-out story. It was the type of evergreen, personal, and comfortably political programming

148 A. FISH

Current wanted. But after reviewing the contract fine print, Mathews refused: "I cannot have you own my home movies," Matthews said to Current (interviewed May 17, 2011). She thought Current's mentality was: "I value your talent, I value your craft, but I am not going to pay you dick for it" (interviewed May 17, 2011). Matthews spoofed Current in a subsequent video, *My First Emmy*, for what she called "bad practices" (interviewed May 17, 2011) regarding their intellectual rights management and compensation practices.

In the spoof, she used the television feed of Gore and Hyatt in 2007 on stage at the Kodak Theater in Los Angeles accepting their Emmy for Interactive Television. However, through a crude edit, "Tom" the CEO of MySpace handed the Emmy to Matthews. She feigned joy and surprise as if she were on stage. Suddenly somebody from off-camera grabs it, with her struggling, saying, "But why should they get it?! I made what is on Current TV!" A text card appears over her fight for compensation and cultural capital: "Democratic Television @ Monarchy Prices." She refused to sell *My First Girlfriend* to Current and instead put it up on various video sites, such as YouTube and blip, where artists are provided more control over their work such as Creative Commons licenses.

Current appropriated strict intellectual property rights management from television's playbook as opposed to encouraging shareable and remixable practices (Lessig 2008). Digital discourse claims that new media work minimizes alienation. However, alienation of producers from media products was the result of Current's all-inclusive rights reservations.

The strictness of these contracts is one of the strongest examples of how the imaginative morality of an open internet met the technical realities of lawsuit-frightened television lawyers. Instead of having a less strict intellectual property agreements and adopting a synergistic and "spreadable" cross-platform approach to content that enrolls the agency of the producer in self-promotion (Jenkins et al. 2013), Current adopted a proprietary model regarding intellectual property. While Current's discourse regarding VC2 was to create a "two-way dialogue" between citizen viewers, citizen producers, and professional chaperones, their legal approach was strictly written to favor the network retaining control over the content. VC2 producers like Matthews elected not to work with Current after having recognized these discursive contradictions.

CEO Joel Hyatt thought it was necessary to attain the rights in perpetuity so as to build a valuable library. According to Current's President of Programming David Neuman, this strict intellectual property rights requirement severely limited Current's capacity to acquire citizen-produced content. Early Current consultant, Michael Rosenblum, thought Hyatt was wrong in this regard, "Joel thought the asset was the library, but the asset was the people. YouTube doesn't own anything and they were valued at $1.8 billion" (interviewed August 31, 2010). By 2011, Current was airing no content from their large and well-protected VC2 library. With Current now defunct, their domain gone and their servers decommissioned, my 16 pods detailing, amongst other things, the struggle of Iraqi refugees and individuals living in divided cities in Nicosia, Cyprus and Belfast are not accessible. Having sold the work to Current, original VC2 producers such as myself cannot legally re-upload our pods or repurpose any of our sold footage in films or television. In fact, legally speaking, they are no longer *our* pods, neither as producers nor as a community. Code is law and in this case proprietary code/law results in the suppression of my contribution to the diversity of opinion on the internet. Any political work my pods were doing to inspire a "two-way dialogue" is over because of the profit-driven, television-centric, proprietary property practices. The digital discourse that networks would improve freelance media work and the convergence myth that bringing the internet and television together would improve politics and generate wealth were proven to be unsupported claims.

CHEMOSPHERE STUDIO

In mid-2007, Current placed a job advertisement on Craigslist for additions to its department tasked with finding VC2 content. Sarah Penna was working as a production assistant for a documentary film and reality television company in Hollywood, World of Wonder, specializing in reality content about celebrity, sex, pop science, and gay culture for television networks Showtime, HBO, and Oxygen. Penna and I were editing our own documentary, *Tantric Tourists*, a reflexive and surreal take on spiritual and sexual seekers which we shot in India in 2005. Internet video and social media were quickly becoming popular and economically powerful from 2005 to 2007 and we were focused on working as scholars, activists, and producers in this emergent creative industry. Current offered an ideal blend of political purpose, financial incentives, scholarly possibilities, an internet-based community, and television distribution. We tailored our pods, *Tantric Tourists* and *Sacred Land Battle*, an investigation into Buddhist and Hindu religious territorial disputes in the Himalayan state of Sikkim, for Current's nascent VC2 aesthetic—short, personal, Aristotelian, with a thoughtful if not happy ending. We submitted our drafts on Current's Leaderboard, a social video site where other users could comment and "vote" for the pod to be purchased by and broadcast on Current. Within days, Current creative executives were emailing and phoning. Apparently, they were desperate for the type of content we created and we were happily surprised by the praise for our nascent skills and/or their dearth of television-grade internet-found content.

After having been discovered in this manner, Penna decided to apply for the permanent position. The next day, Current creative executive Brandon Gross called and asked her if she would meet him at Current's Los Angeles office the following morning. Knowing that I was her co-producer, he asked if I would also come in and do a 5–10-second intro and outro "wrap" for the two pods in their studio, the Chemosphere. We both happily agreed. She eventually got the job, moved to San Francisco, and joined a team of seven outreach workers. Her job was to translate Current's convergence myth that the internet could be the source of elite-refuting television content.

Later that day I ran across the busy intersection in Hollywood's Media District to the Chemosphere studio. The Chemosphere is where Current hosts introduce the VC2 pods and is a studio replica of a spaceship-shaped Hollywood Hills home. The Chemosphere had been a subject of derision for the internet-savvy engineers and "serious" television journalists. Journalists for Current's guerilla journalism program, *Vanguard*, Christof Putzel and Mitch Koss, went out for dinner with the President of Programming David Neuman on the night of the network's launch in April 2005. Neuman asked Putzel what he thought about Max Lugavere and Jason Silva, the handsome Chemosphere hosts and Gap models, who had no production credentials except for their senior thesis film *Textures of Selfhood*, a didactic, psychedelic, and sexual romp through South Beach, Florida. Putzel spoke honestly, "I don't think they reach the audience we are trying to reach" (interviewed June 16, 2011). Neuman immediately retorted, "So everyone has to be like Christof Putzel, the journalist who travels!" (Putzel interview, June 16, 2011). Defending the digital discourse that assumes that with networks comes workforce equality, Neuman scoffed at the elitism of serious television journalism.

Putzel wondered aloud to me why Current didn't give more VC2 producers the experience I had in the Chemosphere, introducing my own work. Plunkett elaborated, "If we are going to be this network that is preaching authenticity and globalism, then we should have people on air that are beacons of that mentality. And I don't think early on we had that" (interviewed September 1, 2010). Neuman thought that the Chemosphere was necessary to ground the chaotic shuffle programming to a predictable television home base. To Putzel, the Chemosphere embodied the pastiche, seduction, and performativity that Current said it hoped to challenge. Despite the powerful digital discourse and the persuasive artifice of the studio, the convergence of internet and television was challenged on-screen and in dialogues with workers.

The Chemosphere was the visual expression of the confusion resulting from Current's convergence myth. "The Chemosphere undermined all that we were doing. Especially those who wanted to see Current as a rebel, a rebellious differentiator, they would see these shiny, preened LA people and we would lose credibility," Brilliant complained (interview May 26, 2010). Putzel agreed that while executives said Current was "getting rid of Hollywood, it didn't, it still had that Hollywood image" (interviewed June 16, 2011). Much of the content from VC2 and *Vanguard* was critical, but editors, graphics artists, and Hollywood hosts sanitized it. Twenty-first-century technopopulism flowed into twentieth-century Hollywood futurism in the Chemosphere studio. No amount of digital discourse could mitigate the result that neither the American public sphere nor Current's shareholder values were going to see diversification via this strategy.

Collective Journalism head Andrew Fitzgerald explained the cultural friction that resulted when the VC2 video content was introduced in the Chemosphere studio:

> I think it was the heterogeneity of the content and presentation ... it existed in two separate worlds that we tried to combine on a daily basis. If you watched the network it was a hard viewing experience because you were being pulled in and out of these different worlds. You kept coming back to this world that was definitely not a part of any of the worlds you dipped into. (interviewed May 26, 2010)

Current had "authentic" content, but how they edited and wrapped it in "evergreen" pods, with slick graphics and hosted outros from photogenic hosts in the distantly hip, alien, and plush Chemosphere studio, shattered that "authenticity." Contradictions resulted from fundamentalist commitments to conflicting perspectives and the lack of transparency

152   A. FISH

in admitting these conflicts. With the absence of transparency, authenticity was also absent and with it the development of the frank dialogue required in a diversified public sphere. With the unlikely expectations of improving both democracy and profitability, convergence was bound to fail. This was evident on the screen as well in Current's offices in both Hollywood and Silicon Valley.

HOLLYWOOD VERSUS SILICON VALLEY

A catechism proceeds like this: San Francisco makes participatory media infrastructure; Los Angeles makes media content. San Francisco creates platforms for social life; Los Angeles performs social life. The amateur is king in San Francisco; the professional artist rules Los Angeles. "Serious" journalists can live anywhere. Current employed media engineers, media producers, and serious journalists who were located in one or other of their two American West Coast offices, in San Francisco or Los Angeles. The conflicts obscured by the convergence myth were dispersed geographically across coastal California. For instance, much of the criticism of the Chemosphere was waged from the professional journalists at Current, those working for the award-winning *Vanguard* program and the platform executives and engineers in the San Francisco internet-focused office. These differing professional affiliations drove conflicts and competitions over resources and the future direction of the network.

Current engineer Dan Linder gave me advice on my research into Current: "The story is how can a TV company centered in Silicon Valley either thrash wildly or creatively reinvent itself?" (interviewed October 11, 2010). COO Joana Earl agreed, "As one of the only cable networks born in Silicon Valley, we are a constant reinvention" (interviewed September 13, 2010). Current Vice President, Aline Allegra wasn't so gentle, "I think the company suffered because it had two different [cultures] … San Francisco had a culture and way of doing things and it was a Silicon Valley company … they saw themselves as an internet company. In Los Angeles we saw ourselves as a TV network and an entertainment company and it was hard for those two cultures to meld in some ways" (interviewed June 12, 2010). In an archetypically digital discursive move, Earl agrees with Allegra's assessment that there were cultural differences but disagrees that it wasn't productive: "There is always a cultural style difference. An engineer from Silicon Valley operates very differently from a producer in Hollywood. There is a natural tension. I think diversity ends up producing better solutions." Most employees, however, thought that the spatial distance of Current's television and internet departments amplified a cultural difference. Vice President of Online Programming, Justin Gunn called this process "the silophication of the company" (interviewed August 4, 2010), where the internet, television, and marketing divisions were not well integrated and took different approaches to the same product. I qualify this geospatial balkanization as structural silophication. No digital discourse can dissuade the development of this professional tribalism. Digital discourse, and more precisely the convergence myth, cannot with sheer technological prowess overcome place-based and material limitations. Technological and professional identities connect with information infrastructure historically located in distinct locations. No amount of digital discourse that the labor in media industries is less alienating, more political, and more profitable will overcome this place-based social reality.

AN INITIAL PUBLIC OFFERING

Throughout its history, Current defined itself as closer to one or the other, its Hollywood or Silicon Valley roots. By 2008, it looked like a new technology bubble around Silicon Valley companies Twitter, Facebook, and YouTube had developed. Current aligned itself with Silicon Valley with its signature move—an IPO. Current's filing for an IPO in 2008 revealed what myths obscure—the lack of profits, an expendable political discourse, and the lack of a robust audience. The IPO showed Current as a business with subservient political aspirations.

To the public, employees, and journalists, Gore portrayed Current as a pro-democratic initiative. To potential investors and venture capitalists, Gore portrayed the network as a risky yet rewarding investment. For one political public, convergence had political potential to transform the elitism of television production. For a business public, convergence is a reason to invest capital. Digital discourse is mobilized to mitigate any contradiction in how work is experienced and politics performed. The human impacts of these mitigations are experienced by the media workers.

The IPO documentation revealed that Current was unprofitable. Despite this, Gore and Hyatt both received a substantial income, around $1 million in salaries and bonuses per year. The IPO explains that both Gore and Hyatt had loaned Current $1million as start-up financing. With a successful IPO, they would be returned this, plus more. SECinvestor. com, which tracks such federal filings, figured Current stock could go for between $13 and $15 a share, making Gore's 3.7 million A shares worth somewhere north of $48 million. The majority of the digital workers at Current barely made a living wage while working in San Francisco, one of the most expensive cities in the world. Freelance citizen video journalists like myself, the core of the political project and also core to the inexpensive content acquisition strategy, made considerably less. These labor and income inequities are facts no digital discourse can effectively mitigate.

Gore was paid and promised these sums because of his role publicly perpetuating the myth of convergence, which helped to secure cable and satellite carriers, skilled freelance and in-house workers, and IPO investors. Gore and Hyatt were committed to retaining creative and economic control over Current through having all of the company's class B shares, which would give them ten votes for every single vote of shareholders with class A stock. This would give Gore the type of "hammer-lock control over the company decried by shareholder rights activists and many of the same unions that supported Gore for years" (Grover 2008). This may have been justified on the grounds that Current was a political project and Gore and Hyatt needed to retain that mission in case of a shareholder mutiny. Current's politics and profit intertwined, and digital discourses such as the convergence myth were rhetorical tools used to achieve and sustain technoliberal power. "That's hardly democratic—with a large D or a small d," stated Charles Elson, a corporate governance expert, "[t]he irony is that this is coming from a Democratic leader" (Grover 2008). For Current, however, these ironies were mitigated through digital discourse that made work less alienated and improved politics, while producing capital for investors. For technoliberal elites, political and economic power can co-occur. For those who work for them, the contradictions of the equality project of democracy and the inequality which results from capitalism cannot be easily mitigated.

Eventually, the IPO was withdrawn and the "democratization" of a company's wealth which an IPO can represent never happened. The year 2008 began with an IPO and ended with a major liquidation of all workers in the VC2 project and the Chemosphere.

The Commercialization of User-generated Content

In 2011, security buzzed me up to Current's 27th floor lobby. In the transition away from the politics of the VC2 project and without the need for a major sound studio with the Chemosphere decommissioned, Current had relocated to a high-rise office in congested downtown Los Angeles. In the corridor were tall *Vanguard* promotional posters of Putzel and Yamaguchi with the words "No Lies" and "No Borders" painted in black across their faces. Across from the leather sofa on which I sat was a large monitor showing Current. A commercial began with a slick narrator saying "It's a Samsung summer road trip featuring Current journalists Max Lugavere and Jason Silva. Their destination? Catalina Island, California, to show how the Samsung Galaxy Tab 10.1 is revolutionizing the way we live." Silva and Lugavere proceeded to have an on-air self-proclaimed "bromance" on the Channel Islands guided by their new tablets.

There was no "journalism" in this commercial, and if there were, "journalists" using their title to add credence to their attempts at selling hardware is unethical. As the most recognizable faces at Current, Silva and Lugavere were kept on a retainer after the 2009 demise of VC2 for just these kinds of collaborative projects with corporations. Silva and Lugavere were most identified with the VC2 project, and therefore any corporate collaboration with these hosts was an attempt to coopt the "authenticity" of citizen video journalism for corporate gain. This advertisement had the authenticity of an infomercial. Another commercial followed. Like the corporatized VC2 pod I just finished watching, this commercial started with a text graphic claiming to be "Viewer-Created Content" with the same narrator from the previous advertisement saying, "Here is a short film about escaping conventions, made by a Current TV viewer, about the new CT Hybrid from Lexus, the most fuel-efficient luxury car available." From my experiences watching hundreds of pods, pitching pods to Current, and discussing pods with VC2 producers, I am confident that pods pitched on luxury cars would be rejected. But in the post-VC2 era, such "pods" were greenlit.

This advertisement was thinly veiled as a VC2 pod about someone "escaping conventions," the owner of Origami Vinyl, a record store in Echo Park, a hip neighborhood in Los Angeles. The ad was produced by Alejandro Heiber, who, according to IMDb, has been producing, directing, and editing films and commercials since 2004, and Salomon Resler, who began his career in 1999 working for the international advertising firm Saatchi and Saatchi in Caracas, Venezuela, and is presently a senior copy writer for DirecTV. The point should be clear. Lugavere, Silva, Heiber, and Resler are not viewer creators but professional salesmen. During the VC2 phase, Current had a program for aspiring commercial producers called VCAM, or Viewer-Created Advertising Message, and it was housed

156   A. FISH

in the advertising department. The journalistic version was VC2 and there was a significant attempt to separate advertising and editorial decision-making. These ads, however, were not promoted as VCAM but as VC2. In these instances, capitalism and democracy are conflated with the surface of democracy attempting to obscure the capitalist machinery. These commercials exhibit the shift at Current from a digital discourse that attempts to mitigate the lack of participation in democracy toward the ideological. Here the sincerity of discourse is consciously used as a mask for an exploitative process. Originally conceived, VC2 was designed to diversify television and be an inexpensive source of content. This dual function created tensions that were never resolved until the politics and with it the digital discourse were eliminated and exchanged for an ideology of capitalism.

Saskia Wilson-Brown, who entered the lobby, saved me from this disturbing ideology. She was once the lead in Current's Outreach department and was now working on web audience curation. She missed the first round of job cuts in November 2008 because she was a "legacy asset" but was let go in November 2009. She returned to her work as an independent film organizer before coming back to Current, where her fiancé now worked. She quickly embraced me, looked at the screen and its commercials, shook her head, pointed at the screen, and said rhetorically, "They call this Viewer-Created Content!?" (interviewed April 20, 2011). The gall with which Current fearlessly peddled its earlier "democratizing" mission for profit production equally stunned Wilson-Brown. She had believed in Gore's original political mission for Current and was one of the last to let go of its possible political potency. We reminisced about the idealistic era of VC2, speculated about whether "media democratization" was all just a sophisticated commercial ruse, and I caught her up on where her ex-colleagues were now working. What we knew was that the politics of user-generated content, or at least the appearance of it, had been commercialized. The commercialization of user-generated content had been observed in video game commentators and others (Postigo, n.d.). The shift from relatively open and amateur to closed and professional forms of media production appears to be a trend throughout the media industries. In Current's earlier period (2005–2009), it was hopeful but not unreasonable to use a digital dialogue that the internet could do both democracy and capitalism. Today, according to law scholar Tim Wu (2010), communications scholar James Curran (2012), and media justice activist and professor

Robert McChesney (2013), the democratic potential of amateur-based internet-supported dialogue is trumped by the capitalist drive toward monopolization of a converged media environment. The professionalization of user-generated content as well as the diasporic life histories of Current employees is evidence of a shift from the honest, if misplaced, digital discourse to a more deceitful ideology.

Diaspora

The commercialization of user-generated content and the professionalization of amateurs were not only happening on the screen in front of me in Current's lobby. Many of Current's employees tasked with finding amateur producers who were fired in 2008 and 2009, or left soon thereafter, were now successfully figuring out ways to sell those now professional producers, and the click-throughs and user data they carry, to corporations. Their commercialization strategy drew from both television and the internet: revenue-sharing deals with video sites like YouTube, thinly veiled commercials, product placement, and "sponsorship" deals.

For example, after being fired from Current in 2008, VC2 Outreach worker Sarah Penna began by working for Phil DeFranco, aka sxephil, the 13th most-subscribed YouTube producer, and proceeded to marry and manage MysteryGuitarMan, the 10th most-subscribed YouTube producer. Penna founded The Cloud Media, a YouTube advertising start-up acquired by Big Frame that "works with online talent doing brand integration, talent development, ad sales and website creation." Prior to becoming the CEO of Big Frame, Steve Raymond was a vice president at NBCUniversal/Comcast. The content managed by this Current alumna is orchestrated to sell merchandise, not improve diversity in the hegemonic public sphere. The political motivation many of these ex-Current employees described to me in 2006–2009 was not observable in their 2010–2013 work practices. Their activism may have migrated to philanthropy but was not integrated with their daily work practices the way it failed to work at Current.

Other examples follow: Joe Brilliant writes on his LinkedIn profile that after Current fired him in 2008 he produced "proof of concept viral video ads illustrating marketing potential of user-generated content" for Butler, Shine, Stern & Partners, an advertising agency. Current creative executive Dan Beckmann started IB5k, a network of freelance video producers that make advertisements for such clients as Kraft and Bank of America. Ezra Cooperstein, head of VC2, founded Maker Studios, a talent pool of the

158   A. FISH

most subscribed YouTube producers. Maker Studios is a "one-stop shop for reach, control, customization, and quality … providing marketers with streamlined opportunities to further their presence" on YouTube (makerstudio.com/advertise). Brandon Gross, the first creative executive I worked with as a VC2 producer at Current, started Urgent Content, Inc. with three other Current alumnis. They described themselves: "As pioneers of branded user-generated media, we help advertisers and their agencies implement content-based marketing 225 campaigns" (urgentcontent.com/about). Gross currently works for YouTube doing the same type of work.

The leading internet video companies and those founded by Current's diaspora—much like the two commercials I saw in Current's high-rise lobby that day—use the form and aesthetic of VC2 in acts of commercialization. This, according to sociologist Patrice Flichy (2007), represents the shift that internet imaginaries often undergo from utopian rhetoric to corporate ideology. In ideology, capitalist domination is hidden or ignored, while the utopian rhetoric persists as a falsity. Indeed, Lugavere and Silva are not journalists. What Penna calls "branded talent" is not "authentic" user-generated content but professionals with no political motivation. This dissonance between the digital discourse and the ideological is palatable for those who worked under the auspices of the former. Departing from our brief lobby meeting, Wilson-Brown said, "Things have changed, and I can't watch it" (interviewed July 1, 2010). Current's convergence myth gave it a repertoire of ways to envision itself simultaneously as a social media entrepreneur interested in the public sphere and a for-profit television network (Fish 2013). After leaving Current, the employees individually exhibit that same capacity to reinvent themselves to suit their needs. As their careers developed, the ideological motive in the pursuit of profit triumphed over the discursive dialogue in the pursuit of the political. The rapidity with which the discursive morphed into the ideological says as much about the future for the type of individual Current hired—young, ambitious, risk-taking, highly educated, financially backed by family—as about the mutability of political discourse within the technoliberal media corporation.

CURRENT'S CONCLUSION: SELL TO AL JAZEERA

What may be Gore's final word on Current may also be the most revealing. Explaining his divestiture, Gore said: "I am incredibly proud of what Current has been able to accomplish. But broadcast media is a business,

TECHNOLIBERALISM AND THE CONVERGENCE MYTH   159

and being an independent content producer in a time of increasing consolidation is a challenge" (Stetler 2013). Convergence was a useful myth but like all justifications for investment, it had its specific temporality.

Gore's position as a purveyor of the convergence myth was necessary for Current to get the lucrative and wide-ranging carriage deals that put the network into millions of American, British, Irish, South African, and Italian homes. It was also necessary to help in the sale to Al Jazeera on the last day of 2012. Satellite carriers such as TimeWarner were looking for a reason to eliminate Current and avoid having to air Al Jazeera English. But Gore used his clout to remind those carriers that they had a regulatory responsibility to broadcast diverse and non-fiction programming. Gore defended Al Jazeera: "Their global reach is unmatched and their coverage of major events like the Arab Spring is thorough, fair and informative" (Stetler 2013). With this defense, Gore preserved Current's sale to Al Jazeera complete with Current's carriage footprint intact. The contradictions were not missed by right-wing FoxNews.com which led with the headline: "Global warming guru Al Gore becomes rich hypocrite with sale of Current TV to Qatar, Inc." For the sale of Current to the Qatar-based television news network for $500 million, Gore would get $100 million.

The usefulness of the convergence myth and the political rhetoric of "independence" had ended and the technoliberal elites had reaped their rewards. For a few moments, the convergence myth helped Current's elites secure investment, content from politically sympathetic producers like myself, and critical awards such as the 2007 Emmy for Interactive Television. During this period, Gore was documented as saying that Current helped along the progressive anti-neoliberal movement and "lifted up the Occupy Movement" with Keith Olbermann and other progressive hosts. When the convergence and the independence myths no longer worked, Gore sold not only to an oil emirate but to an emergent global media conglomeration, Al Jazeera. Current's fickle and nomadic morality had a number of iterations but faced with a lack of profitability, the morality was abandoned into a morass of contradictions.

Originally Current's aspirations to diversify television through the application of the internet was a mitigating discourse, not untrue just unlikely. While the convergence myth was a digital discourse, the larger contradiction was in Western liberal society itself, specifically capitalism, a project that exacerbates inequality, and democracy, a project designed to maximize equality. This contradiction cannot be mitigated only eliminated through the rejection of either democracy or capitalism. Current evacuated

160   A. FISH

the democratic project and when a sustainable capitalist project failed to materialize, the technoliberal elites accepted the consolatory $500 million from the sale to Al Jazeera. This chapter has been about the results of the convergence myth: peculiar hybrids like shuffle television programming and television copyright laws grafted on internet-derived content; a rivalry between television and internet departments; an IPO that reveals the profitable potential of participatory culture; the contradictory commercialization of user-generated content; the ideologically driven life histories of Current employees; and an ethically fraught final sale to Al Jazeera.

The primary contradiction mediated by technological myths in Western liberal society is the copacetic coexistence of capitalism, a system of inequality, within democracy, a system designed to achieve equality. It is this contradiction that digital discourses generally, and the convergence myth in particular, seek to mitigate. Current's convergence myth is an example of a digital discourse that discusses technological progress as beneficial for democracy, business, and work without acknowledging the difficult job of laboring convergence.

Current's convergence myth presented the political potentials of networked labor while obscuring how social and economic capital was unequally distributed throughout the production chain (Fish and Srinivasan 2012). As Dwyer notes, "[c]onvergence discourses [emerge within] discursive frameworks of neoliberalism and technological determinism" (Dwyer 2010, 3). While not ideological, convergence myths are nevertheless embedded within actual existing technocapitalism. Current's convergence myth is an example of a digital discourse that requests citizen and worker obedience to democratic capitalism, while ignoring the contradictions of democracy/capitalism. Digital discourse attempts to mitigate the contradictions of politics-as-work, sewing together capitalism and democracy with the thread of technology. Current shows that democracy/capitalism may not cohere.

REFERENCES

Boltanski, L., and E. Chiapello. 2005. The New Spirit of Capitalism. *International Journal of Politics, Culture and Society* 18: 161.
Brooks, J., and I.A. Boal. 1995. Introduction. In *Resisting the Virtual Life: The Culture and Politics of Information*, ed. J. Brook and I.A. Boal. San Francisco: City Lights.

Campbell-Kelly, M., and W. Aspray. 1996. *Computer: A History of the Information Machine.* New York: Basic Books.

Coleman, E.G., and A. Golub. 2008. Hacker Practice: Moral Genres and the Cultural Articulation of Liberalism. *Anthropological Theory* 8(3): 255–277.

Curran, J. 2012. Reinterpreting the Internet. In *Misinterpreting the Internet*, ed. James Curran, Des Freedman, and Natalie Fenton. London: Routledge.

Current. 2011. Al Gore Welcomes Cenk Uygur and the Young Turks to Current TV. Accessed March 22, 2012. http://current.com/shows/the-young-turks/videos/al-gore-welcomes-cenk-uygur-andthe-young-turks-to-current-tv

Dornfeld, B. 1998. *Producing Public Television.* Princeton: Princeton University Press.

Dwyer, T. 2010. *Media Convergence.* Maidenhead: Open University Press.

Fish, A. 2007. *Secular Iraqi Refugees.* Current TV.

———. 2008. *Divided Cyprus.* Current TV.

———. 2013. Participatory Television: Convergence, Crowdsourcing, and Neoliberalism. *Communication, Culture and Critique* 6(3): 372–295.

Fish, A. and R. Srinivasan. 2012. Digital Labor Is the New Killer App. *New Media and Society.* 14(1): 135–150.

Fisher, E. 2010. Contemporary Technology Discourse and the Legitimation of Capitalism. *European Journal of Social Theory* 13(2): 229–252.

Flichy, P. 2007. *The Internet Imaginaire.* Cambridge: MIT Press.

Gillespie, T. 2010. The Politics of 'Platform'. *New Media & Society* 12(3): 347–364.

Gore, A. 1991. Infrastructure for the Global Village. *Scientific American*, 152. Accessed December 5, 2015. http://www.scientificamerican.com/article/infrastructure-for-the-global-villa/

———. 1994. Speech Delivered at the Information Superhighway Summit at UCLA January 11, 1994. Accessed March 22, 2012. http://www.uibk.ac.at/voeb/texte/vor9401.html

———. 2007. *The Assault on Reason.* London: Penguin Press.

Grover, R. 2008. Al Gore's Convenient IPO. *Bloomberg Businessweek.* Accessed October 12, 2013. http://www.businessweek.com/stories/2008-03-06/al-gores-convenient-ipobusinessweek-business-news-stock-market-and-financial-advice

Harper, J. 2008. Current TV Plans to 'Hack' Debates. *The Washington Times.* September 19. Accessed March 22, 2012. http://www.washingtontimes.com/news/2008/sep/19/current-tv-plans-to-hack-debates/

Holmes, D. 2013. What Can We Learn from the Brief Wonderous Life of Current TV? *Pandodaily.* Accessed December 5, 2015. http://pandodaily.com/2013/01/03/what-can-we-learn-from-the-brief-wondrous-life-of-current-tv/

Howe, J. 2008. *Crowdsourcing: Why the Power of the Crowd Is Driving the Future of Business.* New York: Crown Business.

162 A. FISH

Itzkoff, D. 2011. Plot Twist? If Viewers Say So, Let It Be. *New York Times*. Accessed December 5, 2015. http://www.nytimes.com/2011/02/11/arts/television/11karma.html?_r=0

Jenkins, H. 2006. *Convergence Culture*. New York: New York University Press.

Jenkins, H., S. Ford, and J. Green. 2013. *Spreadable Media: Creating Value and Meaning in a Networked Culture*. New York: New York University Press.

Kelty, C.M. 2008. *Two Bits: The Cultural Significance of Free Software and the Internet*. Durham: Duke University Press.

Lacy, S. 2008. *Once You're Lucky, Twice You're Good: The Rebirth of Silicon Valley and the Rise of Web 2.0*. New York: Gotham Books.

Lessig, L. 2008. *Remix: Making Art and Commerce Thrive in the Hybrid Economy*. New York: Penguin Press.

Levi-Strauss, C. 1978. *Myth and Meaning*. New York: Routledge & Kegan Paul, U.K, Taylor & Francis Group.

Maxwell, R., and T. Miller. 2011. Old, New and Middle-Aged Media Convergence. *Cultural Studies* 25(4–5): 585–603.

McCarthy, C. 2008. Current TV to Broadcast Diggs, Twitters on Election Night. *CNET*. Accessed March 21, 2012. http://news.cnet.com/8301-13577_3-10078556-36.html

McChesney, R. 2013. *Digital Disconnect: How Capitalism Is Turning the Internet Against Democracy*. New York: New Press.

McGirt, E. 2007. Al Gore's $100 Million Makeover. *Fast Company*. Accessed December 5, 2015. http://www.fastcompany.com/60067/al-gores-100-million-makeover

Morozov, E. 2011. *The Net Delusion: The Dark Side of Internet Freedom*. Jackson, TN: Public Affairs Books.

———. 2013. *To Save Everything, Click Here: The Folly of Technological Solutionism*. New York: Public Affairs.

Noll, M. 2003. The Myth of Convergence. *The International Journal on Media Management* 5(1).

Ortner, S.B. 2013. *Not Hollywood*. Durham, NC: Duke University Press.

Perin, C. 2006. *Shouldering the Risks: The Culture of Control in the Nuclear Power Industry*. New Haven, CT: Princeton Press.

Peterson, L. 2007. New Current.com Creates Integrated TV-Screen Experience. *OnlineMediaDaily*. Accessed December 5, 2015. http://www.mediapost.com/publications/chapter/69180/#ixzz2Qp0FAtNS

Peterson, M.A. 2003. *Anthropology and Mass Communication: Media and Myth in the New Millenium*. Oxford: Berghahn.

Pool, I. 1984. *Technologies of Freedom*. Cambridge: Harvard University Press.

Postill, J. 2008. *Media and Nation Building: How the Iban Became Malaysian*. Oxford: Berghahn.

Rao, L. 2009. Current TV Staff Suffer a 'Major Bloodbath' as 80 Employees Lose Their Jobs. *TechCrunch*. Accessed March 22, 2012. http://techcrunch.com/2009/11/11/current-tv-staff-suffer-a-major-bloodbath-as-80-employees-lose-their-jobs/

Schneider, M. 2009. Current TV to Get a Makeover. *Variety*. Accessed December 5, 2015. http://variety.com/2009/scene/news/current-tv-to-get-makeover-1118011203/

Stetler, B. 2013. Gore Went to Bat for Al Jazeera and Himself. *New York Times*. Accessed October 12, 2013. http://mediadecoder.blogs.nytimes.com/2013/01/03/gore-went-to-bat-for-al-jazeera-and-himself/?_r=0

Wallerstein, I. 1995. *After Liberalism*. New York: New Press.

Wu, T. 2010. *The Master Switch: The Rise and Fall of Information Empires*. New York: Knopf.

CHAPTER 7

Silophication of Media Industries

GRAIN SILOS

Throughout my fieldwork with Current and FSTV, I encountered video producers discussing "silos," "partnerships," and "intersectionality" in order to frame and solve problems. While these framing exercises assist different sectors to cope with the complexity of modernity, they also reveal the contradictions inherent in the capitalist/democratic system that simultaneously requires fluidity in collaboration and employment and fixity in markets, policies, and personnel. The discursive frames such as silos and intersectionality are mechanisms to rationalize employment directives in a changing and complex work world.

The agricultural grain "silo" has become a metaphor to describe separated departments within organizations (Neebe 1987). Silophication "refers to feelings of disconnection—the left hand not knowing what the other is doing, stuckness, isolation and powerlessness, lack of trust, respect, collaboration, and collegiality" (Cilliers and Greyvenstein 2012, 9). Anthropologist and journalist Gillian Tett uses the term silophication in her financial journalism, critical of how regulators' and bankers' silophication led to an absence of information-sharing and the presence of a global financial crisis (2008, 2009). Tett also uses the phrase "silo-busting," which I relate to media reformers' conceptions of "intersectionality," a term first used in critical race theory. Media reform and television producers use the term to discuss silo-busting. Silo-busting and intersectionality are two attempts made by media reform broadcasters to overcome

© The Author(s) 2017
A. Fish, *Technoliberalism and the End of Participatory Culture in the United States*, DOI 10.1007/978-3-319-31256-9_7

165

166 A. FISH

the increasing complexities and difficulties of diversifying the American public sphere. These difficulties reveal the contradictions of a democratic system that protects equality and a capitalist system that creates inequality. The contradictions of democratic capitalism are epitomized by the tensions between integration and fragmentation. Or as Tett says, "[W]hile technology is integrating the world in some senses, it is simultaneously creating fragmentation too. Moreover, as innovation speeds up, it keeps creating complex new activities that are only understood by technical 'experts' in a silo" (Tett 2009)."Silos" consistently appeared in my field research with media reform broadcasters. The Media Consortium's Erin Polgreen organized a panel called "Getting out of the Silo: Editing Video as a Community" at the 2011 National Conference for Media Reform. "We are all living in our little *silos*," said Don Rojas, the general manager of FSTV, explaining how a possible partner rejected his overture for collaboration. It's "the *silophication* of the company," said Justin Gunn, vice president of programming at Current, of the process by which internet, television, and marketing divisions were not well integrated, while taking different approaches to the same product.

Tett refers to two mutually reinforcing silos, a *mental* silo epitomized by monological and non-holistic thinking, supported by the second *structural* silo of employees' physical separation (Tett 2009). The type of silophication that negatively impacts media reform broadcasters and other social movements is a combination of both silo forms. The phenomenon of the mental silo has been identified by a range of scholars. Going by the name of the "filter bubble" (Pariser 2011), which fosters the "myth of digital democracy" (Hindman 2009), mental silos appear to be reinforced by personalization algorithms and by the innate safety of sameness in risk-prone fields of cultural production.

Mental silos evolve because of structural components. Structural silos are the results of the hierarchical organization of the firm, resulting in a lack of collaboration within the firm. As anthropologist Thomas Malaby (2009) and sociologist Andrew Ross (2003) have recognized, companies can modify their office cultures and use social technologies to transcend structural silos. Business organizations have been known to reject hierarchy in exchange for the semi-lateral flow of information across the firm (Stark 2009). As Google, Facebook, and other Silicon Valley companies have shown, it is possible to institutionalize through space and practice ways of addressing structural silos. Media reform organizations and television networks attempt to eliminate mental and structural silos through intersectionality, partnership, and other forms of silo-busting. These solutions, however, contradict some of the more radically transformative values held by project participants. These discreet and empirical examples of contradiction are metonyms for problems of complexity impacting information sectors throughout global modernity.

STRUCTURAL SILOS

The first example of structural silos comes from the television news network Current. "Engineering stakeholders, creative stakeholders ... the designers are also there for visual layout ... and maybe [virtual world creator] Will Wright is in the room and they are describing what they need and we are turning that into a technical specification," is how Current engineer Dan Linder described a meeting for Current show *Bar Karma* (interviewed October 11, 2010). Yet what Linder called a copacetic "collaborative process" belies inherent tensions. Current's television and internet departments competed for limited resources, and the emphasis on one or the other shifted throughout its history.

> Current marketer Joe Brilliant did not appreciate Current's silo-busting, "We had a really good web crew but we always had to sit at the table with the TV company. ... the TV held back the web [crew] being a full fledge web 2.0 company. No other web company had to worry about a TV network." (interviewed May 26, 2010)

Competition between the internet and television divisions illustrates the frictions within internet and television companies like Current. While the interviewees attempted to have different shareholders "sit at the table," an opposite process was at work as departments were structurally siloed.

"I want it to be this color, I want it to feel like this, I want it to sound like this, and at this point in the experience I want you to go 'wooo,'" Current Vice President Justin Gunn said as he portrayed a creative producer in a brainstorming session, waving his hands in paired waves (interviewed August 4, 2010). Gunn contrasted this against a computer engineer who asked, "What is the feature set?" he said with a slightly nerdy and irritated tone (interviewed August 4, 2010). Gunn continued:

168   A. FISH

Those are fundamentally opposing ways of designing a product. You've got people in the same building, working on ostensibly the same product, coming at it from two different approaches. One has the vision for what it should look and sound and feel like and the other [is focused] on the list of features. (interviewed August 4, 2010) *Bar Karma* producer Jimmy Goldblum said, "everyone is overworked at Current and so people get entrenched in their departments." (interview February 6, 2011)

Gunn called this process "the silophication of the company" (interviewed August 4, 2010) where internet, television, and marketing divisions were not well integrated and taking different approaches to the same product.

To trump the silo curse, improve regulation, and reduce the prevalence of risky investment, Tett argues that bankers and regulators should "be forced to talk about their business with a wide pool of colleagues, including their immediate silo" (2008). The 2011 National Conference for Media Reform (NCMR) and specifically the panel "Getting out of the Silo: Editing Video as a Community" that FSTV participated in were unique examples of silo-busting in the media reform community. Tett suggests that anthropologist-like employees should work at the *intersections* of shared yet disparate cultures of information production and thereby help translate insights from one department to another. Tett's notion of how to "silo-bust" manifests in media reform broadcasters' attempts to create intersectional partnerships. I learned about the emic use of these terms "silo" and "intersectionality" at NCMR—a place where such intersectional solutions to silophication are addressed.

Media reform broadcasters use the term intersectionality in their work. The notion of "intersectionality" was described by the panel founder and Managing Director of the Media Consortium, Erin Polgreen who was "looking to create an intersectional narrative of collaboration" (email to author). On that panel, FSTV producer Eric Galatas's advice for collaborators was to "find the points of *intersection*." The term intersectionality was deployed among intense discussions of partnerships and therefore offers an aperture to how social movements frame or model collaborations. An analysis of the partnerships reveals how collaborations are formed to transcend silophication.

On the panel, Galatas told the stories of partnership at the 1999 WTO protests in Seattle and the protests against the 2011 Wisconsin Budget Repair Bill. He followed with a story of FSTV's coverage of the Homeless

Marathon that resulted in the Mayor of Fresno responding to the media coverage of homelessness. He described the US Social Forum in Detroit that was the first formal collaboration with the Media Consortium, a meta-group for media reformers. He offered FSTV's unique communication affordance to FSTV's partners, television: "Like the collaboration we were doing with Al Jazeera here in the United States ... FSTV is in a unique situation because with a large television footprint, we can help organizations that do not have a footprint gain access" (statement on April 9, 2011). These media actions were expensive ordeals, requiring partners to share resources and labor. Galatas said he hoped to be doing more collaborations with "people in this room" highlighting that this panel was not only an opportunity to tell inspirational stories but to also conduct important intersectional work. Galatas's concluding advice was to encourage Media Consortium partners to use FSTV's television platform: "[t]elevision is not dead, not yet, and we have this real estate, and we might as well use it" (statement on April 9, 2011). In concluding his remarks, Galatas's advice for collaborators was to "find the *points of intersection*" and "operate in good faith—help others achieve their goals." Galatas echoed Polgreen's written description of the goals of the panel, to find "intersectionality," with his notion of "points of intersection."

Intersectionality is a complex term used by scholars to describe the multidimensionality of a problem. The term was first used in critical race theory to articulate how examinations of gender also require examination of race. Class, disability, and other socio-cultural elements then intersect with the original problem (Crenshaw 1989). This definition of intersectionality refers to the centripetal formation of subject oppression, with the individual at the center and a suite of external forces impacting subject formation. The expansion of the definition of intersectionality that I am presenting is centrifugally formed. This iteration of intersectional theory expands the concept to include the agency of the individuals at the intersectional point. For example, Researchers Patrizia Zanoni and Maddy Janssens (2007) use intersectional theory while emphasizing minority employee agency to transform the structures within which they are suspended. At the center of this centrifugal intersection is a subject, group, value, or idea from which numerous social movements radiate. Traditional centripetal intersectionality starts with oppressive forces on the individual. On the other hand, the intersectional partnerships I observed with FSTV are centrifugal, a value radiates out from the force of numerous partnerships.

And yet, intersectional partnerships are not without their aesthetic and legal complications. The promotional video Galatas proceeded to show exhibits the potentials and problems of partnerships and content ownership. The video promotes FSTV through the use of Al Jazeera English footage from the January 25, 2011 Egyptian Revolution. FSTV did not send any reporters to Tahrir Square. FSTV's partner, *Democracy Now!*, sent Sharif Abdel Kouddous. But through the process of intersectional resource-sharing necessary at this level of insurgent broadcasting, FSTV was able to coopt the work of Al Jazeera English and *Democracy Now!* into their fundraising campaign.

The video presents clips of Al Jazeera English with FSTV's Rojas saying: "Free Speech TV was the only television network to broadcast Al Jazeera's news feeds uninterrupted during the revolution in Egypt" (statement on April 9, 2011). Rojas introduced another clip on the video by saying, "and we were there at the frontlines in Madison, Wisconsin" which preceded a clip of a protester, ending with the chant "this is what democracy looks like" (ibid.). This legal appropriation of Al Jazeera English footage by FSTV reveals how intellectual property issues are implicated within intersectional partnerships.

This process leads to some aesthetic confusions in terms of proprietary branding. When FSTV airs Al Jazeera English or *Democracy Now!* they do so while retaining the original network's branding. To this they add their sans-serif Free Speech logo. This creates a dizzying visual artifact of multiple ownerships and speaks directly to the challenges of partnership and proprietary content. Each organization needs to brand its content to justify its mission and budget but also needs to share content across partners' proprietary platforms. Here, the screen becomes a nexus for intersectionality.

A useful concept related to centrifugal intersectionality is the term "nexus." The term was developed within activist network theory to explain how media activist organizations coalesce on specific topics. Considering the synergies among Vancouver's media activist field, Hackett and Carroll state that "[M]edia activism appears as a nexus, connecting a whole range of activist struggles—in part through the organizational and individual linkages …, in part through a politics of left and alternative community development-efforts of some groups…and the capacity-building work of others" (2006, 185). Hackett and Carroll (2006) identify media activism as the node that links together community development and capacity building. The result of successful centrifugal intersectionality within the media reform movement consists of the development of partnerships—groups forming working and practice-based collaborations.

Media reform constitutes a field, in the Bourdieusian sense, capable of competing with other ideologically based fields in the pursuit of influencing the hegemonic public sphere and their diversifying voice. Drawing from Bourdieu, Hackett and Carroll (2006) state, "Media ... comprise a field, subject to its own self-transformation as social interests as diverse as corporate owners, journalists, advertisers and media reform activists jostle over possible futures" (2006, 40; Postill 2010). Bourdieusian field theory (Bourdieu 1993) facilitates a description of the media field as constituted by various fields internally and externally competitive with other fields. These fields constitute a larger field—the media reform broadcasting field, if you will. In this calculation, the media reform movement, corporate television networks, and internet service providers, to name a few actors, compete within their specific fields and with one another in the hopes of influencing the hegemonic public sphere.

According to Tett, one way to solve the "silo curse" is to employ "cultural translators" who can inform specialized knowledge workers about the big picture of their work. In the case study of media reform broadcasters, individuals like Polgreen and organizations like the Media Consortium and Free Press, the organization that hosted NCMR, are examples of cultural translators. Media reformers, working with and commenting on the federal regulation and corporate control of media systems are like financial regulators, subjects of technological craft specialization and increasing scale and breadth of the networks within which they work. They form meta-groups like the Media Consortium and attend conferences together in the hopes of overcoming the atomization and burden of information overload and precarity in the networked society.

The 2011 NCMR provided a sideways or lateral research/activism alongside media reform broadcasters (Boellstorff 2003; Maurer 2005; Nelson 2009). Partnerships and panels are the result of lateral networking among loose and strong ties of affiliated people (Granovetter 1973). Conferences allow computer hackers to "collectively enact, make visible, and subsequently celebrate many elements of their quotidian technological lifeworld" (Coleman 2010, 50). The NCMR panel was an expression of the lateral and collaborative partnering ethos of media reform broadcasters. The horizontality of such partnerships within politically progressive

172   A. FISH

American culture is also documented in the anti-corporate globalization movement (Juris 2008), hacker activism (Coleman 2011), and was instigated in the Occupy Wall Street Movement by anthropologist David Graeber.

The last morning of the 2011 NCMR, one of my informants invited me to what they called a "power breakfast." A video camera rested on a high tripod above two semi-private tables overlooking Boston harbor through tall glass windows that shed morning light on flutes of parfait and silver pitchers of coffee. Magazine editors, television producers, community media activists, major funders, radio DJs, and progressive television personalities quickly gave their name in an audible wave around the tables. Jay Harris, long-time publisher of the magazine *Mother Jones*, presented two timely issues that were cause for celebration and alarm. He wanted to celebrate a success that needed repeating—the powerful media presence and measurable impact it had in promoting the protests against the 2011 Wisconsin Budget Repair Bill. For that, we needed to generate an institutional history of the media practices that worked—for example, the rapid response of video organizations like the UpTake who successfully coordinated with print journalists at *In These Times*. Harris next proposed that we discuss the shared budget problems. There was not as much agreement, as can be expected, about what to do about the always alarming situation but engaged debate ensued about fundraising, the upcoming 2012 US Presidential election, and ever increasing media consolidation around corporate mergers. We agreed to partner. By partnership, they were referring to the community formed by media reform broadcasters, a recursive public that collectively reflects upon and self-fashions actions to reform the grounds of its very productivity (Kelty 2008). At the center of these partnership is a centrifugal intersectionality based on public media and its reformation. In this process, these partners would silo-bust.

Partnership is usually the tool for the underfunded and those organized to work for social justice. Partnership is a middle-range theory, between unincorporated or involuntary participation, and fully incorporated and economically motivated mergers. Partnership is a powerful tactic to resist hegemonic power, and thus codes an antagonistic relationship to vertically arranged power structures—while at the same time resisting the temporal transformation into hierarchy. Partnership requires a horizontally ordered strategy for internal practical formation. The lateral pooling of resources—sometimes with potential competitors, as I saw that morning—proves that, in the social justice realm, at least in public, the efficacy of the mission trumps the funding operation (sometimes to the point of compromising the efficacy). Despite the fact that many of these organizations compete for a fixed share of philanthropic funds, what was agreed upon was a commitment to partner, share resources, silo-bust, and attack the problem vigorously from the skill sets dispersed throughout the group.

The lateral collaboration I viewed at the breakfast was not an example of a networked and organized public (Fish et al. 2011). This was not internet-enabled participation. Email is the most sophisticated 'new' media system in this context. These collaborators are all technically literate and use very sophisticated technologies in their broadcast and start-up professional lives. However, they are not dependent upon digital peer-to-peer networks for the sharing of code, complex video uploading systems, or sophisticated medical record aggregation databases for their partnership. Rather, embodied meetings and simple text-based communications suffice. They set ad hoc goals and tasks and produce tools, data, and methods that are generative as opposed to being tethered to proprietary protocols (Zittrain 2008).

FSTV's Don Rojas is a major supporter of partnership, even reaching out to potential competitors, such as LinkTV, the other progressive, nonfiction, public interest television network in the USA. Rojas says:

> In the long-term it does not make any sense for us to be fractured. And I am a big proponent of collaboration and *partnership*. We offered them [LinkTV] our election feed. They first accepted it then at the last moment they didn't go along with it ... We are all living in our little *silos*, but I believe we won't be able to survive the long term, now that the political climate has shifted so far to the right. We need an antidote to Fox. But we can't do it alone. We need to work in collaborative ways but driven by a mission to bring a balance to the media landscape that is more and more driven by corporate media. So that is our long-range vision. It is probably a little naïve considering the current situation we are in, but that is the only road we can take to survive, we have to band together our meager resources. (interviewed November 8, 2010)

Rojas addresses the important points in partnership and expresses the collaborative ethos necessary for partnerships to be successful. Pooling best practices and models is the only way to compete with an extremely effective and profitable Fox News. Nevertheless, in order for these partnerships to occur, each partner needs to transcend the silos within which they are suspended. Conferences, shared meals, projects, email lists—but most

174 A. FISH

importantly friendships forged over politics, practices, and time—make partnerships possible.

Another way of looking at partnership is through the work of a significant member of FSTV's board of directors who co-wrote and published a book during my fieldwork. *Beyond the Echo Chamber: Reshaping Politics Through Networked Progressive Media* (Clark and Van Slyke 2010) by Jessica Clark and Tracy Van Slyke (the FSTV board member) is a strategy guide about how four levels of internet-enabled networks have impacts on progressive journalism, political commentary, and activist organizing: (1) networked users; (2) self-organized networks; (3) institutional networks; and (4) networks of institutions. The utility of this book for this project is that it reveals the partnership's ideals-in-practice as conceived by a key member of FSTV and the media reform broadcasting community.

Clark and Van Slyke's fourth category, "networks of institutions," explores the lateral relationships between institutions, or what might be called partnerships. The key example comes from the Media Consortium, the journalism meta-organization in which both authors are intimately involved, along with FSTV, Free Press, and Current's *Young Turks*. The Media Consortium serves as an institution for meetings, conference calls, and email lists that coordinates messaging and projects across a number of progressive partners. The Media Consortium is centrifugal; intersectionality made material.

Partnerships are central to media reform organizing. Professors Robert Hackett and William Carroll (2006) interviewed 54 media activists in Vancouver, Canada. They asked the media activists to identify groups they saw as actual or potential collaborators. The most frequent potential allies are other media activists. They found this citation somewhat surprising as these affined groups compete for limited economic resources. They claim "partnerships between organizations with a history of 'turf wars' are probably less likely. Groups that continually compete for the same project funding and clientele are likely either to die, or to shift their mandate to a less contested organizational niche" (Hackett and Carroll 2006, 151). Considering the limited amount of human and economic resources, and public attention, the media reform movement can sustain "not much more than 100 national public interest groups" (Hackett and Carroll 2006, 151). My informants in the media reform movement, all competing in the same field for the same resources (Bourdieu 1993), acknowledged this competitiveness for diminishing resources, and yet they seemed willing, at least in some instances, to forgo such competition for success in partnered initiatives.

Partnerships are necessary in the not-for-profit sector. In the for-profit sector the concept of collaboration is quite distinct, complicated as it is by how economic relations alter social relations. While Current, because of its for-profit status, is firmly situated within the profit logic, FSTV and its partners continue to resist the reduction of social to economic relations and continue to do their non-profit business in horizontally arranged partnerships. The tactics of intersectionality and partnerships are methods of overcoming the silophication of media reform broadcasting groups. This is an example on the discursive level of cultural interventions mobilized to create instances of openness and access into the hegemonic public sphere (Habermas 1991; Fraser 1992; Fish 2012).

CONCLUSION

What does it mean that the financial, activism, and media sectors each try to solve problems of silophication through intersectionality and partnerships? Tett makes a convincing argument that complexity and job specialization are the reasons for increasing silophication in the financial industries. Silophication is symptomatic of modernity, impacting practices as diverse as television production, social activism, and media reform. But how complexity and job specialization directly impact media reform broadcasters is distinct from how it affects financial regulators and UK bankers.

Media reform activists conceptualize each allied partner as capable of transcending isolation through the centrifugal power of their outwardly applicable competencies. Subject formation results in coalition building. Partnering, formal social enterprise to formal social enterprise, is an undertheorized though widely practiced act. Comparing partnering to how formal social enterprises seed and provoke the development of organized publics (Fish et al. 2011), allows for a more robust theory of participation and collaboration. Identifying, standardizing, and harvesting these centrifugal powers are a challenge structured by the time/spaces of their synchronicity. Both real-time and in-person intersectionality are necessary for calibration and the interoperability of partners across fields of cultural production. In these instances of centrifugal intersectionality are aspirational designs for the disillusionment of silos.

A key question remains: how do these intersectional practices evince the tensions between (siloed) stability and (intersectional) fluidity? Stability as well as fluidity of markets, policies, and personnel are important in global capitalism. For example, neoliberal subject formation requires reskillabil-

176 A. FISH

ity, global mobility, and the instability of temporary precarity. At the same time, competent and committed workers, focused on performing specific tasks, are a premium for corporations and non-profits alike.

Silophication is a result of the fixity that occurs in attempts to rationalize, command, and control workers and informational global processes. Financial regulators need to have this silo-like market stability, bureaucratic order, and other standards for command and control governmentality. At the same time, however, siloed and inefficient information exchange results in stagnation, and worse, ignorance of upcoming catastrophes. Financiers, attempting to improve the fluidity of capital aggregation, are stymied by silophication as they need stability and flexibility simultaneously, and at different times. This contradiction of capitalism is the reason for the conundrum of the silo.

Media reformers have a more critical relationship to the present manifestations of capitalism and the state—and are much less concerned with the stability of each. Media reformers are foremost democracy activists. They advocate for progress and cultural change. They celebrate the plurality of media content and owners in order to diversify the American public sphere. Publicly they are social liberals affirming the importance of a large government and its regulatory oversight on media corporations. Publicly, media reformers do not advocate for the federalization of media industries or the overthrow of capitalism. They work within the capitalist mode of accumulation, commodification, and bureaucratized forms of work. Privately, however, the media reformers I spoke with often expressed post-capitalist or socialist aspirations. For example, my primary confidant, FSTV's General Manager Don Rojas, for instance, was the press secretary for the Marxist Prime Minister of Grenada, Maurice Bishop. When US Marines invaded the island in 1983, he was flown to the USSR where he met Fidel Castro and other Marxist political leaders. I partook of many pro-socialist dialogues with Rojas. Other interview subjects, Thom Hartmann, Giselle Diaz Campagna, and Jon Nichols of the *Nation* magazine, each expound affinity with socialism while successfully working within capitalist media industries. Each of these individuals requires market and employment stability while sometimes publicly and often privately emphasizing their affinities with the radical transformations necessary for a post-capitalist society. Intersectionality is one practice that these public progressives and private socialist media reformers use in their public work to make media more democratic within the capitalist system. Thus, the contradictions of capitalism, between the stability of democracy/capitalism and the radical fluidity necessary for a break from democracy/capitalism, are part of the work of media reformers. These contradictions are mediated in a work world with different complexities.

Media reform work is complex. It is difficult to diversify the voices heard in the hegemonic public sphere (Fraser 1992; Fish 2012). The hegemonic public sphere is constituted by a variety of social practices such as governmental telecommunication policies, overlapping networked communication technologies with differing affordances, and a diversity of populations with different communication modalities. The media reform worker needs to grasp this complexity. However, compared to the financial regulator who has a sophisticated array of internal legal practices and the investment banker with a rich algorithmic skill set to master, both requiring intense craft specialization, the media reformer is an activist whose work internally is less complex involving collaborating with partners to organize people, campaigns, and actions. There is complexity in media reform, but that complexity is not internal to the corporate structure as it is with finance, but is externalized in the complexity of the socio-technical affordances that constitute the hegemonic public sphere. The complexity that leads to the silophication of the media reformer is a result of the external chaos of the hegemonic public sphere, constituted by policy, technology, cultural practices, and competing fields of cultural production.

The problem for media workers is not job specificity but job diversity that forces media workers and media reformers to be siloed. It is not that my informants are doing one job well; they are doing many jobs as best as they can but usually not as well as they would like. Unlike the financial regulator, investor, and banker, today's media worker and media reformer does not do only one specific job to the neglect of understanding the work of colleagues, but rather, these media workers do the job of a number of people. This multitasking, hyphenated work world (Caldwell 2008; Deuze 2007), forces media workers not only to topically understand their own work but also how other divisions work. This distracted work is the result of precarity in information labor, itself a result of the offshoring of employee responsibility from the employer to the employee, a hallmark of neoliberal information work (Sassen 1998). It is also a result of underfunding in the non-profit and mission-driven sectors that leaves departments with overtaxed workers. Intersectionality and partnership are two interlocking ways the non-profit and mission-driven media reform

178   A. FISH

broadcaster attempts to overcome these limitations of neoliberal information labor.

Because media workers perform numerous jobs within their non-profit firms, they seek to share and borrow resources from other individuals and organizations. Thus partnering is a way of sharing resources while at the same time remaining an autonomous formal social enterprise, with its own distinctions and competencies (Fish et al. 2011). This distinction and autonomy is essential for organizations' funding practice. And yet, many of the organizations within media reform, or in progressive media, are funded by a small set of philanthropic foundations and wealthy donors. Partnering and silo-busting are also encouraged by funders who want to see maximum return on their political investment portfolio. Thus, media reform organizations need to remain individualized and unique while enacting as well as performing intersectionality with their allied and sometimes competitive colleagues. These efforts make evident the difficulties of social liberalism in the era of corporate and neo-liberalism.

REFERENCES

Boellstorff, T. 2003. Dubbing Culture: Indonesian Gay and Lesbi Subjectivities and Ethnography in an Already Globalized World. *American Ethnologist* 30(2): 225–242.

Bourdieu, P. 1993. *The Field of Cultural Production*. New York: Columbia University Press.

Caldwell, J.T. 2008. *Production Culture: Industrial Reflexivity and Critical Practice in Film and Television*. Durham: Duke University Press.

Cilliers, F., and H. Greyvenstein. 2012. The Impact of Silo Mentality on Team Identity: An Organizational Case Study. *SA Journal of Psychology* 38(2): 993.

Clark, J., and T. Van Slyke. 2010. *Beyond the Echo Chamber: Reshaping Politics Through Networked Progressive Media*. New York: New Press.

Coleman, E.G. 2010. Hacking In-Person: The Ritual Character of Conferences and the Distillation of a Life-World. *Anthropological Quarterly*, Winter.

———. 2011. Hacker Politics and Publics. *Public Culture* 23(3): 511–516.

Crenshaw, K. 1989. Demarginalizing the Intersection of Race and Sex: A Black Feminist Critique of Antidiscrimination Doctrine, Feminist Theory and Antiracist Politics. *University of Chicago Legal Forum*, 139–167.

Deuze, M. 2007. *Media Work*. Cambridge: Polity.

Fish, A., L.F.R. Murillo, L. Nguyen, A. Panofsky, and C. Kelty. 2011. Birds of the Internet: A Field Guide to Understanding Action, Organization, and the Governance of Participation. *The Journal of Cultural Economy* 4(2): 157–187.

Granovetter, M.S. 1973. The Strength of Weak Ties. *American Journal of Sociology* 78(6): 1360–1380.

Hackett, R.A., and W.K. Carroll. 2006. *Remaking Media: The Struggle to Democratize Public Communication.* New York: Routledge.

Hindman, M. 2009. *The Myth of the Digital Divide.* Princeton: Princeton University Press.

Juris, J.S. 2008. *Networking Futures: The Movements Against Corporate Globalization.* Durham: Duke University Press.

Kelty, C.M. 2008. *Two Bits: The Cultural Significance of Free Software and the Internet.* Durham: Duke University Press.

Malaby, T. 2009. *Making Virtual Worlds: Linden Lab and Second Life.* Ithaca: Cornell University Press.

Maurer, B. 2005. *Mutual Life, Limited.* Princeton: Princeton University Press.

Nelson, D. 2009. *Reckoning.* Durham: Duke University Press.

Pariser, E. 2011. *Filter Bubble: What the Internet Is Hiding from You.* New York: Penguin Press.

Postill, J. 2010. Introduction: Theorising Media and Practice. In *Theorising Media and Practice,* ed. B. Bräuchler and J. Postill. Oxford: Berghahn Books.

Ross, A. 2003. *No Collar: The Humane Workforce and Its Hidden Costs.* New York: Basic Books.

Sassen, S. 1998. *Globalization and Its Disconnects.* New York: New Press.

Stark, D. 2009. *The Sense of Dissonance: Accounts of Worth in Economic Life.* Princeton and Oxford: Princeton University Press.

Tett, G. 2008. How Talking Can Help Cut the Risk of a Lemming Fall. *Financial Times.* May 16. http://www.ft.com/intl/cms/s/0/e040ef72-22df-11dd-93a9-000077b07658.html#axzz1u23EtNca

———. 2009. Waking Up to the 'Silo Curse' Is Far from the End of the Problem. *Financial Times.* October 9. http://www.ft.com/intl/cms/s/0/6d1de780-b469-11de-bec8-00144feab49a.html

Zanoni, P., and M. Janssens. 2007. Minority Employees Engaging with (Diversity) Management: An Analysis of Control, Agency, and Micro-Emancipation. *Journal of Management Studies* 44(8): 1371–1397.

Zittrain, J. 2008. *The Future of the Internet and How to Stop It.* New Haven, CT: Yale University Press.

CHAPTER 8

Neoliberalism and Terminal Video

In the past several years, internet video has become big business with major studios and technology companies investing millions in talent and multichannel networks. Based on interviews with those leading the explosive internet video industry, this chapter investigates the liberal politics—or the lack thereof—of several multichannel internet and video networks and examines the practices of self-branding executed by video entrepreneurs. By 2015, the corporate liberalism that used to regulate television was now out-dated. This chapter charts how earlier desires that internet video constitute a socially liberal public sphere for participatory politics and amateur production have been replaced by a gold rush of acquisition, conglomeration, and monopolization. Internet video is less an open, generative, and democratized platform and increasingly one dominated by the logic of capital. From this world a new type of independent and intimate talent has emerged to make internet video profitable. In this chapter, the self-entrepreneurialism of internet video microcelebrities is linked to the macroeconomics of conglomeration.

This chapter is designed to synthesize two linked trends, one toward entrepreneurial subjectivity in the production of online videos, and the other toward the aggregation of these videos into conglomerated companies. A detailed history of select multichannel networks provides an aperture for observing how these two forces, one working on the individual level and the other on the institutional level, come together. This synthesis represents the efforts of an emergent industry struggling to construct

© The Author(s) 2017
A. Fish, *Technoliberalism and the End of Participatory Culture in the United States*, DOI 10.1007/978-3-319-31256-9_8

181

182   A. FISH

itself in the images of what it sees as the future (data and the internet) and the past (television).

THE RISE OF MULTICHANNEL NETWORKS

For most of its early days since its origins in 2005, YouTube lacked a robust business strategy. But a successful plan appears to have been forged through the development of intermediate businesses or multichannel networks (MCNs). Representing the "missing middle" of online businesses, YouTube defines MCNs as businesses which offer "product, programming, funding, cross-promotion, partner management, digital rights management, monetization/sales, and/or audience development" (YouTube Help) in exchange for a percentage of ad revenue. Part talent agency, advertising company, production assistant, and accountant—and considering the young age of many clients, likely also a part-time parent—MCNs have become major businesses since 2011, when Google acquired Next New Networks, helping YouTube achieve prosperity.

MCNs also are significant players for the consolidation of one-time independent and non-commercialized media. The singular goal of MCNs is to assist producers in monetizing their content. Professionalization is achieved through ever-improving production aesthetics, consistent video serialization, audience engagement, and compliance with sponsors and agents. These services they call "360 degree management" for their "influencers." When these practices coalesce into millions of views and thousands of subscribers, these "influencers" apply to be aggregated into MCNs. This chapter discusses how between 2011 and 2014 traditional multinational corporations like Disney, AT&T, and Comcast purchased most major MCNs. The idealistic founders of YouTube were replaced by experienced players from old media, agents from Creative Artists Agency, senior VPs from Viacom, NBCUniversal, News Corp., and so on. In this way, internet video, instead of being a space for resistance, became a place conducive to the development of mainstream productivity. While political content does exist on YouTube and does receive millions of views, few of the producers of such content receive the incubation provided by MCNs. Instead, MCNs focus their promotional energies on content that is commercially friendly and youth-orientated.

The section below provides a brief overview of the history of select MCNs encountered during fieldwork. It illustrates how earlier digital discourses, reactive discourses, and convergence myths fuel not alternative and independent television, but the cooptation of outsider productivity into insider profit.

As a system that encourages users' self-presentation strategies that combine entrepreneurialism with marketing and advertising techniques, social media links well with the dominant economic system of neoliberalism (Marwick 2013). Neoliberalism advocates a free and open market, enhanced privatization, deregulation, and limited government control of the economy. Each person is a free trader and every social interaction is a contract. There has been a rise in individualization, risk-taking, and entrepreneurial behavior since the late 1990s within the creative, cultural, and media industries (Neff 2012). By exploring the experiences of people who worked in the internet start-up companies during the so-called dotcom boom in the USA, sociologist Gina Neff (2012) emphasizes the intertwinement of risk-taking with personal hopes and desires.

But risk-taking rarely results in significant YouTube celebrity status—which does not equate to financial substance. Connor Manning, an LGBT vlogger with 70,000 subscribers on YouTube, is not a professional vlogger. Instead he works at the Baltimore Aquarium. Gaby Dunn, who along with her friend Allison Raskin has a channel, Just Between Us, which has half a million subscribers, needs to find additional work as a courier. While some YouTubers like PewDiePie and Jenna Marbles are worth millions—and the executives of the MCNs worth several million more—the vast majority of YouTubers are not. Dunn and Raskin's semi-professional lives online "often means grappling daily with the cognitive dissonance of a full comments section and an empty wallet" (Dunn 2015). This empty middle, with wealth pooling for the few elite and the majority struggling to make ends meet, mirrors the middle class in the US economy more generally and follows the winner-takes-all principle of internet economics of scale. The MCN Dunn and Raskin work with, Collective Digital Studios, takes 30% of their revenue. When the largest contract they acquired is but $6000, their take-home pay is indeed paltry. The vast numbers of YouTube aspirants make it a buyer's economy that tilts to favor the MCNs who have the capacity to promote specific YouTubers to astronomical success. The disparity in wealth distribution is exacerbated by access to the means to game the discovery and promotional system online: "there's a flawed distribution of wealth because a small handful of creators have YouTube's structural support—appearances on the popular page, for instance, and boosts in visibility and views" (Dunn 2015). There is no longer a meritocracy on YouTube, you are either in or out.

184 A. FISH

As a bisexual activist, Dunn herself is both economically and politically motivated, which puts her in a good position to be able to perform from a state of passion and authenticity that remains the stock in trade of successful YouTubers. This authenticity, however, must be occasionally violated in order to generate funds. When Just Between Us produces "branded content," which is another way of saying making videos with product placement, they "make money but lose subscribers" (Dunn 2015). For the majority of those seeking fame and fortune on YouTube, the culture that has developed on the platform rejects the commodification of the self. Despite the audience's hunger for authenticity being at cross-purposes with how the majority of YouTube producers endeavor to support themselves, they still must comport themselves as self-entrepreneurs. Cynically, Dunn (2015) recommends,

> Aspiring vloggers may want to think about getting business degrees, because that's what being famous online is: It's protecting your assets, budgeting, figuring out production costs, and rationing out money to employees— whether that's yourself or a camera crew. The numbers on your social media accounts may never match those in your bank account. The internet may always be equated with The Future, but for most social media stars, it ends up being a stepping stone to the same old metrics of success (if you're lucky).

Affect economies rely upon the management of emotion in ways not dissimilar to ways people are hailed to comport themselves within neoliberalism. Media studies scholar Alice Marwick explores how neoliberalism unfolds in the business of social media "which idealize[s] and reward[s] a particular persona: highly visible, entrepreneurial, and self-configured to be watched and consumed by others" (2013, 13). Drawing on Michel Foucault's concept of "technologies of the self," defined as a specific matrix of practical reason through which people learn to transform themselves in order to achieve a desired state (1988, 18), Marwick explains how social media make people regulate and alter their behavior along neoliberal principles. Online networks help individuals obtain a particular status, reputation, and popularity by using self-presentation strategies such as life-streaming, self-branding, and micro-celebrity (Marwick 2013). Thus, social media teaches users how to prosper in a consumer society "where status is predicated on the cultural logic of celebrity, according to which the highest value is given to mediation, visibility, and attention" (Marwick 2013, 14). These ideas have implications for YouTube users whose idiotic performances have brought great public attention and recognizability within online communities. If they were not intending to become micro-celebrities, but gain accidental notoriety because of the shareability of their content, they soon might be hailed to comport themselves in a neo-liberal manner in order to reap the personal and financial rewards of being a central node in the affective economy. The self-governing *polis* of private citizens gives way to the *agora* of public self-commercialization. Engaged in video production, this neoliberal subjectivity produces the risky, fun, affective, and cheap content on which MCNs are built. Based on inter-views with MCN agents, I describe below how MCNs frame the ideal producer in terms of neoliberal subjectivity.

NEXT NEW NETWORKS

> Cute kittens and toddlers may be YouTube's bread and butter, but Google's video portal needs more than that to encroach on the goliath that is cable TV. But instead of shelling out for the rights to premium content from cable networks, YouTube is hoping it can nudge its existing community toward making high quality videos. (Kincaid 2011)

Each year since its acquisition, business journalists have described how YouTube fails to turn a profit. To become profitable, YouTube has focused on MCNs. To do this, Google invested in curating and incentivizing spe-cific producers, styles of production, and MCNs. For a time, YouTube did not invest in individual producers or video production companies. Such interventions were against the spirit of crowdsourcing that required a hands-off approach. Providing the platform was enough, the users would do the rest in accordance with their own creative proclivities, was the idea. In 2010, when Google's CEO Eric Schmidt was asked if YouTube would purchase video start-ups, he said, "[y]ou never say never. We've tried to not cross that line." "We're always debating these things," Schmidt added, "the good news right now is, there's enough of these little digital studios that can raise capital" (Miller and Stelter 2010). This *laissez-faire* approach was about to change just a year later with Google's purchase of Next New Networks.

The two most-watched videos on YouTube in 2010 were made by Next New Networks' (N3) video creators: the *Bed Intruder Song* by the Gregory Brothers had 60 million views and a parody of a song by Ke$ha. The *Bed Intruder Song* was a catchy auto-tune of a television news interview with Antoine Dodson, a black gay man, describing to a reporter how a rapist snuck into his sister's bedroom through a window. Based on these successes, YouTube decided to purchase N3 in 2011 for a mere $27 million and transform it into a laboratory and incubator for YouTube talent called Next Lab. Next Lab kicked off Next Up, a talent search with a $35,000 production budget for a bounty. The winner, Franchesca Ramsey, producer of such videos as *Shit White Girls say...to Black Girls*, bought better equipment, was schooled on how to properly make a video, and saw her subscriptions quadruple (Paynter 2013). Because of the success, Next Lab expanded Next Up with talent searches for the next trainer, chef, vlogger, comic, or education guru. Winners received the grant along with coaching sessions from Next Lab. Thus, YouTube acquired N3 and transformed it into an educational service for video entrepreneurs not into an in-house MCN. This was following Schmidt's concern that YouTube not own the content. YouTube appears to work closely with specific MCNs who do the business of talent development and deal-making while netting significant but undisclosed revenue from profit-sharing deals.

Tim Shey was the founder and president of N3, the most popular MCN in 2010, when I met him at the N3 office in New York in 2010. It was reason to celebrate, they had just hit a billion collective pages and N3's purchase by Google/YouTube was still five months away. On joining YouTube, Shey became director of YouTube's Next Lab and YouTube Spaces. His notable accomplishment toward achieving the goal of professionalizing YouTube talent was the buildout of YouTube Spaces in Los Angeles, London, Tokyo, and New York. As of late 2015, he was the head of Scripted, a YouTube Originals network (YouTube Spaces). Previous to N3 and eventually Google, he had worked at Proteus, where he was responsible for the first-ever nationwide interactive TV broadcast using mobile phones during FOX's Super Bowl XXXVI. He has helped to produce interactive ads for AT&T, Sony, Sprint, *Newsweek*, ExxonMobil, *The Washington Post*, Gibson, Motorola, HBO, ABC, Discovery, and FOX. Shey identifies as a television and advertising person, working his way from interactive television, through mobile, and eventually to original web content. He rejects the discourse that the internet is disrupting television. Instead, he sees or tries to engineer continuity from television business and narrative models to internet video.

"I've never been very good at being a rebel or a revolutionary or anything like that," Shey said (interviewed October 1, 2010). "I am always looking for those connections that say that nothing is really new." The first slide of N3's corporate presentation was still in the docket four years later and it read: "we want to combine the best of the web with the best of TV." Shey continued, "We never try to say we are revolutionizing TV because we are actually just trying to figure out how does TV work in this new medium? How do you have to reinvent TV a little bit to make it work? But you don't want to throw everything away." To illustrate the continuity between TV and the internet, Shey told the story of *Winky Dink and You* a show from 1953 to 1957 that encouraged children to touch and draw on their television screens in ways kids swipe and draw on iPads. A protective vinyl sheet would cover the screen, allowing kids to sketch commercial products directly onto the TV surface. The program ended because of consumer pressure, either because impoverished youths applied their grease pencils directly onto the screen without the expensive vinyl, or concerns that children were absorbing X-rays from close proximity to the TV screen. Shey provided this historical vignette as proof that there are more similarities than differences between older television and newer social media. His job was to smooth the transition from television to the internet by finding producers who could do television—and television advertising on the internet.

I came to N3 with Heather Knight, a social roboticist who had adopted a little robot and wanted to show it to N3. I brought up the roboticist-cum-technocynic Jaron Lanier who had just published an article in *The New York Times* about why we should not let engineers dominate the future. Shey pointed to a brainstorming wall of tables, graphs, lines, and words—the remains of a brainstorming session wherein N3 were pitching one of the "really big video portals" to abandon algorithms and instead have people "take the front-page back." It makes sense that a TV guy would want a return to curation, taste, and what he called "the opposite of YouTube." However, this was not what was happening and their brainstorming session never materialized into a working prototype as the engineers remain in charge. I asked Shey how he felt about this tendency that went against his skill set as a creative as opposed to a technical guy. Surprisingly, he thought it was a good thing that the "product guys" or the engineers were in charge, saying at least they were "pure," meaning they were free from internal conflict, so they could be decisive. Shey was ever faithful to corporate trends and technology knowing that despite the emergent powers of the engineers, his service, finding entertaining talent, would remain core to the transformation of the internet into television.

188   A. FISH

REVISION 3

The MCN Revision 3 grew out of Digg, one of the first social media sites to provide to users a platform for the "surfacing" of content and the opportunity to vote on which of this content would make Digg's highly viewed homepage. I spoke with the Chairman and CEO of Revision 3, Jay Adelson. In comparing it to Current, Adelson called Digg not the democratization of content but "the democratization of editorial and distribution" (interviewed November 10, 2010). As such, Digg is a good example of a networked public sphere and for this reason Current attempted to purchase Digg in 2009 (Lacy 2008). Failing this, Current built its own replica of Digg in current.com. Digg had never focused on empowering amateur media producers. Revision 3 was produced by professionals. Digg, however, was a pioneer in providing the powers of curation and voting to users. The relationship between Current and Digg was not just professional as Adelson lived next door to Current COO Joana Earl with whom he shared opinions about the power of social media and algorithms to help the selection, if not the production, of video content.

A confidential 2006 PowerPoint situating Revision 3 within the history of telecommunication was written by the founders of Revision 3, Adelson and the COO and VP of Programming David Prager (Revision 3 2006). In it, they discussed cable television, which enabled niche programming, as the first revision of television. Cable catered to the "most common denominator." The second revision was internet video with "no business model, no loyalty, no audience." The third revision comes with the convergence of internet video and personal and mobile devices that enable a "mass, loyal audience to shift to on demand, niche content." Advertising follows. This most recent revision, Revision 3, "is designed to capitalize on personalized programming. First inviting viewers to 'kill your television' and then to view their 'television, revised.'"

In this investor-facing document, Revision 3 hoped to position itself at the crux of this third revision.

In an interview, I posed to Adelson the thesis that the third revision would not be dominated by amateurs but by professionals. It will not be a phase marked by independence but by conglomeration. Adelson agreed,

> because the rational for all of these transitions, more toward professional or semi-professional content, is all connected with the money. ... I think Joana (Earl, former COO of Current) would say, and I would agree, that

if you enable the people to create the content, then in theory what would be the result, after some sort of algorithmic voting process, would be better quality content. The problem is that sounds really good on paper, or on a white board, or in a presentation but the reality is that creation of content does require talent. And once you are talented and once you've filtered out the talented from the untalented, how do you call that amateur? This is the Catch-22, what you end up doing is finding your next generation of professional video producers, and, by the way, that is a great process for finding great content. But to call it amateur or user-generated is a stretch. So once you've embraced the reality of that, and gone through the process long enough to realize that that is what you've created, you need to embrace the truth, which is: we believe the public can create content professionally and therefore we are curators of content, and we might provide tools for people to become professionals, but we are basically not saying 'the future will be televised' from my mother but that the future will be televised by a larger group of professionals. ... Where you allow the public to vote they are going to err toward quality, and quality is the non-amateur stuff. (interviewed November 10, 2010)

According to Adelson, because of audiences' preferences for quality content, the accrual of improving skills, and the industrial need for labor, innovation, and content, amateurs are professionalized over time. Any business model based on user-generated content is inherently temporary because these users will become prosumers, and potentially professionals. Content curation becomes talent scouting; business models based on user-generated content are inherently incubators for professional content. Technological changes including increased networked connectivity, the drop in production costs, and digital convergence exacerbate this transition from amateur to professional. In this scenario, user-generated content companies need to "embrace the reality" that they are incubating talent for future exploitation. While "democratization" sounds socially liberal when presented to politically minded video entrepreneurs, in effect, it is a digital discourse.

Adelson's perspective depoliticizes participatory media, claiming that the democratization of content creation is always a temporary intervention and one necessarily and intimately linked to the eventual "maturing" of an industry around professionals and latent, not explicit, participation. Another perspective, based on agonistic politics, sees amateur content production as a way of providing a platform for citizens with all types of production competencies to voice their concerns with evocative videographical

190 A. FISH

media. MCNs, however, do not engage in this public sphere engineering. They empower the "next generation" of video-makers not to combat injustice but to produce content for brands. MCNs celebrate producers who "engage" their audience and "interact with their community." In this "democratization of editorial and distribution," audiences are mobilized to show their support through voting and providing feedback, but not through the production of explicitly political content.

Adelson uses history to make his points. His teleology by which amateurs become professionals also is at work on information infrastructures whose control is going in a similar direction towards increasing monopolization. Adelson sees this transformation not as a closure, however, but as an opening and an expansion of the potential class of professional producers. "Broadcast sets of economies," like radio and broadcast television, are characterized by a "one-to-many" relationship by which elite producers speak to passive audiences, according to Adelson. The next stage, "categorical television," is tailored to niche programming without altering the fundamental logic of broadcasting. Adelson saw early internet video much like "categorical television," a diversification of programming options but again not a disruption. The third phase is indeed a radical departure because of data and personalization of the "semantic web." Using personal data, coming from ubiquitous computing and pervasive social media use, it is possible for any content to find any audience, a true many-to-many system, as Adelson posits: "... there is enough data coming in from the public, and there is enough distribution of the internet, that it further amplifies those hundreds of categories to an unlimited number of categories." Imagining the possibilities for an internet video start-up in the era of semantic web and social analytics, Adelson says,

> You are now no longer a domestic medium, you are an international medium, and you are a real-time, changing medium, and communities of 50,000 can justify the production of content because content production has dropped, and distribution of content has been disintermediated from the networks and from the cable networks to the public internet, and not only are you no longer limited by the number of categories for content but you've gone from a broadcasting medium to a bi-directional medium. And that is revision three and that is why we call it Revision 3. (interviewed November 10, 2010)

Adelson believes that not only are internet video companies beginning to make this vision a reality but television is beginning to imitate the internet: "You can see evidence for this in how broadcast and cable are trying to become what internet television is already—they say, 'on our Twitter feed right now is blah.' That is really broadcast imitating the internet and not the other way around."

And while television apes the internet, the internet prepares to offer experience to audiences commonly associated with television.

> As the lean-back experience basically becomes connected to the internet. Now applications on the television set and applications on the set-top box, which by the way, there is a war going on that is fricking hilarious to watch, those applications have really disrupted cable, and you can imagine those broadcast outlets are totally terrified by what this means. And the only reason things are slowing down, the only reason this hasn't been a faster disruption is that the advertising marketplace is too slow to change. We all knew it was disrupted five years before it really was. I think the television industry is going to be a slow death over a decade where the advertisers start to learn how to use these mediums properly and Revision 3 is at the lead of that. ... The question is, are they going to be early or late to the game? (interviewed November 10, 2010)

This disruption is a "result of technology" according to Adelson, and only advertising stands in the way. To avoid being "late to the game," television networks like CNBC which purchased CNET, not only to gain a niche technology audience which they can synergize with their television programming on business and technology, but for prebroadcast access to the information CNET's journalists gather about the digital future of television.

As the co-founder of Digg and Revision 3, Adelson had much to gain from disruptions to "categorical television" brought on by the internet and social analytics and the many-to-many possibilities of the internet. Revision 3 was purchased by Discovery Communications in 2012 for $30–40 million, a company that made $4.4 billion in revenue that year on assets including Discovery Channel, TLC, Animal Planet, and OWN. Revision 3 has become a key component of the Discovery Digital Network that also includes former Current personality, Jason Silva, and his technoutopian series, *Shots of Awe*.

192 A. FISH

BLIP TV AND MAKER STUDIOS

Blip has changed much since its founding in 2005. Initially it was a distribution platform for independent web producers. Users would post content on Blip and automatically have it also uploaded to Facebook, Yahoo, and iTunes and thereby they would syndicate their content across the online video ecology. It offered a sales force to help bring ads and monetization to the content. In 2011, Blip moved away from this model and redesigned itself as an aggregator of already successful web series. In August 2013, Blip was acquired by Maker Studios that, in turn, was acquired by Disney in 2014. The user agreement changed and in order to use the platform uploaders had to demonstrate that they were part of a successful series. These transformations illustrate how internet video began with a digital discourse of empowerment throughout technology only to later become more television-like.

Blip's original 2005 manifesto emphasized democratization, sharing, and collaboration, empowering users to share in the revenue possible with internet video:

> You deserve to make money from your hard work. That's why blip.tv has built an open advertising marketplace where you can pick the video advertising company that works best for you. If you've got a hit show, we'll even go out and meet with media buyers directly to get you a real, honest-to-goodness high-end sponsorship. We share everything 50/50. ...We'll take care of the servers, the software, the workflow, the advertising and the distribution. Your focus should be on creativity. (Bogatin 2006)

After reaching over three billion video views 2011, the site underwent a major renovation. They rebranded with a new logo, dropping the ".TV" and becoming simply "Blip." With the stylistic modification came a different business philosophy, with Blip embracing "its destiny as a video destination with a redesign that put the most popular blip.tv web series front and center." In 2012, came Blip Studios, and the company worked directly to connect talent to brands to create increasingly professional content. Steve Woolf, VP of Content, became President of Blip Studios. In April 2013, Blip turned on preroll advertising for all of its videos. Now compulsory, previously advertising was "entirely voluntarily." This increasing emphasis on ad-based revenue led up to an acquisition of Blip by one of the major talent agencies, Maker Studios, in August 2013.

Following the acquisition, Blip sought to cut server costs, and make more explicit its focus on professional content. In May, 2014, Blip warned long-time users that they were removing unsuccessful content. The message read: "After many years of being an open platform, Blip is now taking its mission to bring the best original web series to our audience more seriously. To accomplish this, it is essential that we fully support producers who are dedicated to their craft and are committed to making their shows successful" (DeMoss 2014).

David DeMoss, a long-time uploader, who was subjected to the purge, was furious, claiming they were "trying to become a TV network … it was not open for rational discussion, or subject to any form of outside criticism. It was meant to be accepted, meekly and mutely, by we poor provincials. A great many of us did just that, because the message was clear and unequivocal" (2014). They whittled down the tens of thousands of active producer accounts on Blip to the roughly 4000 they feel are best suited to build the biggest audiences. "It's all internal and it's not a science," Woolf said of Blip's new curation process, "it's an art" (Cohen 2013). In "An Important Update from Blip Regarding Account Removals," "After many years of being an open platform, Blip is now taking its mission to bring the best original web series to our audience more seriously" (Blip).

I met Steve Woolf, Senior Vice President of Content, at Blip's office near the ocean and among galleries and artist studios in Santa Monica, CA. Steve is presently Global Head of Networks at AwesomenessTV, where he manages business and talent for AwesomenessTV's MCNs. Woolf is a New Yorker who studied painting and coding and previously worked as writer for films. He and his wife, Zadi Diaz, had witnessed first hand many of the changes in video industry since 2005. That year, there were two business models for internet video, licensing agreements with advertisers, and revenue-sharing deals. With licensing agreements, content producers sold the commercial rights to the content to companies who neither owned the content outright nor the intellectual property. Revenue sharing was Blip's business model that was entirely different with the content producers and the platform hosting the content working together to secure advertising deals. Profits would be shared, sometimes 50/50, sometimes 80/20. Under the name Epic Fu, Woolf and Diaz were experienced licensers, having worked with N3, Revision 3, and for a time were in discussions with Current to bring their content to TV. Epic Fu—according to Woolf, the name means "an epic fuck you to traditional ways of doing things"—featured Diaz as a host talking about technology and contemporary events.

He encourages Blip producers to "think of your show as a business, as a start-up. What is the way you can optimize your revenue while still growing your audience, and maintaining control?" (interviewed April 17, 2011). He proceeded to give an example of a content producer who released their work first on a private site, then YouTube, then other sites while using the Blip player. This example of self-entrepreneurialism—either through licensing or revenue sharing—results in industry sustaining payment for producers, and is preferable to "branding" which Woolf sees as being "unhealthy" for the business. "The industry needs an identity," according to Woolf, and branding—which consists of content simply sponsored by corporations (aka "commercials"), is not the identity he wants to see propagated.

But while content should first and foremost try to entertain rather than sell, individual producers must conceptualize themselves as sales people. In an interview later that week, Dina Kaplan, co-founder of Blip, agreed saying:

> We encourage producers to think of themselves as entrepreneurs. The successful producers view their show as a start-up. So they focus on product, which is the show. But they also focus a ton of energy on marketing. All of our top shows do an incredible job of communication with their audience. It is safe to say they spend half their time communicating with their audience and half their time on production. That means if someone comments on their video, they are commenting back, on Twitter, Facebook, all social media. ... Don't rely on your agent but you are always the best agent for yourself. There is no one better to help you than you. You are going to be the best marketer for your content. ... Once you upload, your work is not done, it has only begun. You got to market the heck out of it, go to SXSW and work it! (interviewed April 20, 2011)

Kaplan called Blip the "first merit-based network in the world." Producers accrue merit if they "have an ability to network," she laughs, continuing: "So we love the idea that with Blip if you have an idea, talent, and drive and a lot of gumption, you can gain an audience of tens of millions of people today and you can make a living, more than a living." Earlier in the discussion, Kaplan claimed that Blip was politically motivated. The co-founders wanted Blip to be a platform for producers who might be "covering a rally in China" so there was a "slight tinge of political interest" and also a platform for "independence [where] no networks executives controlled what audiences could hear, think, and consume. We want our shows to make money, that is a core part of the Blip TV model. And we are not going to find advertising for that kind of content. We are very open-minded politically but closed-minded in the sense that we are a business and we want our producers to be commercially minded." (interviewed April 20, 2011) Clearly, the closed-minded self-entrepreneurial drive dominates the open-minded political motivation.

In September 2013, Blip was acquired by Maker Studios, a subsidiary of Disney, for $10 million. The deal gave Blip's investors an exit while providing Maker Studios with a few valuable producers such as My Damn Channel, Channel Awesome, and Ray William Johnson. In the acquisition, Ray William Johnson returned to Maker Studios, a company he had previously left because of "thuggish negotiation tactics" put on him to sign a contract which gave Maker Studios a 40% share of his channel's AdSense revenue and 50% of his show's intellectual property rights (Ray William Johnson 2012).

Maker Studios is a multichannel network and talent agency co-founded by Lisa Donovan, her brother, Ben, former CEO Danny Zappin, Scott Katz, and popular producers Kassem G, Shay Carl, and Philip DeFranco. It evolved from The Station, which involved Shane Dawson and others. While founded by young and idealistic YouTubers, all Maker Studios' management personnel come from major media corporations. CEO Ynon Kreiz was Chairman and CEO of Endemol Group, the world's largest television production company, which produced *Big Brother* and *Deal or No Deal*. Courtney Holt, Chief Strategy Officer, served as an advisor to News Corp. Digital and as President of Myspace Music (like News Corp., also owned by Rupert Murdoch). Key personnel, board members, and new hires provide an insight into where the company considers its growth heading. Maker Studios clearly sees itself competing as a major television-esque network in its own right in the near future.

Via custom preroll, channel targeting, sponsorship, and media strategy, Maker Studios connects talent and companies like Sony Pictures, WB, Mattel, KIA, Target, Clorox, Pepsi, Old Navy, and EA. Digital discourse features prominently on its webpage, "Maker is a talent first, technology-driven media company." Technology is among the five tabs on the Marker homepage. The Technology page features Maker Max, Insights, Offers, Royalties, Tax and Payment, Forums, Referrals, Video Manager, and Support. Most of these pages describe applications that enable Maker Studios to parse social analytics and better understand their audience and income. Maker Studios also provides a convenient way for Makers to file their taxes online. Maker Studios continues the trend observed with Blip towards professionalization, self-entrepreneurialism, and depoliticization.

196   A. FISH

On March 24, 2014, Maker Studios was purchased by The Walt Disney Company for $500 million, which will become $950 million, when and if milestones are reached. A few months earlier, the purchase of Blip by Maker Studios resulted in an increased consolidation of internet video talent, branding, and distribution.

BIG FRAME

The website for another major MCN, AwesomenessTV, provides an insight into the importance of social analytics for these businesses. The initial splash page asks: "Are you ready to be a star? Get started by entering your birthday." Followed by "Get Discovered by Hollywood." As role model for any would-be star, the page features the Janoskians, a band of Australian pranksters, whose YouTube trailer features them puking five times (impressively, each vomit is a different color!). The visitor is provided no other options than uploading their birthday. Scrolling down, the visitor sees the pictures and stories of successful talent. On reaching the bottom of the page, the same request for birthday information is requested. No other links are provided from the home page. After providing one's birth date, a request is made for one's name, address, PayPal account name, and YouTube account address. Once the YouTube account information is provided, AwesomenessTV requests permission to view the applicant's personal information on YouTube. "AwesomenessTV would like to … manage your YouTube account," the visitor is warned. Fully automated, a legal contract follows giving AwesomenessTV the exclusive rights to sell advertising, collect revenues, and sell brand integration on your channel. In exchange, the user will be paid 70% of net revenue plus a 15% sales commission. The user will retain ownership over the content. This process acquires a good deal of personal information about aspirants with little to no commitment to professional development. This automated process enables AwesomenessTV to acquire the rights to profit on both emergent and established producers with little overhead costs. The approach made AwesomenessTV valuable.

The acquisition of Blip by Maker Studios, and Maker Studios by Disney, in 2014, was preceded by the acquisition of AwesomenessTV by DreamWorks in 2013. The mini-major studio, DreamWorks Animation, announced the acquisition of Awesomeness TV on May 1, 2013 for $33 million in cash, acquiring a company with over 55,000 channels, aggregating over 15 million subscribers and 800 million views. Hearst Corporation—one of the largest media companies in the world with newspapers, magazines, 39 TV stations, and set-top boxes like Roku—purchased 25% of AwesomenessTV from Disney in December, 2014. This would make AwesomenessTV's value around $325 million. The deal is "yet another example of traditional media buying its way into the digital-first media world fueled by smartphone-watching millennials," said Manatt Digital Media CEO Peter Csathy. The trend, he added, "ain't slowing down anytime soon" (Spangler 2014). Earlier in 2014, Hearst invested $250 million in Vice Media.

DreamWorks CEO, Jeffrey Katzenberg said, "AwesomenessTV is one of the fastest growing content channels on the internet today and our acquisition of this groundbreaking venture will bring incredible momentum to our digital strategy" (DreamWorks 2013). In this capacity, AwesomenessTV will become a talent and cross-promotional subsidiary for DreamWorks and Hearst. Potential exists for the content to translate to television. AwesomenessTV produced a preteen program on television network Nickelodeon, featuring user-generated content incubated on AwesomenessTV's YouTube channel.

In April 2014, DreamWorks' AwesomenessTV acquired Big Frame, a small MCN for $15 million. Big Frame's talent includes Mystery Guitar Man and DStorm. Big Frame will feed talent to DreamWorks' AwesomenessTV. Big Frame was co-founded by Sarah Penna, who started her career in reality television with World of Wonder, and worked in viewer-created content for Current, before producing for Phil DeFranco. In July 2011, she founded Big Frame with Steve Raymond, who was previously a vice president of social media platforms for Viacom and vice president of product development for NBCUniversal. In addition to Penna, a number of other former Current employees worked for Big Frame; Jen Oliver was head of talent development at Big Frame and was also a production manager and associate producer at Current. Ben Stein was director of development at Big Frame and left after acquisition to join the MCN Fullscreen as a senior director. Previous to these positions, Stein was a creative executive for VC2 and producer of the *Rotten Tomatoes Show* both at Current.

Penna reflected on the differences of working in internet video instead of television. Penna's career and my own career in media developed together as we worked to produce a number of short documentaries for Current between 2005 and 2007. As co-producers for Current in its formative years, she and I were often frustrated by Current's inability to work as seamlessly as YouTube was already working in 2005. In 2009, she said, "It is ironic that I was so frustrated with the web component of Current to go into the web world but I love it. I will not go back to TV. [There is] so much more unknown [and] innovation. I think of TV and it is so clunky, plaster-casted, and iron-gated. It is a little fluid. But the web is mean and lean and we are always under the gun and super low budget. You have to be really creative, everybody wears a bunch of hats, [there is] so much talent, and everyone wants to be a part of it as opposed to TV with its sense of entitlement (interviewed November 9, 2009). Embodying the concept of "venture labor" (Neff 2012), that job risk is good and fun, Penna claimed that the precarity of internet video and how it lacks job specificity are exciting. She is convinced that this state of excitement is necessary if the talent of internet video is going to rightfully reject the "entitlement" of television. This interview was conducted in 2009, before being purchased by a mainstream studio whose $15 million may have created the job security and specificity she once resisted.

One of Penna's expertises is "brand integration"—an industry term for product placement which she considers a "little less subtle and more creative" for some of "the biggest brands in the world" such as Kellogg's, Sony, GE, Pepsi, L'Oréal, Sanio, and Nestlé. "I have a little cognitive dissonance about these things. But I feel, I encourage all the artists I work with to use it as a production budget ... put it back into your production value, buy a nicer camera. ... also [I] work with them really closely so they don't look like sell-outs." Since acquisition by AwesomenessTV, Penna had a child and started a new project, Awestruck, a talent agency for mommy vloggers. In this way, Penna has made her real-life situation as a mother into a business opportunity. Indeed, she is not only a behind-the-scene manager of talent "so that they don't look like sell-outs" but also talent herself. Her channel named after her son, Jonah Penna, has over 300,000 views and 26,000 subscribers. Scholars are skeptical, "mommy blogs reveal a simultaneous commodification and depoliticization of motherhood" (Van Cleaf 2014, 247). As one of few women involved in technology companies, Penna is often consulted on issues regarding gender disparity. Her advice: "Think of yourself as an entrepreneur first, and a woman second ... there are so many doors that can be opened because you're a female entrepreneur, so don't see it as a handicap" (Draper 2013). For Penna, business comes first, with the personal life secondary and complementary. This commodification of their private life is something Penna and her husband Joe, aka Mystery Guitar Man, engage in. Joe made a video of his marriage proposal garnering

2,900,000 views and at least several thousand dollars from YouTube and their wedding was a who's who of YouTube talent and was featured in several other high-profile videos.

Penna contrasts real against fake views. Web series not on YouTube have "no metrics for counting views, false view counts, impressions, [etc. They] don't know the demographic, users are spread across multiplatforms. You can't subscribe to a web series." She contrasts this to YouTube vloggers and MCNs: "But you can subscribe to Mystery Guitar Man and every Tuesday and Thursday I get an email, a Facebook update, a phone alert, my app buzzes, I can go to his channel, and my subscription box. Six ways. There is no way I will miss when my favorite YouTuber uploads something." Her job was working with what she called "influencers," people who have "a very large and very real social media presence" and are willing to monetize it. Joe, iJustine, and Phil DeFranco are her examples of who "can get people to do things." She celebrates a 12-year-old in LA who sees Mystery Guitar Man's hair gel and wants to use the same brand.

Not only can YouTubers stay in contact in more ways, they also acquire more ornate social analytics about their user base:

They are used to being able to pull down content if it is doing badly, they are used to regulating and monitoring, they monitor by the hour how many subscribers they get. No one else has that influence in that sphere. No one else in the media industry has that. Nielsen? Have you ever known anybody with a Nielsen's box in their house or whatever the hell they use? Nielsen ratings are based off of 30 people. Movies have their box office but you don't know who is buying those tickets. You don't enter your name, your age, where you live. You do not enter that when you buy a movie ticket. When you sign up for YouTube, you enter that and we get that data. For advertisers and Hollywood, that is invaluable. So the move is deeper into YouTube." (interviewed November 9, 2009)

Being an "influencer" or a YouTube talent is preferred because as a partner on the most ubiquitous video platform they have numerous ways of capturing and retaining a commodified audience. Furthermore, this social embeddedness results in more social analytics about viewers that are important metrics when attracting advertisers and brands. These social analytics are the result of the genre of increasingly ornate and professionalized vlogging managed by Penna. She enables vlogging affect to connect to brand affect in professional relationships. While MCNs are figuring out

200 A. FISH

how to capitalize on this genre, they are also undergoing a process of consolidation.

Video in the Era of Neoliberalism and Conglomeration

Media studies scholar Patrick Vonderau (2016) identifies how MCNs attempt to emulate new and old industries. Those industries are television whose success was measured by the principles of aggregation and social media platforms that grew by the exploitation of data. MCNs attempt to scale through aggregation of content producers under a single umbrella company, many of these companies became aggregates themselves—subsidiaries of multinational conglomerates. As Adelson and Penna state above, they also mine social media data about their audiences in order to tailor content for them but to also be in a better position to link brands to viewers.

From the perspective of older conglomerate media firms who had bought shares in MCNs, this period represents a phase of emerging confidence, transmedia synergy, and stability after a tenuous moment in which the internet was disrupting older business models based on access to studio talent and distribution of copyright content. Established media institutions—advertising agencies, talent agencies, television studios, software companies—were surprised by the sudden attention shifting from television to the internet. Some failures and some successes followed as they attempted to recalibrate and regain their centrality. New stars, video genres like vlogging, and business networks emerged. Older business models like licensing no longer worked the way they had previously. Brand sponsorship and product integration gained new life. Revenue sharing emerged as a way of incentivizing and sustaining labor.

But by 2014, it was clear that while young millionaires were being minted, and employment opportunities were created for a savvy bunch of musicians, video editors, comedians, social media managers, and sundry cyber-personalities, this phase did not represent a permanent rupture with established media institutions. Rather, the history of the business of internet video is a narrative marked by an efficient and comprehensive process of cooptation. In the process, YouTube and MCNs found a profitable business model in connecting brands central to global capitalism to low-budget, lowest-common denominator, and advertising-friendly programming for teens and preteens. The world's biggest multinational media companies were able to gain a strong position in this emergent industry. This phase of conglomeration signifies a consolidation of this sector of user-generated innovation by older entrenched players in the media business and global capitalism. From a critical perspective, this phase of conglomeration represents a highly capitalized monopolization of the attention economy around apolitical content. Categories of alternative and independent media became meaningless in these instances of willful cooptation. Critical, alternative, and independent media continue to exist on YouTube and other video platforms but are not supported by the capital and transplatform promotional powers of the youth and advertising-friendly MCNs that dominate YouTube and the video attention economy. Furthermore, conglomeration, monopolization, and cooptation of internet-based programming into television-like networks represents a transformation of the internet from an open, generative, and democratized platform into one increasingly dominated by the logic of capital. If MCNs are the new television networks and YouTube is the new television—and YouTube is not a regulated entity like cable television—then how will we secure equity in future internet broadcasting?

REFERENCES

Blip. An Important Update from Blip Regarding Account Removals. Blip. Accessed December 5, 2015. http://support.blip.tv/entries/23277196-An-Important-Update-from-Blip-Regarding-Account-Removals

Bogatin, D. 2006. Bliptv vs. YouTube? Founder Talks 'The Real Deal' in Exclusive Interview. *ZDNet*. Accessed December 5, 2015. http://www.zdnet.com/article/blip-tv-vs-youtube-founder-talks-the-real-deal-in-exclusive-interview/

Cohen, J. 2013. Blip Institutes Application Process, Emphasizes Quality Over Quantity. *Tubefilter*. Accessed December 5, 2015. http://www.tubefilter.com/2013/03/05/blip-application-web-series/

Draper, J. 2013. Don't Call Me Kiddo: Founder Sarah Penna of Big Frame Is Taking YouTube to the Major Leagues. *Forbes*. Accessed December 5, 2015. http://www.forbes.com/sites/jessedraper/2013/05/06/dont-call-me-kiddo-founder-sarah-penna-of-big-frame-is-taking-youtubers-to-the-major-leagues/

Dunn, G. 2015. Too Liked to Fail: Get Rich or Die Vlogging. The Sad Economics of Internet Fame. *Fusion*. Accessed December 15, 2015. http://fusion.net/story/244545/famous-and-broke-on-youtube-instagram-social-media/

202   A. FISH

Foucault, M. 1988. Technologies of the Self. In *A Seminar with Michel Foucault*, ed. L.H. Martin, H. Gutman, and P.H. Boston. Massachusetts: University of Massachusetts Press.

Revision3. 2006. Revision3 Brief. *Venturebeat*. Accessed December 5, 2015. http://venturebeat.com/wp-content/uploads/2006/09/revision3_brief.pdf

Johnson, R.W. 2012. Why I Left Maker Studios. *New Media Rock Stars*. Accessed December 5, 2015. http://newmediarockstars.com/2012/12/why-i-left-maker-studios/

Kincaid, J. 2011. YouTube Acquires Next New Networks. *TechCrunch*. Accessed December 5, 2015. http://techcrunch.com/2011/03/07/youtube-acquires-next-new-networks-introduces-youtube-next-training-squad/

Lacy, S. 2008. *Once You're Lucky, Twice You're Good: The Rebirth of Silicon Valley and the Rise of Web 2.0*. New York: Gotham Books.

Marwick, A. 2013. *Status Update: Celebrity, Publicity, and Branding in the Social Media Age*. New Haven and London: Yale University Press.

Miller, C.C., and B. Stelter. 2010. YouTube Said to Seek a Producer of Web Video. *New York Times*. Accessed December 5, 2015. http://techcrunch.com/2011/03/07/youtube-acquires-next-new-networks-introduces-youtube-next-training-squad/

Neff, G. 2012. *Venture Labor: Work and the Burden of Risk in Innovative Industries*. Cambridge: MIT Press.

Paynter, B. 2013. How YouTube's Next Lab Can Quadruple a Channel's Subscriptions. *Fast Company*. Accessed December 5, 2015. http://www.fastcompany.com/3002442/innovation-agents/how-youtubes-next-lab-can-quadruple-channels-subscribers

Spangler, T. 2014. Why Hearst Thinks AwesomenessTV Is Worth 325 Million. *Variety*. Accessed December 5, 2015. http://variety.com/2014/digital/news/why-hearst-thinks-awesomenesstv-is-worth-325-million-1201377964/

Vonderau, P. 2016. The Video Bubble: Multi-Channel Networks and the Transformation of YouTube. *Convergence*, 22(3).

YouTube. Creators. Accessed December 5, 2015. http://www.youtube.com/yt/creators/mcns.html

———. Help. Accessed December 5, 2015. https://support.google.com/youtube/answer/2737059

———. Spaces. Accessed December 5, 2015. http://www.youtube.com/yt/space/

CHAPTER 9

Toward the Beginning of a New Participatory Culture

A 2015 survey discovered that nine out of ten people engage in "binge watching," defined as watching more than three episodes of a TV program in one day (TiVo 2015). This new form of consumption is made possible by the internet as well as regulation protecting the business operations of streaming video companies. One form of this protectionism is network neutrality, which was defended in a historic ruling in February 2015. In it, the Federal Communications Commission (FCC) reclassified broadband internet service as a utility. This socially liberal ruling was split along party lines, with three Democrats voting for it and two Republicans voting against it. This judgment deepened the jurisprudential concept of network neutrality, which forbids internet service providers from prioritizing certain content in a fast lane and denigrating other content to a slow lane. FCC Chairman Tom Wheeler said the ruling would preserve the internet as a "core of free expression and democratic principles" (Ruiz and Lohr 2015). In his neoliberal dissenting opinion, Republican FCC commissioner Ajit Pai accused the Democrats of using big government to disrupt competitive business. Cable television and telecommunications companies agreed with Pai, claiming the reclassification would undermine competition and reduce the incentive to innovate. While the cable television industry derides the decision, internet video companies like Netflix likely celebrate it as it enables them to continue to dominate broadband without considerable regulation. Netflix urged the FCC toward this decision but also hoped that there could be a non-regulatory intervention, one based on market principles (Johnson 2014). Netflix has much to gain.

© The Author(s) 2017
A. Fish, *Technoliberalism and the End of Participatory Culture in the United States*, DOI 10.1007/978-3-319-31256-9_9

203

In 2010, video and audio streaming accounted for 35% of broadband use at peak time in North America. In 2015, it accounts for over 70%, with Netflix taking 37.1% and YouTube 17.9% of their share (Sandvine 2015). While the internet may be regulated in terms that are agnostic to content, that mode of regulation may achieve the opposite of what it is designed to do. For with the dominance of the internet by billion-dollar video-streaming companies, on a platform that cannot be regulated to prioritize any content, we will see the rise not of amateur disruption from below but a different form of video power and corporate hegemony.

Those representing the cable television companies may object to the rise of internet video companies but their rise signifies the dominance of a corporate liberal approach which is enshrined by a regulatory and capitalist system that has kept them in power for a significant portion of the twentieth century. The varieties of liberalism shift through time but capital stays central. Socially liberal approaches to content can meet neoliberal approaches to the regulation of distribution platforms. Corporate liberal approaches to regulation institutionalize capital's control over broadband provisions and result in a neoliberal non-existence of a regulatory social safety net for socially liberal content. While neoliberalism dominates some sectors of internet video, it also appears that the present media ecology for participatory television remains in a period of corporate liberalism, in which the state is sanctioning certain industries for growth through regulation. Despite its clear significance, we should be cautious not to make too much of the network neutrality ruling.

Such protectionism is not the neoliberal future that cynical Marxists envision. It is more in line with the bank bailouts, following the global financial crisis of 2008. In this situation, the federal government—negating its overriding principle of neoliberal deregulation and austerity—used its clout and its citizens' taxes to bail out certain banks, many of which were major contributors to former US President Obama's election campaign. It is this cozy corporate liberal relationship between the federal government and not all but certain major corporations that appears to characterize the present state of media democracy. Socially liberal content, of course, is left to fend for itself in the Darwinian marketplace. Despite the challenges, some succeed, consider the cases of Vice.

Former NBA Champion Dennis Rodman shooting hoops with North Korean leader Kim Jong Ill. A heavy metal band in Baghdad. A personal story about being a part of the so-called Islamic State. This is Vice Media, a video company with over a billion views online, a cable news series on

HBO, 800 employees, and 3500 freelance workers in 36 companies. With these assets they are able to advance left and counter-cultural content and an adventurous aesthetic across all screens—television, internet video, and mobile.

Vice was founded in Montreal in 1994 by Shane Smith, a hard-drinking bon vivant salesman, Surosh Alvi, a recovered heroin addict and son of Pakistani professors, and Gavin McInnes, a prankster who has become a regular right-wing contributor on Fox News. The Canadian software millionaire, Richard Szalwinski, was duped into looking into the magazine when Smith fraudulently claimed that Szalwinski was buying their magazine (Widdicombe 2013). He liked what he saw and invested a few hundred thousand dollars and helped the company build a cutting-edge website, Viceland.com. In 1999, Vice moved to Brooklyn and tried to capitalize on the technology investment bubble in Silicon Alley. The bust happened, and bloated with a record label, ad sales, a website, and international expansion ambitions they had to downsize. From then on it was "punk-rock capitalism," according to Alvi, a scrappy approach that refused to invest on debt (Widdicombe 2013).

From its early days, Vice has been fortunate to ride the wave of technological change that transformed media production. "We became a magazine when the barriers to making a magazine effectively became nonexistent," Smith intoned, "[y]ou could do desktop publishing on a Mac and print for cheap. Now you get a digicam and a Mac, and you can have something broadcast on the net within 15 minutes" (Wilkinson 2008). The 2006 DVD, the *Vice Guide to Travel*, was an important milestone in this guerilla production routine. It featured 15 episodes financed by a Viacom executive and included Alvi visiting the gun markets of Pakistan, Smith shooting radioactive boars in Chernobyl, and visits to North Korea and the slums of Rio. In that same year, Vice transitioned to online video with VBS.tv. With this transition came a political maturing. Smith details this historical trajectory: "In the beginning, there was this era online of 'let's just be cool and criticize everything,' and we were very guilty of that. But as Josey Wales says, 'There comes a point when it is time to get busy living or it is a time to get busy dying'" (Adams 2013). By living, Smith means bringing in millions of dollars of investment and making a global business, while at the same time ramping up political engagement.

Not unlike TVTV in the early 1970s, and our work at Current in the 2000s, Vice reporters become characters in their videos. The aesthetic is, according to one of the founders, "do stupid in a smart way and smart

206   A. FISH

in a stupid way" (Widdicombe 2013). "Instead of writing about prostitutes," Alvi describes the original idea, "We were going to get prostitutes to write for us" (Widdicombe ibid.). The content is compelling, what Smith calls "immersive" journalism or what I've called "performative nonfiction" (Fish 2007), which transforms the reporter into a character. In this style, the reporter lets the audience know what they are feeling and thinking. Their desires as well as their foibles drive the action. Subjectivity is objectified. Vice is unafraid to touch the taboo subjects of sex, drugs, and violence in a self-aware, intimate, outsider, sometimes sexist, and frivolous manner. This results in Vice being criticized for blurring the lines between editorial and sponsorship, which Smith roundly rejects as false (Sandle 2013).

Today Vice has an Emmy-winning series on HBO as well as Vice News, an online video news series, which is constituted by footage donated or collected by their global editorial team. While they are happy to use crowdsourced footage, it is important to note that Vice is not viewer-created content in the model of Current. Vice is editorial and professional. Their audience is 64% male, 41% is 25–34 years old, 40% earn $100 K or more a year, and 74% have attended college (Vice Digital 2014). This demographic is coveted by both old and new media. Acquiring a 5% stake, Rupert Murdoch's Twenty-first Century Fox invested $70 million in Vice in 2013. After a visit to their Williamsburg headquarters, he tweeted: "Who's heard of Vice Media? Wild, interesting effort to interest millennials who don't read or watch established media. Global success" (Sandle 2013). A year later, A&E Networks, a composite of Disney and Hearst Corporation, acquired 10% of the company for $250 million. Recent partners include Intel, Unilever, Budweiser, Smirnoff, Samsung GE, Nike, Levi's, Microsoft, and Ford. Major conglomerates taking a stake in a growing company is necessary, according to Smith. "CNN had to go with Time Warner, MTV went to Viacom, and ESPN went to Disney," he said, "Why? Because to be a global media brand takes a lot of money; connections with advertisers in all these countries is incredibly expensive" (Sandle 2013).

What is remarkable about Vice is that it is economically liberal while producing socially liberal content. Smith wants to cater to a politically conscious youth: "young people are starting to find a voice, and they are not looking to the traditional media to reflect that. CNN was made by the Gulf War. I think the economic crisis will prove to be our Gulf War. It is making young people very angry and we want to be the voice of that anger" (Adams 2013). Smith used to be a "real leftist, working for Greenpeace and all that" (Adams ibid.). More recently, however, Smith does not align with either party: "Are my politics Democrat or Republican? I think both are horrific. And it doesn't matter anyway. Money runs America, money runs everything" (Wilkinson 2008). Not Democratic nor Republican, Vice is neither exclusively a television nor internet video company. While they appear very forward-leaning in terms of internet video, they do want a television network. "I want to build the next CNN. With Vice, it is in my grasp," exclaimed Smith (Adams 2013). In this manner, Vice exemplifies an ideal wherein a media company can accept millions of dollars in investment in order to leverage its socially liberal content onto television sets and internet-connected monitors around the world. Vice began as amateurs and they have retained that raw aesthetic and gained a political momentum in the process of professionalization.

I conclude this book with this vignette on Vice because the company embodies the resourcefulness of the technoliberal subject. Similar to the trends observable in multichannel networks (MCNs) examined in Chap. 8, Vice has aestheticized subjectivity in their content production. Like the vloggers that work for Fullscreen and other MCNs, Vice reporters' personal "authenticity" is central to the success of the company. On a theoretical level, authenticity is key to entrepreneurial or neoliberal subjectivity wherein personal traits are marketable assets (Marwick 2013). Vice's success is the result of the branding of a raw, "punk-rock," and an outsider aesthetic. Its success is also the consequence of an ethical mobility, while the content is often quite political it represents the spectacularization of politics: "doing smart in a stupid way." Vice has no dedication to a single liberalism and is able to mobilize socially liberal content and the neoliberal subjectivity of its journalists with economic liberalism. The result is a company with the flexibility in terms of content, editing, and infrastructure so as not to be troubled by political ideals while remaining within a liberal rubric. In this way, Vice embodies the technoliberal spirit of today, a DIY punk-rock capitalism, with fidelity to profit, self-authenticity, and freedom only. While this is a form of liberalism, it is a depoliticized manifestation.

As described above, Vice is liberal agnostic, putting together discourse, money, and technology in such a way so as to achieve their auteuresque vision of immersive storytelling across platforms. Few if any of the cases explored in this book embody a pure liberalism; all must conflate economic realities, political objectives, compromises with regulatory appa-

208   A. FISH

ratuses and networked communication technology companies to achieve an always truncated goal. In this book, I've attempted to explain a typology of liberalism through examples from the history and culture of video production. None of the liberalisms described in this book are incommensurable.

As the literary legacy of Scottish philosopher Adam Smith's œuvre exhibits, liberalism is riddled with simultaneities and historical oscillations. Seemingly paradoxical notions occur side-by-side or follow each other. Individualism and social solidarity coexist throughout the varieties of liberal pragmatics. The rich moral world described in Smith's two major treatises, the socially liberal, *The Theory of Moral Sentiments* (1759), and the economic liberal, *The Wealth of Nations* (1776), speak to the diversity of liberalisms, and a writer grappling with classification and philosophical paradox. This old problem is renewed by new technical-regulatory environments. Sometimes the participants in these public experiments in paradox know what they are doing. Sometimes not.

The guerilla television movement from the 1970s to 2000s, including FSTV, knew its socially liberal focus and its marginal status. Lacking their hubris and with a vision to democratize television, Current was cognizant of their effort in moral engineering. Vice presents yet another model for liberal situatedness. The remit for Vice's HBO documentary series, *Vice*, as spoken by Smith in the opening gambit is to "expose the absurdity of the modern condition." They mediate and therefore mitigate through video and networked systems, the paradoxical nature of contemporary digital capitalism. Their programs expose the simultaneity and visual excesses of modernity.

The modern condition is ripe in paradox, from power asymmetry, income inequality, and double standards regarding race and gender. This book has been about one small, rather elite population of media producers attempting to mitigate the absurdity of their present moment. They did this through justifying discourses, a practical emphasis on tools, and a faith in networked communication. The digital discourse of Vice, at the moment, tames these contradictions with ever ephemeral authenticity. The two Mr. Smiths, Shane and Adam, have figured out a way to mediate overlapping practices of individual entitlement and social empathy. How social institutions regard both self and other slides historically on a scale. Technoliberalism and its mechanism, digital discourse, are the means by which people synthesize economic and moral philosophy in the company of networked computers and market systems.

TOWARD THE BEGINNING OF A NEW PARTICIPATORY CULTURE 209

This book has looked at the history and culture of the amateur insurgency attempting to renovate television into a system more responsive to the diverse needs of a democracy. For some, it was not about transforming the discourse on television, it was about transforming the form of television to be more responsive to the needs of civil society. For others, content was king and access to television was a way of advocating against hegemonic society. In no case was the impact of the resistance straightforward. In many instances, what looked like a successful inclusion of amateur video content on mainstream television quickly became a form of commodification and appropriation. Inconsistencies and other difficulties plagued the television activists. A look at how independent and activist television producers endeavored to convert or gain access to television reveals the complex relationship between media activism and corporate information infrastructure.

Video power is the capacity to be seen on television or the internet, it fluctuates depending upon the political climate, the access to production and distribution platforms, and the cultural will of the moment. This book has analyzed the historical trajectory of video power as it shifts through time. I have attempted to categorize this process through discussions of the varieties of liberalism, broadly conceived as both the social liberal pursuit of justice and equality and economic liberal advocacy for free markets and individualism. Several theories were developed to specify these liberal incarnations. For instance, proformers are media reform broadcasters who use new technologies and advocate for regulation in order to expand access to public media productivity. As such, they are socially liberal subjects caught in a world of economic liberalism. Proformations, like all subjects of this book, carry with them a digital discourse, a hope that new technologies will mitigate the contradictions of liberalism, and bring about a liberalism fitting on both social and economic terms—with the manifestation of this liberalism different for everyone. Technoliberalism requires a willful reinterpretation of the history of the internet so that it appears to achieve the social liberal values of emancipatory politics in a neoliberal regulatory context. Technoliberalism claims to achieve social liberation through technology and the empowerment of self-entrepreneurialism. The contradictions of social liberation through personal practice, and equality through capitalism, are mitigated by a digital discourse that ameliorates these paradoxes through a system of metaphors and mythological hyperboles.

As each film and video production technology and each new distribution system developed, a new set of discourses arose to frame amateur and

210   A. FISH

political video production. For instance, in the marketing of film production equipment in the 1950s, amateurs were central to marketing discourse. With the plenitude of cable and satellite television emerging in the 1970s and 1980s, amateurs felt that they would have the access they deserve. In all instances, as the market for the technology matured, amateur and political involvement, as well as the discourse of the amateur, shifted, with the elite retaining the best position to exploit the modifications made possible by the new technologies. After each transition, the potential for amateur media production to diversify the public sphere, while once celebrated, is conveniently negated or ignored. Like other media industries, the sequential iterations of television follow what law expert Tim Wu (2010) calls "the Cycle," wherein an industry begins with amateur openness and ends with professional closure. What is fought for in the moments of openness and closure is video power. This book has drawn the ebbs and flows of the cycle of video power.

What is at stake here is the fate of participatory and public cultures within a rapacious form of digital capitalism. The television and internet video networks TVTV, Current, FSTV, Vice, and others speak to a relationship to capital that is mediated by technology and regulation and is motivated by both the social and the entrepreneurial. These organizations drive to sustain and enrich capital, and efforts are made for cultural relevance. This is a culture of media production, with its unique worldview, field of socio-technical practice, public audience, and regulatory ecology. It is shaped by the entanglements of amateurs and professionals, consumer electronics, and broadcast network technologies. These are technoliberals who flexibly use technologies and digital discourse within a range of liberal registers in the pursuit of self-justification and social gain.

This book is an artifact of its time, when "convergence" and the "disruption" of legacy-conglomerated industries of sound, television, and film seemed evident. This unique culture of media production is not new, it is not something that appeared with Netscape and was perfected with Google. I have struggled to define a more recent version of liberalism, technoliberalism, responsible for a discourse specific to the design and participatory affordances of video networks. Technoliberalism codes a specific relationship to digitally mediated free markets, subjectivity, and collective self-organization. As such, it draws from a philosophical past in liberalism, itself not a static and singular entity. Liberalism's roots are in the Western Enlightenment concepts of rights, responsibilities, self-control, and the public sphere—liberal ideals deeply integrated with the

TOWARD THE BEGINNING OF A NEW PARTICIPATORY CULTURE 211

political economies of the communication technologies of their time—
first print and reading, and now participatory digital culture. This book
has been an attempt to classify a version of liberalism that is co-created in
the interaction with affordable film and video cameras, small-scale television production, and the hopes surrounding networked distribution
of visual content. Many individual instances throughout the history of
amateur-made film, television, and internet video dovetail with notions
of participatory culture as a creative collision of old and new technologies
(Jenkins 2006). Historically viewed, however, the fluctuating nature of
amateur and hegemonically challenging video power is exposed as effer-
vescent. It is through history that empowerment and power asymmetries
are exposed. Moments of openness reveal the instances of the "closure"
of the video commons in the second decade of the twenty-first century.
There is no doubt that new video encoding technology, the absence or
presence of regulation, and innovative practices developed by those often
on the edge of hegemony or legality will bring about another moment of
networked visibility. It is with these future video guerillas that this book's
findings should be put to work in creating new apertures for disruption
and revolution.

The varieties of liberalism, like those of capitalism and democracy,
appear more or less commensurable depending on who you are. For the
poor, without capital that can be used to acquire political clout, the dis-
sonances resulting from the convergence of capitalism and democracy can
be intense. For the relatively well-off, capitalist democracy and democratic
capitalism are not contradictory. The two systems work well together.
For the most part, while they may occasionally work on behalf of the
impoverished other, the subjects in this book are from this affluent category. It is for them that a liberalism of gradations, of difference in type
but not in kind, makes the most sense. The predominantly white, educated, employed, and urban workers at Vice, YouTube, Current, FSTV,
and TVTV may have to endure precarious pay but they have the luxury
of constituting their identity from a wealth of options, of deciding to be
political or not, to work in a capitalist system or not. For others, who are
subjected to the capitalist system while excluded from the democratic process, there is a stark contrast between the progressive pursuits of a social
liberalism that might have a measurable impact on their lives and a debili-
tating neoliberalism under which they live. It is this population that most
desperately needs video power in order to be able to add their voice to the
hegemonic public sphere.

REFERENCES

Adams, T. 2013. Shane Smith: 'I Want to Build the Next CNN—It's Within My Grasp.' *The Guardian*. Accessed December 16, 2015. http://www.theguardian.com/media/2013/mar/23/shane-smith-vice-interview

Fish, A. 2007. Television, Ecotourism, and the Videocamera: Performative Non-Fiction and Auto-Cinematography. *Flow Journal* 5: 5. Accessed December 15, 2015. http://flowtv.org/2007/01/television-ecotourism-and-the-videocamera-performative-non-fiction-and-auto-cinematography/

Jenkins, H. 2006. *Convergence Culture*. New York: New York University Press.

Johnson, T. 2014. Netflix Makes Case for Rigorous 'Title II' Approach to Net Neutrality. *Variety*. Accessed December 16, 2015. http://variety.com/2014/biz/news/netflix-makes-case-for-rigorous-title-ii-approach-to-net-neutrality-1201263425/

Marwick, A. 2013. *Status Update: Celebrity, Publicity, and Branding in the Social Media Age*. New Haven and London: Yale University Press.

Ruiz, R., and S. Lohr. 2015. F.C.C. Approves Net Neutrality Rules, Classifying Broadband Internet Service as a Utility. *New York Times*. Accessed December 16, 2015. http://www.nytimes.com/2015/02/27/technology/net-neutrality-fcc-vote-internet-utility.html

Sandle, P. 2013. Vice Media Uses Gonzo Sensibility to Win Online. *Reuters*. Accessed December 16, 2015. http://www.reuters.com/article/us-vicemedia-idUSBRE9A30R620131105

Sandvine. 2015. Over 70% of North American Traffic Is Now Streaming Video and Audio. Accessed December 16, 2015. https://www.sandvine.com/pr/2015/12/7/sandvine-over-70-of-north-american-traffic-is-now-streaming-video-and-audio.html

Smith, A. 1759. *The Theory of Moral Sentiments*.

———. 1776. *The Wealth of Nations*.

TiVo. 2015. Original Streamed Series Top Binge Viewing Survey for First Time. *Tivo*. Accessed December 16, 2015. http://pr.tivo.com/manual-releases/2015/Original-Streamed-Series-Top-Binge-Viewing-Survey

Widdicombe, L. 2013. The Bad-Boy Brand. *The New Yorker*. Accessed December 16, 2015. http://www.newyorker.com/magazine/2013/04/08/the-bad-boy-brand

Wilkinson, C. 2008. The Vice Squad. *The Guardian*. Accessed December 16, 2015. http://www.theguardian.com/media/2008/mar/30/pressandpublishing.tvandradioarts

Wu, T. 2010. *The Master Switch: The Rise and Fall of Information Empires*. New York: Knopf.

INDEX

A
access model, 72–5
Adelson, Jay, 188–91, 200
affect economies, 184
Al Jazeera, 9, 15, 86, 131, 145, 158–60, 169, 170
America's Funniest Home Videos (AFHV), 8, 39, 40, 44
Ant Farm, 30–4
anti-monopoly model, 9, 10, 58, 66–70, 81
assemblage(s), 96, 109, 110, 114, 116, 121, 124
AwesomenessTV, 16, 193, 196–8

B
Bar Karma, 167, 168
Big Frame, 157, 196–200
broadcasting, 3, 4, 8–10, 14, 16, 27, 29, 33, 35–8, 45, 54, 57–9, 61, 62, 64–6, 69, 71, 72, 74–80, 96, 110, 130, 170, 171, 174, 175, 190, 201

C
Cable Communications Act of 1984, 72, 89, 92, 93
cable television, 2, 3, 5, 24–8, 33, 46–8, 70, 75–8, 87, 89, 91, 95, 135, 188, 201, 203, 204
camcorder(s), 5, 8, 35, 37–44, 49, 53
capitalism, 6, 7, 26, 40, 42, 43, 47, 48, 61, 67–9, 88, 89, 91, 94, 101, 102, 108, 109, 111, 114, 115, 117–22, 144, 154, 156, 159, 160, 166, 175–7, 200, 201, 205, 207–11
Citizens United, 122
commercialization, 15, 112, 123, 145, 156–8, 160, 185
commercial model, 8, 57, 59–65, 69, 79, 80

Note: Page numbers followed by 'n' refer to foot notes.

© The Author(s) 2017 213
A. Fish, *Technoliberalism and the End of Participatory Culture in the United States*, DOI 10.1007/978-3-319-31256-9

214 INDEX

computer(s), 2, 3, 8, 14, 31, 32, 48–50, 53, 94, 97, 110, 115, 141, 143, 167, 171, 208
convergence, 6, 7, 14, 15, 17n1, 46–8, 50, 100, 101, 110, 111, 115, 129–60, 182, 188, 189, 210, 211
corporatism, 65, 117
Couldry, Nick, 15, 59, 61, 107
counterhegemony, 31, 94
Current, 9, 10, 12, 14, 15, 57–9, 61–7, 70, 72, 76, 77, 79–81, 111, 129–37, 139–57, 159, 160, 165–8, 175, 191, 193, 197, 198, 205, 206, 208, 210, 211
Cybernetic McLuhanism, 24–35

D
Deep Dish TV, 8, 38, 39, 43, 44, 95
degradation rituals, 108, 116
democracy model, 58, 79–81
democratization, 1, 9, 23, 46, 52, 85, 123, 133, 135, 138, 154, 156, 188–90, 192
Digg, 134, 188, 191
digital discourse(s), 7, 12–15, 31, 39, 47, 51, 107–23, 130, 137–9, 141, 142, 144–51, 153, 154, 156–60, 182, 189, 192, 195, 208–10
Digital Entertainment Network (DEN), 8, 45–7, 50, 51, 133
direct-broadcast satellite (DBS), 36, 72, 77, 89, 95, 96
diversity model, 75, 76
Dornfeld, Barry, 17n1, 87, 131

F
Federal Communications Commission (FCC), 39, 60, 61, 66, 68, 69, 72–4, 76, 89, 91, 95–7, 123, 203

fetish, 108, 113–16, 120
Fisher, Eran, 14, 17n1, 108, 144
flexible microcasting, 44–51
free speech, 9, 10, 58, 65, 66, 69–72, 74, 75, 81, 90–2, 95, 97, 111, 123, 143, 170
free speech model, 70–2, 74
Free Speech TV (FSTV), 9–12, 15, 57–9, 61–8, 70, 72–4, 76–81, 86–103, 132, 165, 166, 168–70, 173–6, 208, 210, 211

G
Gore, Al, 9, 12, 14, 79, 80, 107, 108, 110–16, 120, 122, 123, 130–3, 139–41, 144, 147, 148, 153, 154, 156, 158, 159
governmentality, 11, 59, 86, 176
guardianship model, 57–61, 64, 65, 70–2, 79
Guerilla Television, 24–34, 40, 42, 47, 50, 53, 208

H
hegemony, 8, 42, 52, 88, 94, 102, 103, 139, 204, 211
Hollywood, 3, 5, 22, 44, 45, 72, 111, 139, 144, 145, 149, 151–3, 199

I
individualism, 1, 6, 17, 29, 31, 32, 34, 108, 111, 119, 120, 122, 143, 208, 209
infrastructure(s), 10, 11, 30, 33, 43, 53, 77, 79, 85–91, 94–9, 101–3, 109, 111, 112, 118, 123, 152, 153, 190, 207, 209
initial public offering (IPO), 15, 113, 115, 134, 144, 145, 153, 154, 160

intellectual property, 53, 97, 145, 147–9, 170, 193, 195
internet, 1–5, 7–16, 17n1, 23, 29, 30, 44–51, 53, 54, 58, 63, 66, 75–9, 85–8, 90–2, 94, 97–102, 107–24, 130–8, 140–53, 156–60, 166–8, 171, 181–4, 186–8, 190–3, 196–8, 200, 201, 203–5, 207, 209–11
intersectionality, 15, 165, 167–70, 172, 174–8
I Witness Video, 8, 39, 41, 42, 44

J
Jenkins, Henry, 17n1, 140, 141, 148, 211

K
Kelty, Christopher, 15, 16, 17n1, 94, 97, 102, 121, 139, 142, 172

L
leased access, 72, 89, 92–4
liberalism
    corporate liberalism, 5, 10, 11, 58–60, 69, 71–7, 85–103, 139, 181, 204
    economic liberalism, 5–7, 14, 46, 47, 51, 109, 112, 122, 123, 207–9
    neoliberalism, 4–6, 11, 12, 16, 34, 60–2, 95, 99–103, 107, 121, 122, 138, 159, 160, 175, 177, 178, 181–201, 204, 207, 209, 211
    social liberalism, 5–7, 9, 14, 16, 30, 32, 34, 37, 39, 42, 51, 52, 58, 62–5, 85, 88, 91, 109, 111, 112, 117, 123, 176, 178, 209, 211

technoliberalism, 5–7, 12–14, 16, 107–24, 129–60, 207–10
libertarian paternalism, 58, 59
liberty(ies), 5–7, 85, 111, 123
lifecasting, 44

M
Maker Studios, 16, 157, 158, 192–6
Malaby, Thomas, 6, 7, 120, 166
McChesney, Robert, 17n1, 66, 78–80, 91, 157
McLuhan, Marshall, 24–35
media reform, 8–10, 15, 57, 63, 65–9, 72, 74, 78–81, 86, 87, 90, 91, 95, 165, 166, 168, 169, 171, 172, 174–8, 209
Microsoft, 44–50, 101, 206
moral technical imaginaries, 14, 15, 129–46
multichannel networks (MCNs), 181–6, 188, 190, 193, 195–7, 199–201, 207
myth(s), 13–15, 107, 108, 110, 111, 113–16, 122, 124, 129–60, 166, 182

N
National Conference for Media Reform (NCMR), 10, 68, 79, 87, 90, 166, 168, 171, 172
NBCUniversal, 67, 68, 157, 182, 197
Next New Networks (N3), 16, 182, 185–7, 193

O
Obama, Barack, 12, 13, 74, 107, 108, 110–13, 115–19, 122, 123, 134, 135, 204
open source, 1, 13, 14, 111, 112, 117, 121, 142

216 INDEX

Ortner, Sherry, 17n1, 86, 108, 139
Ouellette, Laurie, 37, 38, 40–3, 52
Oxygen, 8, 46, 47, 50, 149

P

Paper Tiger TV, 38, 43, 44
Parks, Lisa, 8, 46–8
participation, 3–5, 10, 25, 28, 36, 47,
    50, 58, 60, 64, 74, 135–7,
    140–3, 156, 172, 173, 175, 189
partnership, 12, 36, 90, 165, 167–75,
    177
Penna, Sarah, 149, 150, 157, 158,
    197–200
personalization, 47, 48, 51, 102, 166,
    190
populism, 6, 61, 108, 111, 120–2
portapak, 24, 28, 31
professionalization, 3, 21, 35, 133,
    157, 182, 195, 207
proformation(s), 7, 10, 85–90, 92–4,
    97, 99, 209
progressivism, 6, 11, 108, 111, 122
Pseudo.com, 8, 45–7, 51
public
    public, education, and government
        (PEG) channel, 72, 73, 77, 92,
        95, 96
    public interest, 9, 11, 35, 60, 65,
        66, 69–74, 76, 78, 81, 86,
        89–91, 95–8, 173, 174
    public interest model, 68–70
    public resource model, 76–9
    public sphere, 8–10, 15, 16, 23, 28,
        33, 53, 57, 58, 60–5, 71, 72,
        74–81, 87, 91, 92, 99, 101,
        103, 108, 123, 130–8, 141,
        143, 146, 147, 151, 152, 157,
        158, 166, 171, 175–7, 181,
        188, 190, 210, 211
    public sphere model, 9, 57–65, 69,
        80

R

Radical Software, 25, 26, 29, 53
RAND Corporation, 25, 48
reform, 8–10, 15, 57, 58, 63–9, 74,
    78–81, 85–7, 90, 91, 95, 119,
    165, 166, 168, 171, 172, 174,
    175, 177, 178, 209
revision(s), 13, 143, 188, 190
Revolution in a Box, 40
ritual(s), 12, 13, 107–13, 114–16, 124

S

satellite(s), 5, 7–11, 23, 24, 26, 28,
    35–44, 50, 52–4, 61, 70, 72, 73,
    77, 79, 85–9, 91, 93, 95–9,
    101–3, 154, 159, 210
set-asides, 10, 11, 61, 72, 73, 77, 86,
    88, 95–7
Silicon Valley, 5, 16, 32, 49, 102, 111,
    112, 123, 130, 132, 141, 142,
    144, 145, 152–3, 166
silophication, 7, 15, 153, 165–78
Silva, Jason, 150, 155, 158, 191
Smith, Adam, 4, 5, 207, 208
Smith, Shane, 205, 206, 208
streaming, 3, 45, 51, 184, 203, 204

T

technocapitalism, 12–15, 109, 118,
    120–1, 144, 160
technoindividualism, 12, 13, 109,
    119, 120
technology, 2, 4–10, 12–16, 17n1,
    21–3, 27, 28, 30–2, 35–7, 40, 43,
    45–7, 52, 58, 66, 69–71, 73,
    77–81, 85, 88, 91–3, 96–8,
    107–10, 112, 114, 115, 117–23,
    135, 137, 138, 141, 142, 153,
    160, 166, 177, 181, 187, 191–3,
    195, 198, 205, 207–11
technology model, 78–9

technopopulism, 12, 13, 109, 121, 151

technoprogressivism, 14, 15, 111, 113, 121

television, 2, 22, 57, 85, 107, 130, 146–7, 165, 181, 203

Tett, Gillian, 15, 165, 166, 168, 171, 175

Top Value TV (TVTV), 29, 30, 33, 34, 205, 210, 211

Twitter, 2, 4, 29, 99, 100, 130, 134, 140, 146, 153, 191, 194

U

Ultimate TV, 49, 50

V

Vice, 197, 204–8, 210, 211

video, 2–5, 7–9, 12, 13, 15–17, 23–47, 49–54, 57–8, 63–7, 70, 78, 85–103, 110, 116, 117,

129–32, 135, 137–40, 142, 144, 146–51, 154–8, 165, 166, 168, 170, 172, 173, 181–201, 203–11

Videofreex, 8, 27, 30, 33

video power, 1–17, 21–54, 204, 209–11

viewer-created content (VC2), 9, 40, 63, 64, 66, 72, 129–35, 144, 146–51, 154–8, 197, 206

visibility, 16, 17, 54, 183, 184, 211

W

Wallerstein, Immanuel, 109, 123

WebTV, 48–50

Y

YouTube, 1, 16, 29, 30, 45, 53, 99, 139, 141, 146, 148, 149, 153, 157, 158, 182–7, 194, 196, 197, 199–201, 204, 211

CPSIA information can be obtained
at www.ICGtesting.com
Printed in the USA
LVOW04*1556230417
531877LV00006B/18/P